The Policy Vacuum

The Policy Vacuum

Toward a More Professional
Political Science

Robert N. Spadaro
The Chinese University
of Hong Kong

Thomas R. Dye
Florida State University

Robert T. Golembiewski
University of Georgia

Murray S. Stedman
Temple University

L. Harmon Zeigler
University of Oregon

Lexington Books
D.C. Heath and Company
Lexington, Massachusetts
Toronto   London

Library of Congress Cataloging in Publication Data

Main entry under title:
The policy vacuum: toward a more professional political science

1. Policy sciences. 2. Political science. I. Spadaro, Robert N.
JA74.P82   309.2'12   75-3787
ISBN 0-669-99697-1

Copyright © 1975 by D.C. Heath and Company.

Published simultaneously in Canada.

Printed in the United States of America.

International Standard Book Number: 0-669-99697-1

Library of Congress Catalog Card Number: 75-3787

To Margaret and Sumner

Contents

Preface

When I was younger, I entered political science on the rather naive notion that it dealt with politics and public policy. I had been a "professional politician" and as such often wondered why political science academicians had such little impact on the real policy arena and why, when they were consulted, they were called upon essentially to legitimize decisions that already had been formulated. Thus this book represents, in part, an attempt to bridge the gap between academia, politics, and public policy, and to explore the options open to us as political scientists and social scientists while there is still time. For now, political science is jumping aboard the policy bandwagon and there is a considerable contribution that can and must be made to society. Now with Watergate, the energy crisis, and the like relatively behind, with an increasing apathy if indeed not alienation by many to our policy processes, and with the "decline" of the nation-state vis-à-vis international economic and political forces, we must concern ourselves with knowledge and improvement of policy analysis, the policy process, and policy impact.

Yet there is still considerable confusion, polemic, and debate over values, behavioralism, post-behavioralism, and how to be or not to be relevant. Additionally, on the one hand, the policy scholar and student is urged to eclecticism to span many areas whereas others opt for sharpened skills within narrow parameters. Therefore some will lose sight of the forest for the trees whereas others will lose sight of the trees for the forest. Policy institutes have been and are being created, policy majors developed, and at the very least, the word policy being worked into course descriptions—often functional yet occasionally dysfunctional, if in fact not simply fashionable. Thus this book also attempts through *original* contributions rather than "readings" to present the controversy and available options before we become locked in, and at least to pose the immediate questions and bring some sense of central identifying schema to the dialogue. In the process, existing policy models are examined and a new policy model offered, not as an end but as a means, for we still have a long way to go.

I have few acknowledgments to make. In a sense I owe a debt to my former colleagues at Temple whose for the most part (fortunately not all) general confusion over policy analysis motivated the idea of the need for such a book.

I owe a particular debt of gratitude to my wife, who stood by me through the harrowing experience of putting together such a book, and to my daughter, who never doubted. I am grateful for the kind collaboration of my coauthors. Certainly I must acknowledge Thomas R. Dye, my oldest and dearest friend, who has made a significant contribution to both academia and me, and without whose cooperation, participation, and intellectual stimuli this book would not have been possible. Any criticism or defects of this work are mine and certainly not his. I also am indebted to Dr. William Kuhn, mathematics professor—who helped increase my understanding of set theory—and to our secretary, Mrs. Angela Chan. Finally, because politicans and those who shape public policy are in such disrepute, I would like to acknowledge my debt to two of those who truly serve—William W. Scranton and United States Senator Richard S. Schweiker.

Robert N. Spadaro
Hong Kong
May 1975

The Policy Vacuum

1

Public Policy and the Political Scientist: An Overview

Robert N. Spadaro

Political science is a discipline in search of an identity and a raison d'être. Since World War II in America and, to a far lesser extent, in Europe, the field of political science has experienced and is still undergoing considerable change, evolution, metamorphosis, and confusion. Several resulting phases have developed sometimes in important new perspectives and sophistication, particularly in terms of methodology, and sometimes more to be fashionable. Now a state of flux and attention centers on public policy. More precisely, it centers on political science's direction, training, contribution, and degree of commitment on public policy and public policy analysis, and its relationships to the other social sciences and society.

The purpose of this book is to attempt to organize at least the questions of this debate and provide further conceptual clarity to professional political scientists and particularly students of political science in their understanding of where we now stand, where we seem to be heading, and the major problems that we face. The foci of this book, original contributions aligned along central themes rather than "readings," is generally aimed at these questions: (1) the debate over descriptive v. prescriptive policy research; (2) the argument over relevancy in the policy arena; (3) the training of political scientists; (4) new trends in interdisciplinary policy approaches; (5) an examination of current policy models and methodology; (6) the neglected role of policy impact analysis; and (7) the desirable degree of commitment to policy analysis by three key subdisciplinary areas of interest—the basic interaction, in terms of political science, in the policy world: political leaders and political parties, public administration and administrative processes, and pressure groups. Finally, in the concluding chapter, the essay represents an attempt to explain the "how" and "why" factors necessary to understanding the methodological considerations in the systematic formation of policy variables in a "real" policy-making schema.

Thus, we trust the reader will find controversy that should be helpful by comparison to a better understanding of the relationships of political science to public policy and an increased sense of direction and conceptual organization of the continuing dialogue over the political science/public policy interface.

1

Political Science Today and
the Social Sciences

Political science has yet to achieve full maturity as a discipline. Unfortunately, as a field, it often lags behind other social sciences in relation to theoretical and applied research, training, and contribution. One political scientist has observed that political scientists have little knowledge and few skills that are of interest or value to anyone except other political scientists.[1] Part of this criticism probably stems from the inherent research difficulties of what political scientists are trying to study; nevertheless part also is due to the relative lack of consensus on central identifying themes.

Critics within and external to political science, professors, students, and interested laymen, argue for increased/decreased relevancy in relation to government, society, research, and professional associations; more scientism/less scientism; increased/decreased interdisciplinary emphasis; and curriculum revision; these are but some of the more major and germane divisions within political science.

Still many do share one common perspective, although there are alternative approaches and degrees to that perspective, that is that public policy is too important to be left to politicians alone and that political science should be involved with public policy analysis. In turn, if valid this may lead to increased central identifying focus.

In order to understand the divisions within political science and for the purpose here at hand, the resulting divisions and approaches in public policy, a brief review might be useful. For some two thousand years, from Aristotle to approximately World War II days, political scientists were concerned with public policy. The study of politics and policy was deemed as the "queen of the social sciences." Essentially this concern, the traditional approach, was (and remains so today for some) normative in nature. That is, behavioral phenomenon were bypassed in the pursuit of what ought to be. Thus the political scientist was primarily concerned with the study of institutions, laws and regulations, and frameworks of government in terms of what would work best. Therefore, from a policy point of view, the policy ideal or the best policy at least was usually the goal. Where methodology was used it usually tended to be a case study approach. This is still very much the way European political scientists approach public policy. Victor Laski more recently, for example, was one of the principle European scholars to work in this tradition and compare and make important judgments on influences and types of policy.

However, while no arbitrary dates can be set, post-World War II American political scientists, and social scientists in general even earlier, began to develop the "behavioral" approach. The behavioralists devoted their attention to how and why political beings and political phenomenon empirically (as compared to normatively) behaved the way they do. In the process, in developing new concepts, methodological tools, and gathering data, public policy, particularly prescriptive public policy, became to a large extent ignored. Therefore, one important division that remains within political science and now divides opinion on public policy analysis is the argument over normative versus empirical research and prescriptive versus descriptive public policy analysis.

Most political scientists still differ and students are both challenged and harangued consequently on whether values and value judgments should be a proper academic concern. Or to put the argument more simply, some argue what good is empirical research if it does not involve values and norms about society, government, and public policy. Others argue that it is difficult to quantify values and what good are intuitive explanations of society, government, and public policy. Some of this conflict was due to growing pains within the discipline and if better research has emerged, then it has been healthy for political science. However, some of this conflict has also been a product of political infighting for some in the "young guard" also sought to use methodology to establish reputations, supercede the old guard, and advance their careers, while some in the old guard simply refused to engage in the considerable effort necessary to retool and learn new skills. Thus the reader should be aware that these battle lines both academically and pragmatically have important implications for the direction and future of public policy analysis. Moreover, more recently, some in "post-behavioralism" maintain that public policy is the total of political science per se and values must be postulated for societal relevancy regardless of research limitations. They argue that political science fiddles while Rome burns.

The real argument comes down to descriptive versus prescriptive policy studies. Descriptive policy research seeks to explain the cause and consequences of public policy; whereas prescriptive policy research concentrates on the values implicit to public policy. The long-range goal for public policy must be to achieve a high level of integration of values and scientism and a general theory of public policy, but we are still far from these goals.

A Question of Relevancy

Theoretical Versus Applied Policy Research

A further related basic division within political science that has important implications for the future of public policy analysis lies in the debate over theoretical research versus applied research. Many in political science believe that political science must have greater relevancy to society and public policy. Others feel that to do so could corrupt the objective detachment of academic research, and that we just do not know enough about the policy process to make an effective contribution.

The reader should be aware that descriptive policy research is not necessarily theoretical research and prescriptive policy research is not necessarily applied research. The distinction between theoretical and descriptive is that the former means basic research within academia usually and the latter involves empirical research procedures on causes and consequences. Applied indicates direct involvement on, say, studying how a particular agency implemented a specific policy while prescriptive research implies that the values of policy, whether in direct involvement or in general academia, should be formulated or analyzed. This last distinction is an important one since values can be approached traditionally or attempts can be made to empirically analyze values. In short, prescriptive policy research can include both these approaches. Or to return to an earlier point, theoretical policy research could carry over to applied in the general sense by first formulating hypotheses and then testing them in the field. Thus, for example, when Thomas R. Dye urges descriptive policy research, in Chapter 2, he is suggesting empirical procedures *and* also theoretical research as compared to prescriptive and/or applied policy research. In applied research the variables that are subject to governmental manipulation are given priority, whereas theoretical or basic research seeks to explain maximum variance and priority is given the variables explaining the largest proportion of the variance. Robert Lane, writing on applied research, suggests that, "public policy analysis is applied social science in several senses: first in the identification of the need to which the policy is addressed, secondly in the inquiry and to the consequences of government actions, and thirdly in the evaluation of public programs."[2]

Since there are significant limitations on our present state of development in theory, models, and methodology, there are strong arguments against both applied policy and prescriptive research. Nevertheless, the counterarguments are at least equally strong. Research, for example, in these latter two areas could help generate the data and models we need for more sophisticated theoretical knowledge. Then too, the argument for action is compelling.

Knowledge into Action

Professor Harold D. Lasswell has long advocated that the political scientist should be more directly involved in the policy arena and should provide linkages between policymakers and general publics.[3] Professor Yehezkel Dror calls for, "the application of political science to important policy problems."[4] He observed that while there have been political scientists individually and collectively contributing their *personal* views on policy issues, that this is not the same as the systematic application of political science to policy questions.[5]

Political science as an academic discipline alone or when compared to its sister social sciences, particularly economics, has had little and limited impact in the real world of the policy arena. When political scientists have been called into appraisals of policy, it has usually been in the context of legitimizing and rationalizing public actions that have already been decided upon or after the policies are in existence. Rarely has the political scientist, at least in recent times, actually been involved in deciding what policy should be or formulating policy decisions and rarely has he been utilized in real evaluation and impact of policy. It seems strange that political scientists have had little impact into crucial policy matters such as the energy crisis or the Watergate affair. Persons such as Robert Wood and Henry Kissinger have been personally active in government as individuals. Yet we could effectively argue that matters such as Watergate, which involved political structural reforms and variables, could be a pertinent concern for a systematic political science input. In fact, the major policy reports that we have seen in the last several years have been primarily executed by social scientists other than political scientists. For example, James Coleman, of the Coleman Report, is a sociologist. Economists also convene directly in government. Again to illustrate, there is no political science equivalent to the Council of Economic Advisors. In terms of governmental spending sources, life sciences receive approximately $500 million, psychologists alone about $55 million, all of the social sciences receive about $72 million of which political science gets less than $3 million.

There are many now actively engaged in applied research in political science such as the Brookings Institution, Eagleton Institution, the Fels Institute, et al., or the various newly emerged and created policy institutes—sometimes as spinoffs of contiguous departments of political science such as Michigan's Institute of Public Policy Studies. The former essentially concentrate on the processes of applied public policy while the latter tend to also concentrate on processes and theoretical development.

Of course, most advocates of increased involvement in the policy arena ignore the problem of access. Both in conducting research on policymakers and/or engaging in policy formulation, gaining entry can pose a major obstacle particularly since it generally has not been established in the past nor has the political scientist proven systematically that he can indeed make a real contribution. In some sense, this is one reason why political scientists thus far generally have only been personally involved in direct policy involvement and action. Yet the argument of access begs the question, we have to prove that political science can systematically and collectively contribute if that is indeed possible.

We need therefore to aim not only for a general theory of public policy optimally but in the meantime for goal-based empirical theories. In the process, perhaps we can better bridge the gap between values and empiricism. Public policy analysis may and should offer an umbrella to encompass these interests, particularly if there is going to be a payoff to the political scientists' contribution in the real policy arena and world. To some extent, we must begin participating now if time and the other social sciences are not to completely pass us by. Currently when teams of social scientists all gather to engage in policy, the political scientist is usually relegated to examining the processes of policy alone rather than the impact of policy. Most of us have the uneasy notion either way that political science not only should but perhaps more than any other discipline does have something to do with public policy.

Here, before we engage in "knowledge into action," the title of conferences by the Brookings Institution aimed at bridging this gap, Thomas R. Dye argues the point that systematic empirical descriptive policy analysis must be developed before we can make a truly viable contribution to applied knowledge, while Robert T. Golembiewski argues that we should begin immediately to apply our knowledge more to the real world. Murray S. Stedman argues a differing perspective, that since political parties are increasingly ineffective as policy influences, the parties' scholar has less interest in this linkage a priori.

In the concluding chapter, L. Harmon Zeigler with Michael O. Boss, former graduate student in political science working with Zeigler, writing on the "why" and "how" of the systematic formulation of policy variables in a real world schema, educational policy-making in this case, believe that an understanding of values is inherent to understanding public policy.

Policy Models

The General State of Policy Theories and Models

There is a plethora of theories and models for public policy analysis, many spanning disciplinary areas of interest. For example, systems analysis is used in sociology and biology as well as political science. Some, particularly those used in political science, are macro oriented, that is trying to explain aggregate policy phenomenon, while others, such as in sociology or psychology, tend to be more micro oriented, that is concentrating on group and individual behavior. Economists tend to utilize both approaches in their policy analysis.

Thus, current models for policy analysis tend to be either/or, macro/micro, and this basic dichotomy poses a problem of talking past each other. A further dichotomy is also apparent. Policy models usually focus on the functional and programmatic aspects of policy or on decision-making factors involved in specific policies. Or we may argue, one seeks to measure the why and how of a given policy while the second approach seeks to explain why and how policymakers configure in a policy process. A third basic problem and research obstacle is again the separation of descriptive from prescriptive policy research for values are divorced from processes. Finally, by way of introduction, in political science, most policy models we now employ generally only study policy as a function, process, outcome or output. In other words, they focus on what a policy does, how it was manipulated, and implemented. But the impact of that policy, why that policy came into being, and the symbolic and feedback linkages of that policy or policy in general are to a large extent ignored.

Public policy is consequently normally viewed as the *dependent* variable, the product of causes or *independent* variables. Yet public policy should also be treated as an independent variable or cause in itself *leading* to a product or outcome. For policy expectations redefines other resulting variables such as economic capacity or political redistribution to name but a few of the possible and potential new dependent variables. In terms of regression analysis then, where Y (the dependent variable) is predicted by $A + B + C + \ldots$ (the independent variables manipulating Y), policy should be analyzed both ways (a point Dye and Golembiewski also raise later in their chapters). Thus, at best we receive a very limited and marginal understanding of what public policy is all about (and therefore our potential "applied" contribution is by definition limited).

To illustrate, if we were trying to explain a specific welfare policy, it is important to know why policymakers decided the way they did on that policy, how it was implemented, and how resources were allocated, but it is equally important to know or try to know also the impact and success of the policy, the symbolic or intangible results of that policy in perceptions and expectations, and the function of feedback for new welfare policy, which means not only new specific welfare policies but also the general policy environment. For example, how do you cost/benefit analyze intangible results of policy. If one is trying to understand the Great Society programs on poverty, by concentrating on resource allocations they were at least partially successful yet in reality the programs were essentially disasters.

Of course, considering present modeling and methodological limitations, many argue with some justification that that is the best one can do and we better learn to walk before we can engage in other than descriptive research. Yet to some extent this argument is misleading for it assumes that descriptive research must be concerned only with processes and programs of specific policy while it could also be directed to feedback, symbolic, impact, and the paradigm of policy as a whole. In short, it assumes that policy has a limited life cycle, a birth, life, and death, while in reality policy has no arbitrary dates for perceptions, supports, expectations, frustrations, alienation levels, and the like, are both latent and activated long before and possibly long after a specific policy has come and gone. And descriptive research is used for socialization studies, voter studies, political personality studies, et al., which are areas that already indirectly at least attempt to empirically operationalize attitudes and perceptions relating to policy. In Chapter 5 Zeigler discusses the importance of values to policy-making and presents empirical formulation on operationalizing values in a practical policy context.

When the political scientist uses systems analysis for the study of policy, that is, for the moment simply put, that inputs are converted into outputs or policy, he is limited a priori to studying specific programs, the systematic outputs. Yet the policy cycle thus becomes so general (no one yet has really operationalized the systems concept) that it is almost beyond empirical research or so specific in studying outputs that we are in danger of missing the forest for the trees. When the political scientist goes the alternative policy decision-making route, he is essentially limited to the more micro oriented explanation of principal actors which can be very important but still becomes self-containing in terms of all of the parameters that we can associate with the policy phenomena. Either way, most policy models are taxonomic, they attempt to organize categories for public choices yet there now is no commonly accepted policy classificatory schema particularly over time and across systems. In the model that will be developed, it is hypothesized that nonoverlapping taxonomies are available.

These arguments are not meant to suggest that present models lack utility for they are helpful and we are still at early stages of development in policy analysis. However, we should be aware of what they are, what they do, and what they do not do. Later, methodological approaches and limitations will be discussed to show their relationships as tools for operationalizing theories and models of policy analysis.

A Review of Specific Policy
Theories and Models

The most used public policy or quasi-policy models in political science (and to a great extent used in all social sciences though the originators and names may change) are: systems analysis, functional/structuralist analysis, decision analysis, group dynamics, elitist v. pluralistic models, incrementalist v. rational models, and "institutional" analysis (Larry L. Wade in his book on policy describes most of these in detail).[6]

Systems analysis is perhaps the most used and the most conventional. Originally "developed" by European social scientist Vilfredo Pareto, adapted for sociology by Talcott Parsons, widely used by biologists, it was first applied with great utility to political science by David Easton.[7] Simply stated, Easton conceptualized an abstract (as compared to discrete) political system with certain boundaries and intensity of interactions to separate the system from environment in which, similar to a flow process, there are certain inputs (demands, supports) which are converted by government (withinputs, thruputs) to outputs and outcomes (suffice to say policy for the moment). He defined a political system as "those interactions through which *values* are authoratively allocated for a society" (emphasis mine).[8]

Most scholars applying systems analysis to study public policy follow this general framework with variations. Dye, in previous work, poses a useful and similar systematic model for policy that regards outcomes and outputs as an essentially isomorphic relationship while to Easton the specifics of a policy are

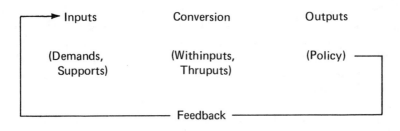

Figure 1-1.

outputs and outcomes are rather the general affects and consequences of public policy.[9] Dye stressed that *value* commitments of the political system are the chief output of that system. Ira Sharkansky applied the systems concept to public administration.[10] The distinctions, useful in understanding the relationships of policy and public administration to which we shall return, are essentially that inputs can be viewed as clientele groups, government in general as a public administrative agency, and outputs as the decisions and policy of that specific agency. A *policy* system, as Randall B. Ripley suggests, can be looked at the same way, as policy statements, policy actions, and policy outcomes.[11]

This deliberately simplified review of systems analysis, especially in relation to policy analysis, by no means exhausts the subject or encompasses all the variations that have stemmed from it, but an important point or two should be clear by now. While these models and systems analyses offer conceptual utility, they tend to be macro oriented, difficult if not impossible to fully operationalize, and end up by almost forcing us to concentrate on specific policy processes and functions. Most conceptualize the potential of symbolic factors but treat them as purely allocations or outcomes with possible feeedback and offer little potential for operationalizing such variables, thus they usually become "dormant" acknowledgments that symbolism may be important. Yet the symbolic and intangible but nevertheless real causes and consequences of policy can be crucial. As if by default, the concept of feedback linkage, relationship to environment or *other* political systems, and values are bypassed. Thus, the values that are studied are "tangible" and material and limited to specific programs by resource priorities and allocations.

The major offshoot of systems analysis, the functional/structural model, developed by Almond and Coleman and later modified by Almond and Powell, suffers primarily from the same limitations for the same reasons.[12] Both models acknowledged that the systems idea while useful was too general and could not really measure the important function of change. Therefore, they respectively concentrated on the functions a system, any system, performs. Briefly stated, the basic model stated that inputs are interest aggregation, interest articulation, political socialization and recruitment, and communications, while the outcomes are policy; rule adjudication, rule-making, and rule enforcement. The later policy model reclassifies public policy into four areas, regulations, allocations, symbols, and extractions (resources). Yet while being more particularistic than the parent systems notion and again offering considerable conceptual utility, nevertheless by still being too general, specific programs and policies become the focal point of study. Symbolic allocations remain vague and limited to outcomes alone.

Institutional policy studies usually concentrate on the structure involved as a measure for policy reform and change. In their recent book on policy, Dolbeare, Dolbeare, and Edelman, discuss problems with getting policy through the U.S. Senate and the structural reforms that would be necessary to accommodate change.[13] Essentially such approaches become institutional case studies.

However, structural reforms lead us to a hoary problem relating to policy. Specifically, are political structure and variables, e.g., party competition or apportionment, or economic structure and variables, e.g., per capita spending or economic base, more important in predicting and determining public policy? Scholars in political science have debated this question rather extensively in the last decade and the controversy is by no means resolved.[14] Dye, in Chapter 2, expands his point of view that economic variables are most significant and accuses most American political scientists of having a bias in favor of political pluralism that he feels is both unrealistic and fails to understand how policy works, particularly in view of new international economic situations.

This contiguously relates to the elitist v. pluralist models for policy explanation, again with important unresolved implications for understanding policy. Briefly stated, elitist theorists such as C. Wright Mills, Floyd Hunter, and Edward C. Banfield reason that a unified homogeneous elite usually really decides policy, often in Peter Bachrach's expression, by "non-decision-making," that is without the public generally even being aware that there was an issue in the first place.[15] Pluralist proponents such as Robert A. Dahl or Nelson A. Polsby find that multiple groups decide policy, which group, depends upon the issue at stake and relative influence.[16] Agger, Swanson, and Goodrich in *The Rulers and the Ruled* suggest that who or how many rule is actually situational.[17] Therefore, depending upon your point of view, these respective simplified policy models and arguments are basic to understanding policy and reflect the still embryonic stage of development that we are in, in relation to full policy clarity.

Curiously, the more micro oriented decision analytical approaches lead us to the same dilemma purposely. While there are ample decision-making models available in law, psychology, sociology, and economics, since they are reasonably similar to political science models in this area, discussion will be limited to those utilized by political scientists.

First, most center on the decisions going into and/or internal to *specific* policies and programs. In other words, the causes and consequences of policies again are the target of analysis, this time in relation to their inherent decisions. However, decisions are as difficult to quantify as values, for that matter, indirectly decisions are or reflect values, and their originators accurately acknowledge the difficulty in operationalization.

One important policy decision-making model is that of Mitchell and Mitchell.[18] The model seeks to classify the problems rather than policies that decisionmakers are trying to solve or resolve. Based upon a *rational*-choice model, they construct six problems, (1) resource mobilization, (2) distribution of benefits, (3) allocation of costs, (4) controls, (5) adaptability and stabilization, and (6) division of labor and role allocation. Another approach to policy classification by decisions is Theodore Lowi's three types, distributive, regulative, and redistributive policies.[19] Robinson and Majak's policy model focuses on the processes of decisions that are made by analyzing "outcome clusters" of public policy into outputs, outcomes, and affects.[20] Outcomes are public policy, outputs, and intermediate decisions, and effects refer to the world external to the political system. Our final example is a decision-making model developed by Agger, Goldrich, and Swanson.[21] The policy *process*, "a series of related events or acts over a period of time," is composed of policy formulation, policy deliberation, organization of political support, authoritative consideration, formulation of the decision, and effectuation of the policy. Effectuation redefines new policies for a linkage is incorporated. Yet in all we still face problems of values, operationalization, and emphasis on only specific policies and processes which takes a long step forward but at an early stage of development again. The emphasis is usually drawn to the *formal* decisionmaker and not necessarily the interaction and overlap of pressure groups, function of change (a decision is not always an arbitrary point in time), or mass publics, and usually on the allocation of policy aspects.

One last but very controversial and important decision-making debate should be quickly reviewed and affords a general illustration of this critique. The incrementalist v. rational decision-making policy models revolve around the type of decision itself. Are formal decisionmakers simply "satisficing," that is routinely engaging in decision-making, or engaging in "rational decision-making," objective means/ends relationships and goals? Most scholars (e.g. Thomas Anton, Aaron Wildavsky, Richard Fenno) believe that governmental decision-making (and so policy generally) is primarily incrementalistic.[22] However, a recent article by Natchez and Bupp suggests that the "incrementalists" are misled by aggregate data and that *within* agencies there is considerable non-routine change in policy(s).[23] Either way, the issue, like others we have already reviewed, has important and yet unresolved implications for our understanding of policy.

Group analysis in terms of policy studies lies somewhere in between and vis-à-vis political science lags behind the relatively more sophisticated models developed by sociologists. In Chapter 3, however, Golembiewski shows some of the more important linkages between the types of group related approaches to policy and public administration. Moreover, as group dynamics relates directly to pressure groups analysis and the operations and influence of pressure groups in the public policy arena, political scientists, e.g., Zeigler, Norman R. Luttbeg, David Truman, have considerably expanded our knowledge.[24] Since Zeigler's chapter directly relates to pressure groups and Stedman's indirectly by discussing brokerage interests in reference to political parties, the only important point to be made here is that pressure groups' policy *potential* spans systems and should be included in any policy model such as the one that will be developed later.

A Brief Summary

Present models of public policy analysis, therefore, primarily concentrate on outcomes or outputs. Policy analysis is thereby usually approached as a process of a system which tends to downgrade what *ought* to be in policy for what *is*, indicates a concern for the *ex post facto* explanation of specific policy, concentrates on *specific* policies rather than on the overall nature of policy, treats policy as the *dependent* variable, essentially bypasses the *symbolic* for tangible or allocative factors of public policy, and only partially tests *feedback linkages*. In this respect, while it is possible to visualize the policy process, it becomes very difficult to operationalize the inherent general characteristics of most policy models. From a methodological prespective, essentially the majority of our policy studies almost a priori become essentially "case" studies, which presents an inherent difficulty in effectively generating hypotheses.

What Is Public Policy:
Perspectives and Definitions

Alternative approaches in addition to models per se also suggest a sense of direction for the political scientist for public policy analysis. Austin Ranney writes that policy involves:

A particular object or set of objects—some designated part of the environment (an aspect of the society of physical world) which is intended to be effective.
　　A desired course of events—a particular sequence of behavior desired on the particular objector set of objects.
　　A selected line of action—a particular set of actions chosen to bring about the desired course of events; in other words, not merely whatever the society happens to be doing toward the set of objects at the moment, but a deliberate selection of one line of action from among several possible lines. A declaration of intent—whether broadcast publicly to all that will listen or communicated

secretly to a special few, some statement by the policy makers as to what they intend to do, how, and why.

An implementation of intent—the actions usually undertaken vis-à-vis the particular set of objects in pursuance of the choices and declaration.[2 5]

Ranney's definition of the nature of policy indicates there may indeed be common denominators to both explain policy as a whole and span specific policies, an important point to which we shall return. However, the interrelationships and interface are almost by definition difficult to conceptualize and more difficult to operationalize. Concentrating on policy processes alone, James Rosenau writes:

Undertakings, unlike policies and decisions, encompass goals and their implementation. Their distinctive quality is that they focus on what government does, *not on how it decides to do it or on what it commits itself to do* . . . (Emphasis mine)[2 6]

Rosenau's intent focuses attention on possibly the more interesting aspects of public policy and yet leaves us still somewhat unclear on how we may compare policies. One recent model (see Figure 1-2), which is included here rather than under our section on models since it develops interesting linkages which will be developed shortly, offers utility by attempting to develop the interaction of policy variables.[2 7] Again we come to the notion that just as there may be common denominators to the nature of policy there may be common denomi-

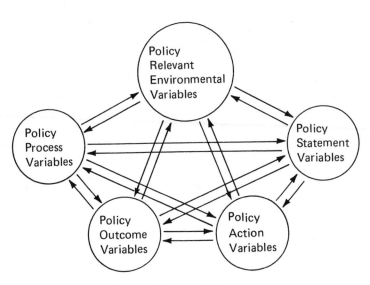

Figure 1-2.

nators within policies. Nevertheless, again it becomes difficult to accurately determine the interactions and interface between variables and across time or on what policy ought to be.

Charles McClelland points out that, "finally outcomes are not determined by initial conditions, but rather by conditions of outflow and inflow over a period of time."[28] Yet we are particularly weak on our data base and empirical procedures for testing feedback linkages and no policy exists in a vacuum. Devices such as resource allocation, cost benefit analysis, program and performance budgeting, operations research, systems analysis, etc., cannot adequately explain the totality of expectations and consequences of policy. The various Great Society programs were more symbolic than tangible, yet most studies of these programs generally try to measure what was accomplished tangibly while the more symbolic frustrations, disappointments, and consequently changed perceptions have been largely ignored. We are thus usually on the horns of a dilemma in studying policy; oftentimes we end up trying to compare apples and oranges. Contiguously, the non-rational or irrational factors in policy-making and policy analysis, in some part because of their inherent methodological and empirical problems and restrictions, also have been generally bypassed. Nevertheless, methodological limitation should not preclude the importance of this type of behavior and perceptions in their effects on policy. In short, when we think about the preceding problem areas we are left with the uneasy impression that we are missing a good deal of the content and repercussions of public policy. Parson's output variables, for example, include opportunity for effectiveness and leadership, operative values, and moral responsibility, which have generally been ignored but can be crucial to a more thorough understanding of policy dynamics.[29]

Therefore, we need to develop theories and/or models that attempt to fill these gaps with the ideal being essentially a general theory of public policy. In the meantime, we need to generate *both* deductive and inductive modes of analysis in modeling and aim for a goal-based empirical model that can integrate values and empirical analysis. I do not mean including values in the purely traditional or intuitive sense but by value analysis, trying to quantify values by methodology, by probability choices and preferences. The descriptive purist, not without justification, will argue that value prescription has no place in descriptive research and *perhaps*, if at all, values can be approached empirically as testing of choices and action indicators. In this case, the purist might finally argue that this latter type of value analysis has nothing to do with prescriptive research.

In other words, as David Hume suggested long ago and as any course in the philosophy of science will attest, facts are separate from values and never the twain shall meet. The prescriptive purist will argue by curiously similar reasoning that values are within *his* province and involve only what is best. If any middle ground exists, it is murky indeed. For example, Lasswell's social process model involves man seeking to optimalize value outcomes through institutions affecting resources.[30] Here, and I readily admit it is a highly debatable point, values are meant to represent a *bridge* between descriptive and prescriptive policy analysis. Therefore, value study is separated into two different steps—first as indicators or belief systems and second as "best" or "worst" type statements. Value analysis and the use of values as a basic variable in the model to come is here viewed as being empirically testable only as priorities and action indicators for policy involvement, that is as S:O:R relationships, for Hume was quite right—values per se cannot be empirically proven. For those who do wish to engage in "best" and "worst" type policy prescriptions, the first step is all the more important for they should know the patient if they want to prescribe the medicine.

Of course, any model in the present state of development of public policy analysis offers more hope in generating hypotheses and increasing conceptual utility rather than in satisfying all or in resulting in a general theory per se.

A Policy Paradigm

While policies may vary across systems and within systems, we may profitably argue there is a policy paradigm, key and central characteristics and variables common to the nature of policy and within specific policies and policy processes.

What is there then that is common to the nature, functioning and processes of public policy? What are common variables that range across and within policy(s) that would tend to further help explain this overall phenomena that we label public policy? What are the boundary lines between what the political scientist can contribute to public policy analysis, if any should exist, as compared to the economist, sociologist, and psychologist? In other words, does the political scientist have a real contribution to offer by virtue of being a political scientist in public policy analysis or should the political scientist simply become say an economist and have done with it. In the exploratory model that follows I hope not to solve these problems but more realistically to generate hypotheses and provide an alternative line of policy direction and analysis.

First of all, we know that certain "sets" (mathematical use defined in the following model) of actors will always have a *latent* potential to formulate and influence policy depending upon systemic differences on the one hand, and on the other, perceived values and stake, levels of arousal and intensity of commitment, and influence potential and power base.

1. Political leaders are indigenous to public policy. Whether they operate in elitist or pluralistic fashion, in one party, two party, multiple party, or no party schemas, through effective or ineffective party policy mechanisms, they possess a latent potential to either shape and decide and/or help direct both the overall nature of public policy and public policy processes.

2. Pressure groups, by whatever name, exist in any milieu. Consequently they too possess, depending upon their comparative power, perceptions, and stake a similar potential. For the purposes of this model we may then include the role of economic elites and variables under pressure group activity, thereby avoiding the immediate quandry of whether economic or political variables most influence public policy. Certainly then, the "multinational" economic forces prevail through sets. The point here is that all possess latent potential to do so through pressure group activity and through political leaders (occasionally causing a "policy gap" which some models ignore).

3. By the same reasoning, public administrators and the administrative process, depending upon the system, type of organization, power base, and degree of administrative discretion, will either help make and decide public policy, influence policy, and/or implement policy. To illustrate, a public administrator might have considerably more potential to influence public policy in a developing nation or say in the U.S.S.R., because of the relatively increased concentration of power and relative absence of alternative inputs, than in the United States. However the potential then varies by degree and not by kind.

4. Due to differences across and within systems, the functions of propaganda and policy communications should be divorced from mass publics in general. The capability for organized propaganda to influence the policy climate or specific policy should be included as a basic and separate variable which is dependant upon systemic differences. By propaganda, it is meant the again latent potential of mass media, government, etc., those possessing the latent influence to shape, sell, or submerge public opinion.

5. Again depending upon which system we are studying or on differences within systems, the public, in terms of *individual* opinion and attitude formation and *aggregate* consensus as separate from pressure group activity which would lie somewhere in between, has a latent potential to effect or be effected by public policy. Therefore, these five sets make up the inputs of policy nature and specific policy(s) and in turn are effected by the policy climate and specific policy(s). Only their relative weights, propensity for action, and structural variables vary. Furthermore, we may hypothesize that these sets are essentially nonoverlapping classifications since their boundaries may be determined by the frequency and intensity of their interactions in comparison to each other.

In addition to the potential influence these five sets will possess, their values and response, and action capability, also obviously vary. Thus any model must incorporate both influence and values which can incorporate responses. As a result, the problems of symbolic as well as tangible policy impact, nonrational and irrational as well as rational behavior, and feedback, can at least be partially reduced and studied for value perceptions encompass these cognitive processes. Also the problem of resource availability and appraisal as well as resource allocation can thereby be included. Any formulation of policy or specific policy is limited to some extent by propensity to spend, consume, and create. However since policies may be unrealistic and/or overestimate or rationalize what can be done on relative resources, these factors are an integral part of value perceptions and policy analysis. Thus while we perhaps cannot quantify values or what is best per se, which are two separate items, we can nevertheless attempt to quantify value perceptions of principal sets through survey research, simulation and gaming, context analysis, and role analysis, including biopsychological and psychorational as well as more verbalized behavior. In other words, we can attempt to either directly study, or replicate conditions for study, the sets that are deemed to be active in policy(s). In the process, we can hope to better quantify the mix of values to actions. In turn, for those who so wish, then, at least some empirical basis is provided for comparative values of what "should be."

Therefore, the two basic variables that become necessary to understand these sets are values and influence; values and influence are both a function of time and are subject to modification by responses to policy outcomes (material and symbolic) and relative policy environment. Again the use of the word "values" is controversial; it is meant here not in the normative sense but as predispositions: outcome/response or S:O:R relationships of those sets and actors within sets. Parenthetically, the political scientist by virtue of his particular skills, tools, and interests should be able to contribute specifically to the study of these variables as they relate to political leaders and partisan politics and public administrators and administrative processes, whereas they share interests with economists, psychologists, etc., on pressure groups, propaganda, and public opinion. This also presents an opportunity to further link subdisciplines within political science since although policy interests will vary across cultures and systems, e.g., comparative politics, American government, urban, international relations, public administration, etc., each perspective can blend into varying perspectives on similar goals and research. Obviously none of these academic areas are self-exclusive, for each can profit from interdisciplinary attention and from the point of view of the political scientist, within disciplinary interests.

A Quantum Dynamics Policy Model

The word quantum stems from the Latin "how much." Here quantum theory will be utilized as an analogy for policy dynamics. The equation $e = hf$, formulated by Max Planck (Nobel Prize-winning German physicist), states that energy (e) in terms of units equals Planck's constant (h), the proportional relation between quantum energy and frequency, times the frequency, f. For a quantum policy model, e means policy as energy, h means proportionate policy structure, and f the frequency or input/output of our sets. Frequency, of course, is not continuous or equal appearing in quantum theory or in public policy either. Thus, our analogy suggests that policy (or non-policy) is not a product, but a dynamic of change, over time, allocation, and source for feedback, which is related to type and fit of policy structure through which operate any one or combination of sets, rarely evenly but in discontinuous action reflecting potential, intensity, and change. Policy analysis, then, should not be analyzed by studying it as if it were a constant process leading to a result but as a function of change over time, so that to study any given point is really a "slice" in time and action and that action varies and covaries by sets.

This is not an exercise in mathematical semantics but a means to convey the dynamics of policy and a way to show the relationships of sets to policy and policy to sets. Set theory is simply an exercise in logic. In effect, the operationable procedures are then to quantify the "how much" of their involvement and interaction.

Set theory involves two methods stating the elements of a set.[31] The roster method lists all members in a set where for example, *PL* (political leaders) = $(P_1, P_2, \ldots P_N)$ or in other words a finite set, P_1 = Person 1, Person 2 is P_2 through P_N or the total set. The defining property method indicates a property that the objects having this property, and only those having this property, are members of the set, or where *V* (values) would then be the shared values of political leaders, so V_{PL} would be read the values of political leaders is the set of those elements *V* such that they are shared values held by political leaders. Obviously, not all political leaders will share one common value or to the same degree, rather we mean the *prevailing* consensus. Influence then will be the sum or union of that which political leaders can bring to bear on policy. It too will vary according to political, academic, and sociological variables. Yet there will be a resulting net prevailing influence to effect policy. To use an example, pressure groups' values and influence will vary across and within systems. Next, those that effect or are effected by policy will depend upon those which are activated by values and their relative influence. Thus, there will be variance within and between sets and therefore we are talking about prevailing mean scores. Thus, for our purposes, PL = political leaders, PA = public administrators, PG = pressure groups, PR = propaganda and PO = public opinion. The defining property method then can be used to define *V*, values and *I*, influence.

$FPL = f(V_{PL}, I_{PL})$ where *FPL* stands for the frequency function of political leaders and where: $\qquad(1.1)$

V_{PL} = the values of political leaders toward and as a consequence of public policy

I_{PL} = the potential influence of political leaders on and as a result of public policy

or

$$FPA = f(V_{PA}, I_{PA}) \qquad (1.2)$$

$$FPG = f(V_{PG}, I_{PG}) \tag{1.3}$$

$$FPR = f(V_{PR}, I_{PR}) \tag{1.4}$$

$$FPO = f(V_{PO}, I_{PO}) \tag{1.5}$$

Thus:

PUBLIC POLICY $= f(FPL, FPA, FPG, FPR, FPO)$.

Therefore, this exploratory model can generate hypotheses across and within systems depending on the function of each set's involvement in the first place and by the relationship in terms of properties of each set in the second. Policy can thereby be viewed in a specific context but also in a general contextual sense since these sets both comprise policy and according to their variance make up the total policy environment. Finally, public policy can also be analyzed as an *independent* variable which reflects the function of feedback.

Since values and influence are modified by response we can say, for example, that

$$\left\{ \begin{array}{l} V_{PL} = f(\text{Public Policy}, V_{PA}, I_{PA}, V_{PG}, V_{PR}, I_{PR}, V_{PO}, I_{PO}) \\ I_{PL} = f(\text{Public Policy}). \end{array} \right\}$$

In our next section, the problems of methodology and quantifying values and influence are discussed.

Methodology and Policy Analysis

A Phenomenal Problem

The social scientist and certainly the political scientist have come a long way in the sharpening and refinement of their methodological skills, empirical testing, and computer analysis. Yet they still have a comparatively long way to go before they can feel completely confident that their operationalization of knowledge of human behavior and political and policy phenomenon is satisfactory, or that they can match, if ever, the research expectations of the "hard" scientists.

Part of the problem lies with the type of knowledge and data with which the political scientist and student of public policy is concerned. The hard scientist, e.g., the chemist, physicist, biologist, has the enormous research advantage of dealing with relatively predictable and "rational" non-human phenomena. He can reasonably expect certain replicatory interactions and patterns of action that are more quantifiable in his studies and analysis. In dealing with human behavior, however, we are dealing with a still vastly unexplored research frontier. Man can be relatively explainable and predictable in the aggregate (i.e., set) and only marginally so in the individual.

To illustrate, we can research how members of a pressure group feel about a certain policy by analyzing the variance of their collective responses, but there is inherent difficulty from a statistical probability point of view in isolating the behavior of any one member of that group. Furthermore, that member can be non-rational or irrational and so we get into research problems in the subconscious area, a still expanding area of knowledge. Moreover, we are just beginning to engage in nonverbal behavioral research. We have not even yet begun to any extent to explore nonverbal behavior or for that matter biopsychological behavior. Once an attitude has been verbalized to the point of response, the original intensity, emotion, and time of stimulus may have changed or been partially forgotten or clouded. Consequently, since most of our present studies are based on verbalized behavior we may find it even more difficult to understand public policy values and policies if we only engage in ex post facto studies. Little attention has also been paid to stimuli such as gossip, rumor, humor, policy symbols, and energy arousal levels, particularly in relation to formulating and changing policy values. Finally, there are in reality no limits to policy, where it begins and ends. Decision-making and attitude and value formation are a complex process of interactions, stimuli, and responses. Kurt Lewin, for example, conceptualized his "funnel of causality" (very useful in voting studies), that the decision itself is really the spout of the funnel and the influences on that decision go backward in time in ever widening fashion depending upon one's life spaces or "valences."[3][2] But this is what can make policy analysis exciting as well as frustrating, the opportunity and the challenge are fresh and potentially vastly rewarding.

A Problem of Scaling

One immediate problem, in terms of general methodology, is the limitation placed upon understanding human phenomena by data. Unlike the hard sciences, most of the data which the social scientist has to work are limited to nominal and ordinal scaling. To refresh the reader's memory, a nominal scale essentially organizes data into either/or, an ordinal scale into more or less, while the more advanced interval and ratio scales assume data that can also be multiplied and divided. As we know, while these mathematical distinctions may seem simplistic and in themselves not limiting, in reality, and in terms of empirical research, if you can only do the first two it is roughly analogous to being able to determine a falling object's relationship to gravity without being able to precisely measure the rate or impact of the fall.

Think of a grading system. A student will either pass or fail, e.g., nominal data; receive an A through F and we know that a B is higher than a D but for the moment not how much more, e.g., ordinal data; but if we know that there are equal appearing intervals of ten between grades, we can now say how much more or less one grade is to another, e.g., interval data; and finally if we know that the entire system is based upon zero to one hundred then we can know how many times each and all grades are compared to one another, e.g., ratio data. If we apply this to human behavior and policy analysis, it would mean that we could, for example, precisely measure perceptions on power, on priorities, on rational utility wins and losses, on symbolic expectations, and on satisfaction, apathy, and alienation. Yet, if we are to *fully* understand, explain, predict, and/or prescribe public policy, this is precisely what must eventually be possible. Therefore, given the very nature of research into human behavior as compared to physical behavior in the hard sciences, perhaps the social scientist and the political scientist face an inherent self-limiting research barrier.

To illustrate, let us assume that a particular public policy benefits some and penalizes others. While we can rank order who got more and who got less, we cannot be completely precise in saying by how much unless we limit our definition to resource allocation and manipulation. Or if we are to study the use of power in shaping policy, we cannot precisely say how one group or broker perceives values in *exactly* the same way another group or broker does. If we are also to be concerned with prescriptive public policy analysis, then to some extent our value judgments and prescribed values must also be essentially less than initially completely rational and potentially intuitive.

Yet these limitations on current state of knowledge and research capability do not preclude or vitiate the necessity for increased attention to descriptive policy analysis and prescriptive *empirical* policy analysis. For other social sciences are making inroads and advances in these directions and political science could well nigh be left behind (again) and there *are* ways and means now available or immediately available to study public policy. And to know when and where an object falls and have at least some idea how, can be important in relation to policy.

The Methodological Arsenal

While there are specific areas of public policy and policy analysis that the political scientist qua political scientist can affectively concentrate upon and for which he is particularly well equipped, to think about the quantum dynamics policy model in the preceding section, nevertheless his methodology in so doing is not unique from the general methodological arsenal indigenous to most social sciences. In fact, the majority of our current methodologies were originated in other sciences before political science, which is all the more reason now that the political scientist should try to lead the way. Gaming was developed in the 1940s in economics and by the military, content analysis by sociologists and economists as well as by political scientists, laboratory simulation essentially by sociologists, predisposition/response models and field studies by psychologists, and survey design by virtually all disciplines. The political scientist can claim methodological distinction, however, in the way he utilizes methodology, by the kind of questions with which he is concerned and formulates, and because of the phenomenon and goals in which he is interested. Thus, while the political scientist may draw from the same methodological arsenal utilized by social scientists in general, he has and will have to develop theories, models, and methodological expertise for public policy analysis for his own goals (and not simply become say an economist as some suggest, a point to which we shall return). Moreover, since many methodological tools and models were "borrowed" from other sciences, particularly those in relation to the natural sciences, they occasionally are not as effective as they could be since they were designed for other purposes. Therefore the political scientist, where necessary, should again seek to develop new skills that best meet his methodological needs.

Several methodologies in particular, assuming refinement and sophistication continue, are worth closer examination in relation to policy analysis. Simulation and gaming can and are used to study probability choices and value priorities. Gaming can develop the systematic formulation of values and decisions in a policy context or for policy planning. Simulation can offer analysis of respondents who are not aware that they are the basis for study or if aware, can be controlled for stimuli and response. Embryonic use of television, one-way mirrors, and correlating galvonic skin responses and kinetics to formal behavior also suggests a fruitful addition to simulation to gather additional data and knowledge of priorities and reactions to values and perceptions of both policy inputs and outcomes. Role theory and role playing are naturally related. It would be particularly beneficial, if we can gain increasing access, to have politicians, public administrators, and pressure group leaders actually engage in role playing under observation. Even without such direct access, and it is very difficult to gain such access (including security problems), the more we can understand of roles in policy, the relationship of what ought to be and what actually is, the more effective we can be as social scientists and political scientists.

Survey design already has an important and sophisticated heritage in methodology. Yet we must also find ways to conduct surveys while the decision-making process and policy in the first instance, and immediate response to perceive policy outcome in the second instance, are actually occurring rather than ex post facto. Again this poses an immediate and serious problem of access. To be fair, however, part of the problem is created by political scientists in particular since we have deliberately ignored the real world in many cases for too long. Content analysis, although in some current disregard, has utility in examining the implications of values in prior documentation and communications. Case studies will also continue to play an important and useful role in policy analysis. They should simply not be the *only* research tool.

Political scientists are also developing perceptual and personality studies of actors directly involved in the policy arena. Work such as that by Lewis Anthony Dexter, Robert E. Lane, or J. David Barber on politicians, or John C. Wahlke and Donald R. Mathews on legislative roles, or Deil Wright and Rufus Miles on public administrators can yield important insights on why policy decisionmakers are the way they are and arrive at their value and belief systems in the first place.[33] This is obviously important for such insights help determine why one policy is preferred over another or how power to determine policy is used. In one recent study, findings indicated that by matching perceptions of elected politicians vis-à-vis senior career public administrators, both sets of actors tend to view each other with suspicion, marginal reciprocal understanding, and conflict on perceived roles, although they agree on general policy goals. Furthermore, each sample claimed that they best represented the public interest and each indicated that they operated by different time referents, politicians on a short-time basis and administrators on a more long-range level. If this particular exploratory research is true, then public policy is going to be confused, perhaps inefficient, and less than rational almost by definition.[34]

Additionally, operations research, PPBS, cost/benefit analysis, cybernetics and information systems, beyond the purview of our present discussion, can reasonably assess inputs/ouputs of specific policy(s), while newer horizons in methodology such as the potential in body kinetics, psychodrama, role playing, and informal communications, in addition to needed refinements in our present methodological tools, offer exciting promise in further increasing our understanding of both descriptive and prescriptive public policy. What relation, for example, is there between body kinetics and perceptions when verbalizing opinions to a particular policy? Or how can we utilize our observations of phenomenon at the place in time that the individual is most actively committed to the policy process and policy value formation?

Currently, we are also in the third generation of computers. The fourth generation, when it arrives, may geometrically increase our research potential. Meantime, the newer computer programs such as MAC (Multiple Analysis Interaction) and AID (Automatic Interaction Detector) have been developed to help overcome the problems of data and scaling limitations by essentially matching relatively mathematically sophisticated programs to less rigorous data assumptions.

Summary

The political scientist has a considerable methodological arsenal now to pursue more sophisticated descriptive and prescriptive policy analysis and research with considerably more potential in relatively unexplored new tools and skills. Time is on our side. Symbolism, feedback, and values in policy can at least be explored and reasonably tested if for no other reason than to generate new hypotheses and data (a point Zeigler makes in Chapter 5). In short, we should seek a higher level of integration in policy analysis.

Relevancy, the Political Scientist, and the Social Sciences

The call for relevancy actually encompasses many arguments, not only theoretical v. applied and descriptive v. prescriptive research, which have already been touched upon and to which we shall return in the following chapters, but also in relation to professional associations and publications, training and skills, and interdisciplinary and intradisciplinary orientation. In brief, political science and the political scientist, faculty and students, stand at various crossroads in time and need new directions pursuant to public policy and public policy analysis.

Relevancy by Association

The professional associations of political scientists, such as the American Political Science Association or the various regional and local associations and ad hoc conferences, have only infrequently concerned themselves with applied policy research and/or real policy involvement. The abortive 1950 American Political Science Association report on "reforming political parties" (which Stedman discusses in Chapter 4) was one of the relatively few attempts at systematic involvement and its subsequent repudiation was a function of its lack of quality rather than an argument against involvement per se. For that matter, it is only fairly recently that policy qua policy has been included as a major and pertinent topic in our meetings. Also, nonpolitical scientists, such as fellow social scientists in general, and policymakers from government and pressure groups are only occasionally asked to participate and are mostly excluded from general membership. Other social sciences, particularly economics, and associations related to political science such as the American Society for Public Administration, incorporate much more direct interaction with policymakers. The ASPA, as an example, includes policymakers, representatives from civic groups, and public administrators in its membership, its seminars, and its research publications. Furthermore, in the area of publications, the leading political science journals again generally exclude nonpracticing professional political scientists from their editorial boards and from publication. Of course, pure academic research by definition helps exclude nonprofessionals and accomplishes a vital purpose in the subsequent exchange and dialogue of academic ideas in itself and nonprofessional political scientists have not to date exactly beaten down the doors by offering high quality research for publication but many of us would agree that we would benefit by trying to incorporate more involvement with policy-making types in both our associations and research. Golembiewski, in Chapter 3, writes that there is such a need and that such involvement has paid handsome dividends between scholars of public administration and public administrators and between business schools and business life. Robert Lane mentions an interesting idea, that the APSA should provide a kind of information brokerage system on policy matters including data on research needs of government people and their research availability and capacity.[35]

Naturally I am not advocating involvement by cause, partisanship, or polemic. Some in our professional associations now would turn them into advocate roles which would in all probability result in more fragmentation, division, and increased impotency. However, this danger can be minimized by mature consensus and cannot preclude the increased dividends that rational interaction has to offer. Indirectly, rational involvement would help answer the problem of access, theoretical and applied, to policymakers discussed earlier. It might also be feasible to consider direct incentives to consider exploring ways for the political scientist to receive academic credit and incentives over and above publications and individual leaves of absence for participating in policy affairs. Dror writes that the political scientist should help make the policymaker more rational and this possibility is greatly enhanced through contact, or at least by generating new data for policy analysis.[36] Perhaps we should also consider organizing policy "task forces" for those with mutual interest to study and/or relate to policy affairs. Finally, we should at least consider encouraging other social scientists into contributing more to our associations, publications, and task forces.

Relevancy in the Training of
a Political Scientist

The urge to jump aboard the policy bandwagon is well near irresistable. Public policy, by whatever name, policy sciences, public policy, policy analysis, etc., is "in" for the seventies and eighties. New departments bearing these labels, new policy-oriented programs, new institutes, new consortiums, new majors, new interdisciplinary programs, new courses, and at the very least attaching and incorporating policy to existing courses and programs have swept political science. Moreover, the books, journals, and articles of political science have also become increasingly policy oriented. Several more recently created publications such as the *Policy Studies Journal* (begun in 1971) are devoted exclusively to policy questions.

Nevertheless, while the direction is healthy, many in political science have the uneasy feeling that the quantum leap is being made into new training and emphases without careful analysis and preexamination. Currently training and emphases seem to fall into two disparate areas, almost as if in polarization. On one hand, the political scientist and particularly the student is expected to qualify, if not become expert, in economics, sociology, psychology, engineering, law, or whatever, since there is no general consensus, in a broad interdisciplinary fashion. On the other hand, political scientists, and particularly the student, is expected to become highly specialized. For example, they are expected to become and perhaps devote their lives to housing policy or health delivery administration or ecology or welfare policy and, in the process, whatever happened to the political scientist. It has been previously suggested that a problem already has existed in that policy researchers often talk past each other. Thus, either way we may produce a generation of amateur economists, biologists, mathematicians, and the like who know a little something about a lot of interdisciplinary areas or highly specialized experts in very limited areas. Either way, political science may be further disintegrated and lose conceptual focus.

Most current "policy" programs require a year or so of economics, roughly a year in quantitative analysis, perhaps some biology, some planning, some engineering, or psychology, or accounting, or the like. Most generally first require core training followed by training in specific policy areas. Here, Dye, Golembiewski, and Stedman argue for increased interdisciplinary emphasis and training. There are valid reasons for this eclecticism and for these approaches but there are also dangers in addition to either becoming too amateurish or too specialized. First, they may lead us further from a general theory and possibly methodology for public policy. We again may simply talk past one another. Furthermore, these approaches may tend to blur if not disintegrate subareas within political science such as International Relations, American Government, Political Theory, etc., which have already led to a certain degree of myopia in relation to the whole of political science.

Still, policy training and policy exposure is germane and crucial; the question becomes how can we best accomplish these purposes. One interesting possibility has been suggested, that for these and dissertations, a student should be permitted to engage in team policy research. The student would engage in policy research with other students with a similar policy research purpose. Another possibility might be to extend this idea further and allow an option for its student to work with fellow students in other disciplines on a common policy paper and so incorporate appropriate interdisciplinary skills and talents toward integrated policy research. Perhaps the feasibility of further plugging students into actual policy slots as participant observers should also be considered.

Intradisciplinary training and foci might also be reviewed. Now a certain sense of xenophobia sets in between those interested in socialization or urban or American or comparative politics, etc. There should be some central paradigm that tends to integrate the parts into the whole of political science. The perspective here is that the study of public policy can profit from varying inputs and intradisciplinary interests and research but that the goals inherent to policy analysis offer an umbrella for differing pursuits and cut across subareas. What we should avoid is simply ceasing to be political scientists in favor of being interdisciplinary eclectics as such. If boundaries are drawn either too narrowly or too broadly then the possibilities of a general theory for public policy will be decreased.

Caveat Emptor

Herbert Simon has warned that public policy could swallow all of political science.[37] Certainly there is accelerating movement in this direction, sometimes functional and sometimes perhaps dysfunctional. The commitment of the political scientist to public policy and public policy analysis must seek greater organization and conceptual clarity. It must be more than fashion or fad. In turn, public policy offers the increased central identifying theme and enlarged raison d'être from which political science can profit, and in the process offer means to bridge intradisciplinary and interdisciplinary gaps.

It has already been suggested where the political scientist can most affectively make his particular academic input and contribution and the spinoff questions of relevancy have been raised. A further important question lies in the extent and degree of commitment to public policy that should be engaged in by political science. Some do indeed argue that public policy *is* political science, the totality of political science. Others believe that political science as a whole or by certain subareas should have little or nothing to do with public policy analysis. Here all agree that political science must engage in greater commitment to public policy, not to the extent of total immersion but rather by increased degree.

All suggest that oftentimes past focus and research have raised the wrong questions, and furthermore, that important linkages have been relatively neglected. In any case, the central linkages of political leaders and parties, public administration and administrative process, and pressure groups, have been specifically incorporated in this volume both to reflect on considerations of our quantum dynamics policy model and to systematically study each area vis-à-vis public policy. Dye writes on policy research parameters, Golembiewski on public administration, Stedman on parties, and Zeigler and Boss on pressure groups, (and the interaction to specific policy formulation) in an empirical setting. Each attempts to show both limitations and new directions in the continuing political science/public policy interface.

There is nevertheless disagreement within the parameters of political science's commitment to public policy, by area, by research, and by degree. Therefore, in the final analysis, we hope that the reader, particularly the student reader, will profit by these arguments in terms of increased conceptual clarity and increased sophistication, and make up his own mind.

Notes

1. Phillip O. Foss, "Policy Analysis and the Political Science Profession," *Policy Studies Journal* 2 (Autumn 1973):69.

2. Robert E. Lane, "Social Science Research and Public Policy," *Policy Studies Journal* (Autumn 1972):103-106.

3. For example see, Harold D. Lasswell, *A Pre-View of Policy Sciences* (New York: American Elseview, 1971).

4. Yehezkel Dror, "Some Diverse Approaches to Policy Analysis," *Policy Studies Journal* 1 (Summer 1973):258-60.

5. Ibid.

6. Larry L. Wade, *The Elements of Public Policy* (Columbus, Ohio: Charles E. Merrill, 1972).

7. See David A. Easton, *A Systems Analysis of Political Life* (New York: Wiley, 1965).

8. Ibid., pp. 343-44.

9. Thomas R. Dye, *Politics in States and Communities* (Englewood Cliffs, New Jersey: Prentice-Hall, 1969), pp. 9-10.

10. See Ira Sharkansky, *Public Administration: Policy-making in Government Agencies* (Chicago: Markham, 1970).

11. Randall Ripley, *The Politics of Economic and Human Resource Development* (Indianapolis, New York: Bobbs-Merrill, 1972).

12. See respectively, Gabriel A. Almond and James S. Coleman, *The Politics of the Developing Areas* (Princeton: Princeton University Press, 1960); Gabriel A. Almond and G. Bingham Powell, Jr., *Comparative Politics: A Developmental Approach* (Boston: Little, Brown, 1966).

13. Kenneth M. Dolbeare, Murray J. Edelman, and Patricia Dolbeare, *Institutions, Policies and Goals: A Reader in American Politics* (Boston: D.C. Heath, 1973).

14. For examples see, Robert L. Lineberry and Edmund P. Fowler, "Reformism and Public Policies in American Cities," *American Political Science Review* (September 1967); Dye, *Politics in States.*

15. C. Wright Mills, *The Power Elite* (London, Oxford, New York: Oxford University Press, 1956); Floyd Hunter, *Community Power Structure* (Chapel Hill, North Carolina: University of North Carolina Press, 1953); Edward C. Banfield and James Q. Wilson, *City Politics* (Cambridge, Mass.: Harvard University Press, 1963); Peter Bachrach and Morton Baratz, "Two Faces of Power," *American Political Science Review* 56 (December 1962):947-53.

16. See Robert A. Dahl, *Who Governs?* (New Haven, Conn.: Yale University Press, 1961) or Nelson A. Polsby, "How to Study Community Power: The Pluralist Alternative," *Journal of Politics* 21 (August 1960):474-84.

17. Robert E. Agger, Daniel Goldrich, and Bert E. Swanson, *The Rulers and the Ruled* (New York: Wiley, 1964).

18. Joyce M. Mitchell, and William C. Mitchell, *Political Analysis and Public Policy* (Chicago: Rand McNally, 1969).

19. Theodore J. Lowi, "American Business, Public Policy, Case-Studies and Political Theory," *World Politics* 16 (July 1964):677-715.

20. James A. Robinson and R. Roger Majak, "The Theory of Decision-Making," in Charlesworth (ed.), *Contemporary Political Analysis*, pp. 184-88.

21. Agger, Goldrich, and Swanson, *Rulers and Ruled*, pp. 40-51.

22. Thomas J. Anton, *The Politics of State Expenditure in Illinois* (Urbana, Ill.: University of Illinois Press, 1966); Aaron B. Wildavsky, *The Politics of the Budgetary Process* (Boston: Little, Brown, 1964); Richard F. Fenno, *The Power of the Purse* (Boston: Little, Brown, 1966).

23. Peter B. Natchez and Irvin C. Bupp, "Policy and Priority in the Budgetary Process," *American Political Science Review* 3 (September 1973):951-63.

24. See Norman R. Luttbeg and L. Harmon Zeigler, "Attitude Consensus and Conflict in an Interest Group: An Assessment of Cohesion," *Public Opinion and Public Policy: Models of Political Linkage* (Homewood, Ill.: Dorsey, 1968) or David Truman, *The Governmental Process* (New York: Alfred A. Knopf, 1951).

25. Austin Ranney (ed.), *Political Science and Public Policy* (Chicago: Markham, 1968), p. 7.

26. James Rosenau, "Public Policy," in Ranney (ed.), *Political Science*, p. 222.

27. Ripley, *Politics of Economic and Human Resource*, p. 15.

28. Charles A. McClelland, "Applications of General Systems Theory in International Relations," in James N. Rosenau (ed.), *International Politics and Foreign Policy* (New York: The Free Press, 1961), p. 414.

29. For a detailed discussion on Parsons see, William C. Mitchell, *Sociological Analysis and Politics* (Englewood Cliffs, New Jersey: Prentice-Hall, 1967), pp. 77-81.

30. Lasswell, *Pre-View of Policy Sciences*, p. 18.

31. For an interesting application of set theory to parties' analysis see, John H. Kessel, *The Goldwater Coalition: Republican Strategies in 1964* (Indianapolis, New York: Bobbs-Merrill, 1968).

32. Kurt Lewin, *Field Theory and Social Science* (New York: Harper, 1951).

33. See Lewis Anthony Dexter, "The Representative in His District," in Nelson W. Polsby, Robert A. Bentler, and Paul A. Smith (eds.), *Politics and Social Life* (Boston: Houghton Mifflin, 1963); Robert E. Lane, *Political Man* (Riverside, New Jersey: The Free Press, 1972); James David Barber, *The Presidential Character* (Englewood Cliffs, New Jersey: Prentice-Hall, 1972); John C. Wahlke, Heinz Eulau, William Buchanan, and LeRoy C. Ferguson, *The Legislative System* (New York: John Wiley, 1962); Donald R. Mathews, *U.S. Senators and Their World* (Chapel Hill, North Carolina: University of North Carolina Press, 1960); Rufus E. Miles, Jr., "Administrative Adaptability to Political Change," *Public Administration Review* (September 1965):221-25; and Deil Wright has been conducting surveys on attitudes of public administrators.

34. Robert N. Spadaro, "Role Perceptions of Politicians Vis-à-vis Public Administrators: Parameters For Public Policy," *The Western Political Quarterly* (December 1973):717-25.

35. Lane, "Social Science Research and Public Policy," pp. 107-11.

36. Dror, "Some Diverse Approaches."

37. Herbert A. Simon, "A Comment on the 'Science of Public Administration'," *Public Administration Review* 7 (Summer 1947):202.

2

Political Science and Public Policy: Challenge to a Discipline

Thomas R. Dye

Policy Analysis in Political Science

Policy analysis is finding out what governments do, why they do it, and what difference it makes. More complex definitions can be found in the academic literature. But they boil down to the same thing—the description and explanation of the causes and consequences of government activity.

Governments do many things—in national defense, foreign relations, education, welfare, health, the environment, police protection, transportation, housing, urban development, taxing, spending, and so on. Indeed, simply finding out what governments are doing in so many different fields is a formidable task. Explaining why governments do what they do, and trying to learn what the consequences and impact of these many diverse activities are for society, may be an impossible task for political science. We shall return to the problems confronting policy-oriented political scientists later in this chapter.

Policy analysis is not really a new concern of political science; Aristotle revealed an interest in the laws of different polities, the forces shaping these laws, and the impact of these laws on society. Yet until recently the major focus of political science has not been on policies themselves, but rather on institutional structures and their philosophical justifications, and on political behaviors and processes.

"Traditional" political science focused its attention primarily on the institutional structure and philosophical justification of government. This involved the study of constitutional arrangements, such as federalism, separation of power, and judicial review; powers and duties of official bodies, such as Congress, president, and courts; intergovernmental relations; and the organization and operation of legislative, executive, and judicial agencies. Traditional studies described the *institutions* in which public policy was formulated. But unfortunately the linkages between important institutional arrangements and the content of public policy were largely unexplored.

Modern "behavioral" political science focused its attention primarily on the processes and behaviors associated with government. This involved the study of the sociological and psychological bases of individual and group political behavior; the determinants of voting and other political activities; the func-

31

tioning of interest groups and political parties; and the description of various processes and behaviors in the legislative, executive and judicial arenas. While this approach described the *processes* by which public policy was determined, it did not deal directly with the linkages between various processes and behaviors and the content of public policy.

In recent years, "behavioralism" has come under attack as "dry," "irrelevant," even "immoral" because it does not confront the really important social issues facing the nation. Unfortunately, many students of politics came to believe that the only alternative to a scientific, behavioral political science was advocacy and activism—a radical vision of a "new" political science. They rejected scientific description, explanation, and understanding in favor of rhetoric, persuasion, organization, and activism. Indeed, the "post-behavior" era was said to include a rejection of scientific methodology because of its irrelevance to contemporary problems confronting American society.

But the new policy analysis movement in political science offers scholars and students the opportunity to address critical policy issues without abandoning our commitment to scientific inquiry. Policy analysis involves the systematic identification of the causes and consequences of government activity, the use of scientific standards of inference, and the search for reliability and generality of knowledge in the form of systematic theory. Perhaps this is not as much "fun" as rhetoric, rap sessions, demonstrations, or confrontations. But policy analysis offers "the thinking man's response" to demands that political science become more "relevant" to the problems of our society.[1]

Policy research can involve investigation of either the causes or consequences of government policies and programs. In studies of the *causes* of public policy, public policies themselves are the "dependent variables" and analysts seek to explain these policies by reference to "independent variables"—social, economic, or political forces in society which are hypothesized as determinants of public policy. Let us label such research as "policy determination" research. In studies of the *consequences* of public policy, public policies are the "independent variables" and the "dependent variables" are social, economic, or political conditions in society which are hypothesized to be affected by public policy. Let us label such research as "policy impact" research.

The new interest in public policy in political science is reflected in new courses and curricula in public policy studies, new graduate programs and research institutes (including the Harvard Graduate Program in Public Policy; the Graduate School of Public Affairs at the University of California at Berkeley; the Institute of Public Policy Studies at the University of Michigan; the Lyndon B. Johnson School of Public Affairs at the University of Texas); new organizations and journals in the discipline (including the Policy Studies Organization and the *Policy Studies Journal*); and a host of articles and books marking the shift of concern in political science from institutions, processes, and behaviors to public policies.

The Myopia of Political Science

Certainly the recent progress in policy studies in political science has been encouraging. Yet there are serious obstacles to the development of a systematic policy science within the discipline of political science. Let me describe two of these obstacles, which I have labeled "the professional and ideological myopia of political science."

Professional Myopia

The professional myopia of political science is the narrow and restricted definition of the boundaries of the discipline—a definition which limits the attention of political scientists to governmental institutions and political processes. The professional preoccupation of political scientists has been with the characteristics of political systems. The result is a professional predisposition to assert the importance of political system characteristics in determining the causes and consequences of public policy. For example, political scientists may explain public policy in terms of successful interest group lobbying, or presidential influence in Congress, or the strength or weakness of government in dealing with state legislators, or the cohesion of the Democratic or Republican parties in Congress, or the extent of malapportionment in the states, or the effects of the security system in congressional committee activity, or the constitutional arrangements limiting or augmenting the powers of congress, courts, or the president. But if political science is to become a *policy science*, political scientists must be prepared to search for the determinants of public policy among economic, social, cultural, historical, and technological factors, as well as political system characteristics. Political scientists must also be prepared to examine the consequences of public policies in areas as diverse as education, welfare, health, housing, the environment, national defense, the economy, and foreign affairs. Clearly, then, for political science to become a policy science, it must discard narrow definitions of what is political. Political scientists must be prepared to examine the full range of forces shaping public policy, whether they are "political" or not.

This preoccupation of political science with governmental institutions and political processes has even produced a defensiveness in the political science literature on public policy—a marked professional reluctance to accept results which show that underlying economic or social or environmental or technological factors are more influential in determining the causes or consequences of public policies than traditional political system characteristics.

Ideological Myopia

The ideological myopia of political science is the prevailing ideological commitment of the discipline to democratic "pluralism." The pluralist ideology which prevades our discipline directs the attention of the political scientist to political participation, electoral processes and behaviors, interest group activity, and party competition, because these processes are highly valued in pluralist political theory. The result is an ideological predisposition of political scientists to assert the importance of participation and competition in determining the causes and consequences of public policies. Yet, despite the importance of participation, competition, and equality as *political values*, we must not make the mistake of assuming that they are influential *determinants of public policy*. Moreover, there is an ideological predisposition among political scientists to believe that democratic-pluralist political systems produce "better" public policies than non-pluralistic systems—quality educational programs, liberal welfare benefits, comprehensive health care, progressive tax schemes, etc.

These professional and ideological predispositions operate to reinforce each other. Political scientists are predisposed to believe that political system characteristics are important determinants of the causes and consequences of public policies; and that competition, participation, and equality in representation produce "good" public policies. Either of these propositions *may* be correct. It is not my intention to dispute them. My point is that a systematic policy science must treat these propositions as *hypotheses* to be tested, not as prior *assumptions*. My plea is for a scientific posture in political science which designs policy research in such a way so as to control, insofar as possible, our predispositions and values.

Some Discomforting Findings—
Cities, States, and Nations

Policy *analysis* is still in its infancy. Most of our findings regarding the causes and consequences of government activity are still very tentative and most of our theories and models are still very underdeveloped. However, some initial studies of the determinants of public policy raise serious doubts about the traditional assumptions of political scientists—assumptions regarding (1) the importance of political system characteristics as determinants of public policy and (2) the influence of democratic pluralist political structures on the content of public policy.

The purpose of this chapter is twofold. First, we will survey some policy research studies involving cities, states, and nations—studies which raise doubts about these traditional assumptions. The really remarkable fact is that different scholars working with different types of political systems—cities, states, and nations—have all produced roughly similar findings regarding the influence of political system characteristics on the content of public policy. Second, we will raise questions concerning the direction of policy research.

Let us turn first to research on public policy in the American *states*, where many of the key issues were first raised. Then we will briefly examine the growing body of research on policy determinants among American *cities*. Finally, we will examine some really thought-provoking research on the determinants of public policy in capitalist and communist *nations*. The exciting prospect in policy research is that someday all of this research will come together; that scholars will begin to test propositions about the behavior of *political systems*—cities, states, and nations; and that truly general theories of government activity can be developed.

Policy Analysis—The American States

Within the discipline of political science, significant advances in policy analysis have occurred in the field of state and local government. Traditionally this field was not renowned for systematic research; instead, it reflected traditional concerns for governmental institutions and administrative arrangements, party competition and voter participation, and structural reforms. But fifty separate state political systems, and hundreds of community political systems, offered scientifically-minded political scientists an excellent opportunity to employ non-experimental comparative research designs in their studies of the linkages between environmental conditions, political systems, and public policies. Fortunately, if only for the sake of analysis, there are marked differences among the American states in economic development levels, in many political system characteristics, and in a significant range of public policies.

The traditional literature in American state politics instructed students that characteristics of state political systems—particularly two-party competition, voter participation, and apportionment—had a direct bearing on public policy. Since political scientists devoted most of their time to studying what happened *within* the political system, it was natural for them to believe that the political processes and institutions which they studied were important determinants of public policy. Moreover, the belief that competition, participation, and equality in representation had important consequences for public policy also squared with the value placed upon these variables in the prevailing pluralist ideology. States with high voter participation, intense party competition, and fair apportionment—usually northern and midwestern states—suggested a normative model of pluralist democracy, which was expected to produce "good" public policies—liberal welfare benefits, generous educational spending, progressive taxation, advanced health and hospital programs, and so on. In contrast, states with low voter participation, absence of party competition, and unfair apportionment—usually southern states—suggested a type of political system which was widely deplored among American political scientists. Moreover, such political systems were believed to produce meager welfare benefits, miserly educational spending, regressive taxation, archaic health and hospital programs, and so on. (It is intellectually fashionable now to regard these beliefs as mere strawmen erected by economic determinists to attack. But at the time these beliefs were central assertions in the state politics literature; assertions which had long been nurtured on the a priori reasoning and case studies of V.O. Key, Jr., Duane Lockhard, John Fenton, and others.[2])

Economic research had suggested very early that the public policies of state and local governments were closely related to their economic resources. Although this economic literature was largely overlooked by political scientists, economists contributed a great deal to the systematic analysis of state and local public policies. Systematic analysis of the economic determinants of state and local government expenditures began with the publication of Solomon Fabricant's *The Trend of Government Activity in the United States Since 1900.*[3] Fabricant found that per capita income, population density, and urbanization explained more than 72 percent of the variation among the states and total state and local spending. Of these three economic variables, he found that *per capita income* showed the strongest relationship to expenditures. Another economist, Glenn Fisher continued Fabricant's analysis of the economic determinants of state and local spending into the 1960s.[4] Fisher added additional economic variables (e.g., percentage of families with less than $2,000 annual income, percentage increase in population, percentage of adult education with less than five years schooling) and was able to explain even more of the interstate differences in state and local spending. Again, like Fabricant, Fisher found that per capita income was the strongest single factor associated with state and local expenditures. Later, economists Sachs and Harris added to this research literature by considering the effect of federal grants-in-aid on state and local government expenditure.[5] They observed that federal grants tended to free the states from the constraints of their own economic resources. Federal grants were "outside money" to state and local government officials, which permitted them to fund programs at levels beyond their own resources. Hence, they noted the decline in the closeness in the relationship in economic resources in state and local spending, particularly in the fields with the heaviest federal involvement: welfare and health.

The traditional state politics literature overlooked this economic research into the determinants of public policy. Nonetheless, some early research in state politics suggested that party competition and voter participation were themselves heavily impacted by economic variables. A number of scholars—Ranney and Kendall, Key, Schlesinger, and Golembiewski, for example[6]—indicated that economic factors affected the level of inter-party competition; they reported statistically significant associations between urbanism, income, industrialization, and classifications of party competition among the states. Knowledge of this linkage between economic forces in the political system *should* have suggested to political scientists that they test to see if competition and participation *independently* affected public policies, or whether both competition and participation and public policy were all determined by economic factors. For example, if it was shown that, in general, wealthy states have more party competition than poor states, then it might turn out that differences in levels of educational spending between competitive and non-competitive states are really a product of the fact that the former are wealthy and the latter are poor. In other words, policy differences between the states might be attributable to wealth rather than to party competition.

When political scientists finally began to shift the focus of their attention to public policy, they immediately challenged many of the traditional notions about the policy impact of some popular political variables—party competition, voter participation, democratic and republican control of state government, and malapportionment. The first hint that these political variables might not be as influential in determining levels of public taxing, spending, benefits, and service, as commonly supposed, came an important research effort by Richard Dawson and James Robinson in 1953. These political scientists examined the linkages between socioeconomic variables (income, urbanization, industrialization), the level of inter-party competition, and nine public welfare policies. They concluded that:

High levels of inter-party competition are highly interrelated both to socio-economic factors and to social welfare legislation, but the degree of inter-party competition does not seem to possess the important intervening influence between socio-economic factors and liberal welfare programs that our original hypothesis and theoretical schemes suggested.[7]

In 1965, I published a comprehensive analysis of public policy in the American states, *Politics, Economics, and the Public.*[8] I described the linkages between four economic development variables (urbanization, industrialization, wealth, and education), four political system characteristics (democratic or republican control of state government, the degree of inter-party competition, the level of voter turn out, and the extent of malapportionment), and over ninety separate policy output measures in education, health, welfare, highways, corrections, taxations, and public regulation. This research produced some findings that were very unsettling for many political scientists (and still are). These four commonly described characteristics of political systems were found to have *less* effect on public policy in the states than environmental variables reflecting the level of economic development. Most of the associations which occur between these political variables and policy outcomes are really a product of the fact that economic development influences *both* political system characteristics and policy outcomes. Of course, I noted several policy areas where political factors remained important, and I also identified certain policy areas where federal programs tended to offset the impact of economic resources on state policies. Yet in the attempt to generalize about the determinants of public policy in the states, I concluded that *on the whole* economic resources were more influential in shaping state policies than any of the political variables previously thought to be important in policy determination. Doubtlessly these findings disturbed scholars who felt more comfortable with the reassuring notion of pluralist democracy that "politics counts."

But the findings themselves—regarded almost as commonplace by economists—were really not as important as the impetus this study gave to the policy analysis movement. A number of scholars were stimulated to systematically reexamine the traditional wisdom of the state politics field. The result was an outpouring of systematic *social science* research which employed rigorous and comparative methods to test propositions about the determinants of public policies, particularly at the state and local levels.[9] New and more sophisticated methodological techniques were introduced;[10] some primitive causal modeling was begun;[11] additional political variables were tested for their policy impact;[12] some policy outputs other than levels of public expenditures and services were examined;[13] changes over time were described and analyzed;[14] some research findings were modified and exceptions to general propositions were described;[15] some more discerning theoretical notions about public policy were developed;[16] and propositions developed at the state level were tested at the municipal level.[17] In short the whole subfield of the discipline of political science grew to maturity in a very short period of time.[18]

State Policy Studies—The Professional Response

Implicit in much of this literature, however, was a noticeable reluctance to accept the view that political system characteristics, particularly those reflecting pluralist values of competition and participation, may possess less policy-relevance than economic resources. Indeed, there appeared to be a great deal of scrambling about by scholars ideologically committed to proving that party competition, voter participation, partisanship, and apportionment do indeed influence public policy.[19] Of course, governmental institutions, administrative arrangements, and political processes may indeed help to determine the content of public policy. This is a question which we must try to answer in our research. But we should not insist that political variables influence policy outcomes simply because our traditional training and wisdom in political science has told us that political variables are important.

Nonetheless, there have been some interesting challenges to the general direction of the findings regarding the influence of economic resources on public policy. Richard Hofferbert studied the relationships between economic resources, political variables, and public policy in the American states from 1890-1960.[20] He detected a slight *decline* in the strengths of relationships between economic resources and policy outcomes over this time period. He reasoned that a generally high level of economic development provides political decisionmakers with greater latitude in policy choices and tends to free them from the restraints imposed by limited resources. While economic resources continued to be the major determinant of public policy, the implication of Hofferbert's study is that in the future the *attitudes of political leaders* may be increasingly important in determining levels of public spending and service.

Other researchers focused their attention on a narrower range of policies which are independently associated with competition and participation. Two widely acclaimed studies—a regression exercise by Cnudde and McCrone and a factor analytic exercise by Sharkansky and Hofferbert[21]—indicate that party competition may indeed have some independent influence in the determination of welfare benefits. In these studies, Key's traditional notion of the liberalizing effects of competition is narrowed to a single set of policy measures—welfare benefits. According to Cnudde and McCrone: "Party competition, then, may not have an appreciable impact on some types of policies, but Key's discussion would lead us to specify the conditions under which it would have its greatest effect: the have-not oriented policy." There is nothing wrong with this, of course. But these findings do not really "contrast" with earlier efforts to generalize about the relative influence of economic resources in determining a broad array of policy variables in education, welfare, health, highways, corrections, taxing, and spending. However ideologically satisfying the results of these studies must have been for democratic pluralists, they do not justify the "conclusion" that "the (economic) model now predominant in state politics literature rests on shakey empirical foundations."

A more promising avenue of research effort may be to search for political system characteristics *other than* competition, participation, partisanship, and apportionment, which may be more influential than these pluralism variables in determination of public policy. Of course this may involve the abandonment of a great deal of traditional literature in the field, but the effort may prove worthwhile. For example, it may turn out that measures of professionalism or reformism in political systems are independently associated with a wide range of public policies. Reformism has been an important political movement in American state and local government for over a century. The reform style of politics emphasizes, among other things, the replacement of political patronage practices with a professional civil service system; the professionalization of government service; the reorganization of government to promote efficiency in responsibility; and a preference for a nonpartisan atmosphere in government (see Chapter 4). At the municipal level, reformism has promoted the manager form of government, nonpartisan election, home rule, at-large constituencies, and comprehensive planning. At the state level, reformism has emphasized a professional state administration, a reduction in the number of separately elected executive officials, civil service coverage of state employees, and a well-paid, well-staffed, professional state legislature. There is some evidence that reformism and professionalism is more influential than pluralism in the determination of a number of important state policies.[22] Further research on the impact of professionalism and reformism in government is certainly indicated.

Another promising avenue of research effort is the search for policy variables *other than* levels of public taxing, spending benefits, and services. Certainly there are many dimensions to the general concept—public policy. It is frequently asserted, albeit seldom demonstrated, that there are important qualitative aspects of public policy which are determined by political factors, rather than economic resources. For example, Fry and Winters undertook to measure the progressivity and regressivity of both taxing and spending in the American states.[23] Certainly the distribution of burdens and benefits among income groups of government taxing and spending is an important qualitative aspect of public policy—one that is not reflected in measures of the level of government taxing, spending benefits, and service. Fry and Winters find that voter participation, civil service coverage, and legislative professionalism have a significant independent effect in bringing about progressivity in the distribution of taxing and spending burdens. They argue erroneously that they have "reversed" the findings of earlier research; but, of course, what they have really done is show that political variables affect the *distribution* of taxing and spending burdens. They have not challenged the original findings about *levels* of public taxing and spending benefits and service. However, a recent re-analysis of Fry and Winters' data cast some doubt on their claim that political variables had a significant independent affect on their distributional measure, or even an effect greater than a state's economic resources. John L. Sullivan contends that Fry and Winters erred in their analysis and that it is "unclear" whether political variables have any affect on the distribution of tax and spending burdens which is independent of wealth.[24] Nonetheless, Fry and Winters' effort deserves praise.

Less praise-worthy, perhaps, has been the assertion that because economic variables fail to explain *all* of the variation in public policy, or even half of the variation in a number of specific policy measures, this fact is itself evidence of the influence of political factors. Unfortunately, my colleague Ira Sharkansky on several occasions has called attention to *un*explained variation in levels of government taxing, spending, benefits, and services in the states.[25] (*Un*explained variation is one minus explained variation; for example, if economic resources explain 63 percent of the variation among the states and per pupil expenditures, the remaining 37 percent is unexplained by economic resources.) Now certainly there is room for continued research on additional determinants of public policy. But social science rarely produces complete explanations of anything, as Spadaro argued previously. Unexplained variation may be a product of poor measurement or a product of the combined effects of thousands of other factors at work in the states. The implication by Sharkansky and others that unexplained variation is evidence of the influence of politics tells us more about the professional and ideological predispositions of political scientists than anything else.

Confusing Systematic and Incremental
Models of Policy Determination

Some years ago Charles Lindbloom observed that public policy develops incrementally.[26] Decisionmakers do not annually review the range of existing and proposed policies, identify societal goals, research the benefits and costs of alternative policies in achieving these goals, rank preferences for each alternative policy, and make a selection on the basis of all relative information. They reduce their task by considering only *increments* of change proposed for next year in programs, policies, and budgets. This descriptive model of the policy-making process found in the writings of Lindbloom, Wildavsky, and Sharkansky is widely known as "incrementalism."[27] Its utility in understanding the policy-making process can hardly be overestimated. Anyone who has any experience with state budget-making can testify to its relevance. And there is comparative systematic evidence in support of incremental decision-making. For example, the single factor that shows the closest relationship to state government expenditures in a current year is the level of expenditures in the recent past. Indeed, expenditure and service levels in the states in a current year correlate quite closely with expenditure levels in the states many decades ago. Doubtlessly, current expenditure and service levels reflect past habits, accommodations, and the conservative orientation of government budget procedures. There is no question that past decisions do have an important independent effect on current decisions; and this fact helps to explain the relationship between past and previous expenditure levels.

Yet, it is important to realize that the incremental model does not conflict with an economic resource model. Both explanatory models can be asserted simultaneously. To say that public policies this year are related to public policies last year does not contradict the statement that public policies this year *and* last year are a product of economic forces. Both explanations are logically correct; they do not contradict each other.

Unfortunately, Ira Sharkansky offered the correlation between current and past expenditures as a refutation of the economic model.[28] Sharkansky noted that current state government expenditures are *more* closely tied to previous state government expenditures than to any other socioeconomic political variable. This is, of course, true. The problem is that he asserted that this finding "contrasts" with those showing the effect of economic resources. But actually the correlation between past expenditures and present expenditures is shaped by the fact that the same environmental resources shape expenditures in both the present and the past. For example, New York and Mississippi were at opposite ends of the rank ordering of the states on levels of public expenditures in the 1970s and the 1890s. During the same periods, these states were also at the opposite ends of rank-ordering of the states on environmental resources. Their environmental resources shaped their relative expenditures in both 1970 and 1890, so, of course, there is a correlation between expenditures in these two time periods.

It is logically incorrect to put previous expenditures together with current environmental conditions in a regression problem on current expenditures. This is because previous expenditures *embody* the effect of the environmental resources against which they are matched within the regression problem. On the basis of partial correlation coefficients in a multiple regression equation with both previous expenditures and current environmental resources, Sharkansky concluded that, "The impact of previous expenditures over current expenditures—most noticeable in a multiple regression and partial correlation analysis with other independent variables—... indicates the great extent to which government expenditures depend upon intragovernmental stimuli rather than on economic, political, or social stimuli from their environment."[29] Economists were quick to note the logical confusion: Robert Harlow writes about Sharkansky's work: "Since ... (environmental forces) were operative for 1961 as well, and since these factors are not likely to be radically different over the two year time span encompassed by the study, they are in a sense represented by, or contained in, the previous expenditure variable ... Using the previous expenditure variable tells us only that there are differences because there were differences."[30] Thus, economic and incremental explanations do not "contrast" with each other. They are both important contributions to our understanding of public policy.

Policy Analysis—American Cities

Systematic studies of the determinants of public policies of cities have become abundant in recent years. While this progress is encouraging, the profusion of materials has made it difficult to grasp the major themes of this literature. One study focuses on the adoption of floridated water supplies; another concerns the adoption of consolidated city-county government; another investigates school desegregation policies; and still another attempts to specify the factors affecting municipal expenditures for planning and amenities. Some sort of framework is required to get a handle on this research—to organize it, summarize it, and see in what direction it is taking us.

Let us attempt to organize this research within a simplified systems model. The systems framework has been frequently employed by scholars as an organizing device in the study of urban public policy, and it can also be used as a framework for categorizing urban policy studies.

The systems model postulates three major categories of phenomenon—environmental inputs, political system characteristics, and policy outputs—and it also postulates four kinds of linkages between these major categories. These are the linkages between: (A) urban environmental variables and the characteristics of political systems, (B) the characteristics of political systems and city policies, (C) urban environmental variables and city policies, and (D) the "impact" of city policies on the urban environment and political system. In the real world, of course, data do not come with labels attached—"inputs," "system characteristics," "outputs," or "impacts." Yet systems theory is helpful in suggesting categories and labels for real world data. And for our purposes, it can provide a framework for organizing urban policy studies.

What generalizations can we derive from various studies on linkage A? In reviewing this literature Brett Hawkins concluded:

Clearly the most frequent pattern relates to the political impact of social differences among people. Indicators of ethnic, religious, and lifestyle differences are associated with the retention of unreformed, politicized, group arbitrating forms—including decentralized, fragmented governments. The same is true where the local economy, sub-communities, population size, and population stability suggest more human diversity and cementing of peoples socioeconomic ties to the community.[31]

Alford and Scoble reached the same conclusions:

Social heterogeneity—the existence of sizable groups with diverse political cultures in demands—favors a more 'politicized', less centralized, less professionalized form because there is not as great a consensus among politically active groups upon the proper goals of city government in a greater need for access in representation from diverse groups.[32]

Of course caution is in order; there are always exceptions and relationships are not so close as to permit an accurate prediction of political system characteristics by simply knowing the characteristics of the environment.

What valid generalizations can be derived about linkage B? At a general level, this research suggests most clearly that the environment is a major determinant of public policy. This is true whether policy is measured strictly in terms of city expenditure patterns, in terms of substantive policy decisions, or in terms of policy typologies. In reviewing the literature linking urban environment to city policies, Brett Hawkins concludes:

. . . large and dense populations and large minority (racial, religious, and ethnic) subpopulations correlate with general city spending and spending for specific purposes. These correlations, while not uniform, suggest that larger, denser, and more heterogeneous environments generate demands for services by various segments of the population and that city governments often respond favorably to these demands. Class characteristics of city populations as well as city resource capacity are not consistently related to policy output is actually demand behaviors of population groups, private elites, or officials.[33]

In short, the relationship between population characteristics and city policies is closer than the relationship between environmental resources and city policies.

What generalizations can be derived from various studies of linkage C? Traditionally, in explaining city policies, political scientists have tended to

A Framework for Categorizing Urban Policy Studies

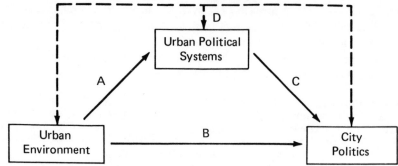

A. Studies of Linkage A. Urban Environment and Political System

Political System Characteristics

Urban Environmental Variables	Form of Government	Partisanship Voting	Governmental Consolidation	Power Structures Political Attitudes
Size	Kessell Schnore & Alford Alford & Scoble Gordon	Cutright Alford & Lee	Hawkins & Dye Dye Hawkins ACIR	Walton Gilbert
Ethnicity	Kessell Gordon Alford & Scoble Wolfinger & Field Schnore & Alford	Wolfinger & Field Cutright Alford & Lee	Hawkins & Dye Dye Hawkins ACIR	Walton Gilbert Wilson & Banfield Wolfinger & Field
Economy	Kessell Gordon Alford & Scoble Schnore & Alford	Cutright Alford & Lee	Hawkins & Dye Dye Hawkins	Walton Gilbert
Social Class	Kessell Gordon Alford & Scoble Schnore & Alford Sherbenov	Cutright Downes Alford & Lee	Hawkins & Dye Dye Hawkins ACIR	Walton Gilbert Wilson & Banfield

C. Studies of Linkage C. Urban Environment and City Policies

City Policies

Urban Environmental Variables	Expenditures and Taxes	Urban Renewal	Planning & Amenities	Health, Education and Welfare
Size	Bahl Brazer Rogers Williams et al. Lineberry & Fowler Booms Froman	Clark	Lineberry Eulau & Eyestone	Dye Froman Derthick Pinard

Figure 2-1. Urban Policy Studies

Ethnicity	Lineberry & Fowler Froman	Clark	Lineberry Eulau & Eyestone Wolfinger & Field	Dye Froman Derthick Pinard
Economy	Bahl Brazer Williams et al. Rogers Booms Froman	Clark	Lineberry Eulau & Eyestone	Dye Froman Derthick Pinard
Social Class	Bahl Brazer Williams et al. Rogers Booms Froman	Clark	Lineberry Eulau & Eyestone	Dye Froman Derthick Pinard

B. Studies of Linkage B. Political System and City Policies

City Policies

Political System Characteristics	Expenditures and Taxes	Urban Renewal	Planning & Amenities	Health, Education & Welfare
Form of Government	Lineberry & Fowler Booms	Duggar		Dye Pinard
Partisanship	Lineberry & Fowler			Dye Pinard
Governmental Consolidation	Hawkins & Dye			
Power Structure		Hawley		
Political Attitudes	Wolfinger & Field Wilson & Banfield	Wilson & Banfield	Eulau & Eyestone	Wilson & Banfield

Figure 2-1. (cont.)

emphasize the importance of what happens within the little black box labeled political system. It was natural for political scientists to assume that what they were studying was important—manager versus mayor or commission form of government, partisan versus nonpartisan elections, powers of mayors and councils, home rule, etc. Yet assumptions about the importance of one's professional work are no substitute for a systematic investigation of the actual linkages between system characteristics and public policy.

It is no easy task to demonstrate the independent effect of political system characteristics on city policies. In general, political scientists have found it difficult to discover political system characteristics that explain variation in city policies, independently of the effects of the urban environment. For example, in a very comprehensive examination of the determinants of city expenditures, total and bi-functional category, involving all cities with a population of 25,000 or more, Chester Rogers concluded that "none of the political variables considered had an influence on policy."[34] All relationships between political and policy variables turned out to be the result of both being related to an environmental variable. The political variables studied included a form of government, partisan versus nonpartisan elections, and at-large versus ward constituencies.

In contrast there are at least three studies of city policy that demonstrated some relationship between the political system and public policy. Lineberry and Fowler suggested that the public policies of reformed cities were less "responsive" to the cities ethnic and social opposition than unreformed cities.[35] Another study suggesting the importance of political system variables in shaping city policies is the work of Heinz Eulau and his associates in their studies of ninety communities in the San Francisco Bay metropolitan region. These researchers identified relationships between the goals, perceptions, and policy positions of city councilmen and public expenditures for planning and amenities. They found that the policy "images" of city councilmen were in accord with public spending patterns. They concluded that "policy development is greatly influenced by the predictions, preferences, orientations and expectations of policy makers."[36] Yet is is important to point out that Eulau and his associates only "assumed" that councilmen's attitudes influenced public policy; they did not systematically test to see if a councilman's attitudes affected city policy *independently* of environmental variables.

In summarizing the literature dealing with linkage C, Brett Hawkins concludes:

The studies described here show that system has a policy impact, but none of them shows that system variables have a bigger impact than environmental variables. However many studies do demonstrate that system is important to policy explanation simultaneously with environmental factors. Urban renewal, enforcement of traffic laws, fluoridation, school desegregation, policy treatment of juvenile offenders, wage garnishment litigation, stages of policy development, and per capita expenditures for services—all of these are to some degree shaped by system variables.[37]

Policy Analysis—Capitalist and Communist Nations

Findings in American states and cities that pluralist political variables—particularly competition, participation, and equity in representation—do not count for much in determining levels of taxing, spending, benefits, and services, are ideologically discomforting for many political scientists. How far can we go in asserting the proposition that *democratic pluralism* is not really an important determinant to public policy? Can we hypothesize that the structure of *national* political systems is not really relevant to the level of benefits and services provided to their citizens? Is it possible that democratic *nations* do not produce noticeably different levels of public spending, services, and benefits than non-democratic nations at the same level of economic development? For example, is it possible that welfare benefits and social security programs in Communist nations are the same as those in capitalist nations with similar economic resources? Is it possible that educational benefits and services in capitalist and Communist nations with similar economic resources are equivalent? Is it possible that environmental resources, rather than the extent of democracy in the political system, are really the determining forces in shaping public policy in nations of the world?

Despite the obvious importance of these questions, systematic cross-national research on public policy is relatively rare in political science. Only recently have political scientists in the field of comparative government actually begun to make systematic comparisons of the levels of taxing, spending, benefits, and services among nations.

One of the first studies to tackle these kinds of questions from a cross-national perspective is Phillips Cutright's study of social security programs in seventy-six nations.[38] Cutright examined national social insurance programs in terms of the extent of coverage in the level of benefits in work injury programs; sickness and maternity programs; old age, invalidism, and death insurance programs; family allowance plans; and unemployment programs. He also examined "political representativeness" in order to assess the importance of democracy in the political system to the social security and welfare programs provided national populations. His hypothesis, of course, was "that governments in nations whose political structures tend to allow for greater accessibility to the people of the governing elite will act to provide greater social security for their population than that provided by governments whose rulers are less accessible to the demands of the population." Such a hypothesis fits neatly with democratic political theory.

But it turned out the political representativeness had relatively little effect on national social security and welfare programs. In spite of very great differences among nations in ideological orientation and type of political system, social security and welfare programs are closely related to levels of economic development. Indeed, Cutright reports that energy consumption by itself accounts for 81 percent of the variation among nations in the extent of coverage and level of benefits provided by national social insurance and welfare programs. Similar social security and welfare programs are found in democratic and non-democratic nations with the same levels of economic development. His findings directly challenged traditional democratic pluralist political wisdom.[39]

It should be noted here that Cutright is a sociologist and not a political scientist.

Perhaps the most systematic cross-national policy study now available is economist Frederic Pryor's *Public Expenditures in Communist and Capitalist Nations.*[40] Pryor examined expenditures for national security, internal security, education, health, welfare, science, interest and investment, and administration, in six communist and six capitalist nations. In generalizing from a myriad of findings, Pryor concludes that Communist and capitalist political systems provide essentially the same types and levels of public expenditures, benefits, and services for their citizens. For example, in education Pryor concludes that:

For total educational production and expenditure the most important determinants appear to be the level of economic development and the proportion of school aged children in the population. Other variables such as those of economic or political systems do not seem to play any significant role in explaining educational expenditures.[41]

For other policy areas as well, factors other than political or economic system characteristics determined policy outcomes.

In an interpretation of his own findings Pryor observed:

Such results can be interpreted in several ways. They suggest to me that the policy dilemmas facing decision-makers of public consumption expenditures are quite similar in all nations, regardless of system. Such policy problems include: the desirability of financing a service through the public rather than the private sector; the proper relationship of different public consumption expenditures to the tax revenues which must be raised; in balancing citizen's demand for particular services with the adjudged interests of the state. If the basic economic circumstances (in Marxist terminology 'productive forces') are similar and if the policy dilemmas are similar, it should not be surprising that the decisions taken are also roughly similar. . . .[42]

Despite these generalizations, however, Pryor recognized the influence of some "political" factors in determining certain expenditure patterns. For example, regarding health and welfare programs, Pryor found that the date of the introduction of the social insurance system correlated with the political mobilization of workers, as reflected in the growth of unionization. However, once social insurance programs were introduced, they appeared to expand incrementally in both Communist and capitalist countries.

The notion that political considerations may be influential in policy *innovation*, particularly in health and welfare programs, is well argued by Arnold Heidenheimer in an essay comparing social policy development in western Europe and the United States.[43] He argues that conservative regimes—Prussia and Austria—first introduced social insurance on paternalistic principles. But liberal governments did not introduce social insurance programs until after the unionization of their work forces. He concludes that "the timing of the introduction of public pensions seem to have been determined by complex relationships between the growth of labor unions, the prevailing ideologies, and the strategies of social demand anticipation on the part of governments." He argues that the working classes in America are concentrated on education as an instrument of social mobility, while the working classes in Europe backed social insurance and welfare programs as an instrument of social equality. These differences in political objectives and strategies, he believes, account for the fact that the American educational system is "ahead" of European systems of education, while the U.S. health and welfare programs are "behind" comparable European ones.

Thus some students of comparative cross-national policy studies believe that public policy outcomes, regardless of political systems, are closely associated with levels of economic development. The energy crisis and "multinationals" clearly add to this lesson. Others apparently believe that political systems do make a difference, independent of the availability of resources. The emerging field of cross-national policy research offers excitement and challenge to political scientists interested in systematic policy analysis.

Democracy and Policy Responsiveness

Are democratic political systems more responsive to socioeconomic conditions than non-democratic systems? A common belief in traditional democratic-pluralist ideology is that competitive, participatory, representative political systems are more responsive in policy decisions to the social and economic conditions affecting their citizens. Presumably, pluralistic democracies—with competitive parties, widespread participation, and representative institutions—extend influence to broader sectors of the population. This widening of influence is supposed to result in a greater tendency to enact the preferences of lower strata of the population into public policy. Thus, among pluralistic democracies, we would expect to find greater congruence between characteristics of the population and public policy than among non-democratic political systems. In short, democratic political systems should be more responsive to socioeconomic conditions affecting their populations than non-democratic systems.

To test these notions about the greater responsiveness of democratic political systems, we can divide nations into those which are democratic and those which are not, and then observe whether there is a closer relationship between socioeconomic conditions affecting the population and public policies in democratic nations than in non-democratic nations. Ideally, we would expect to find closer relationships in democratic nations than in non-democratic nations.

But surprisingly the results of systematic analysis are just the *reverse* of what we would expect on the basis of a priori reasoning from democratic theory. It turns out that relationships between socioeconomic characteristics of national populations and public policies of these nations are closer among Communist nations and autocracies than among democratic nations.[44] Political scientist Larry Wade provides data showing that per capita income is *less* related to health, education, and welfare measures in affluent democracies than in poor democracies or Communist nations or autocracies.[a] For example, per capita income explains over 20 percent of the variation in higher education enrollment in Communist countries and poor democracies, and 40 percent of the variation in autocracies, but only 6 percent of the variation in higher education enrollments in the affluent western democracies. Per capita income explains 72 percent of the variation in physician services among poorer democracies, 26 percent among Communist nations, 37 percent among autocracies, but only 16 percent of the variation in physician services among affluent western democracies. The same differences between democratic and non-democratic nations and Communist and non-Communist nations can be observed in other policy areas. In short, available evidence runs contrary to the proposition that policy outcomes and socioeconomic conditions affecting the population are more closely related in democratic than in non-democratic nations.

Let us pursue the same notion about the greater responsiveness of democratic-pluralist political systems in the American states. We can divide states into

Table 2-1

The Relationships Between Income and Health and Education Measures in Democratic and Non-Democratic Nations

	Amount of Variance Explained by Per Capita Income			
	Physicians per 10,000	Hospital Beds per 10,000	Male Life Expectancy	Enroll. Higher Ed.
Affluent Democracies	16%	0%	9%	6%
Poorer Democracies	72	13	64	21
Communist Nations	26	83	42	20
Autocracy	37	6	41	40

Source: Derived from figures supplied by Larry L. Wade, *The Elements of Public Policy* (Columbus: Charles T. Merrill, 1972). Tables 2.2, 2.3, 2.4. Original data from United Nations, *Statistical Yearbook 1968* and *Yearbook of National Accounts and Statistics 1969.*

[a]His affluent democracies were the United States, Sweden, Switzerland, Canada, Iceland, Denmark, Australia, France, New Zealand, Luxembourg, Belgium, the United Kingdom, West Germany, Finland, and the Netherlands. His Communist states were East Germany, Czechoslovakia, the USSR, Poland, Hungary, Rumania, Bulgaria, Yugoslavia, Cuba, Albania, and China. His poor democracies were Israel, Austria, Italy, Japan, Ireland, Uruguay, Malta, Mexico, Jamaica, Costa Rica, Lebanon, Columbia, the Philippines, Ceylon, and India. His autocracies were Kuwait, Spain, Portugal, South Africa, Nicaragua, Saudi Arabia, El Salvador, Iran, Peru, Jordan, Dominican Republic, Taiwan, Honduras, Paraguay, Bolivia, Liberia, Thailand, Indonesia, Pakistan, South Vietnam, Sudan, Nepal, Haiti, Burma, Afghanistan, and Ethiopia.

Table 2-2

The Relationships Between Income and Welfare and Education Measures in Pluralist and Non-Pluralist States

	Amount of Variance Explained by Median Family Income			
	Per Pupil Expenditures	AFDC Benefits	Per Capita Taxes	Police Protection
Pluralist States	25%	20%	35%	8%
Non-Pluralist States	64%	65%	70%	30%

Source: Data from *Statistical Abstract of the United States 1972.*

those which are more pluralist—states with competitive parties and high voter turnout—and those which are not so pluralist—states with one-party system and low voter turnout. We can then observe whether there is a closer relationship between socioeconomic conditions and public policy in pluralist states, than in the non-pluralist states. On the basis of a priori reasoning from pluralist political theory we would expect to find closer relationships between socioeconomic conditions and public policies in the pluralist states than in the non-pluralist states.

But again systematic analysis reveals that just the reverse is true. It turns out that relationships between socioeconomic conditions and public policies are closer in the non-pluralist states than in the pluralist states. For example, median family income explains only 25 percent of the variance in per pupil expenditures among pluralist states, compared to 64 percent of the variance in per pupil expenditures for non-pluralist states. Median family income explains only 20 percent of the variance in welfare benefits among pluralist states, compared to 65 percent of the variance in welfare benefits among non-pluralist states. This same pattern holds true for other policy measures as well.

In short, there is no empirical evidence that democratic nations are any more responsive to socioeconomic forces which affect their citizens than non-democratic nations, or that pluralist states are any more responsive to socioeconomic conditions affecting their citizens than non-pluralist states.

I am not prepared to argue on the basis of these limited findings that non-democratic nations and non-pluralist states are *more* responsive than democratic nations and pluralist states. My own guess is that the apparent greater responsiveness of non-democratic nations and non-pluralist states is really a product of economic underdevelopment. The democratic nations and pluralist states are generally affluent. This affluence relieves them from some of the constraints of limited economic resources. Once a certain level of affluence is attained, non-economic forces probably play a greater role in the determination of public policy. In contrast, less affluent nations and states are heavily constrained by the availability of economic resources. A high level of economic development provides decisionmakers with greater latitude in policy choices, and tends to free them from restraints imposed by limited resources. Thus, policy measures are closely related to economic variables in poor nations and states, but less closely related to economic variables among more affluent nations and states.

What Political Scientists Must do
to Become Better Policy Analysts

This brief survey of the policy research literature on cities, states, and nations was not designed to demonstrate the merits of economic determinism. Instead, it was designed to challenge political scientists to reexamine many of their professional predispositions and ideological commitments, and to stimulate the development of the genuine policy science. Policy research is still very exploratory; no body of literature can be thought of as "the final word" in understanding public policy. But systematic policy research to date is sufficiently challenging to the traditional professional concerns of political science, and to the long standing assumptions of democratic pluralist ideology, to warrant a serious reconsideration of the traditional assumptions of our discipline.

Specifically, for political science to establish itself as a viable *policy* science, it must at a minimum do the following:

1. First of all, development of a policy science will require an expansion of the traditional boundaries of political science well beyond all previous definitions of these boundaries. Political scientists must be prepared to look beyond governmental institutions and political processes in their search for the causes and consequences of public policy. Political science must become far more interdisciplinary in character—incorporating concepts, methods, and measurements drawn from a wide variety of disciplines, not only in the social sciences but also in the physical and biological sciences.

More importantly political science cannot react defensively—as if it were protecting a vested professional interest—when it is found that economic or social or environmental or technological factors are more influential in determining the causes or consequences of public policies than traditional political system characteristics. A "policy science" derives its importance from what it seeks to study—public policy. The important goal to achieve is the explanation of public policy—its causes and consequences—not the assertion of the primacy of politics (or of economics) in policy formation.

2. Secondly, political scientists must acquire greater scientific objectivity in dealing with variables which are important to democratic and pluralist ideology. Democracy, representativeness, competition, participation, equality, are not only measurable real-world phenomena, they are also important values. But our

commitment to these values—to representative political institutions; to stable, developed democracies; to competition, bargaining, and compromise as a mode of decision-making; to the dispersal of power and influence; to high levels of political participation; and to social and political equality—are really moral commitments to a democratic form of government. The legitimacy of democracy should not depend upon the policy outcomes which it produces; but rather, to the fact that this form of governance maximizes opportunities for individual participation in the formation of public policy. This form of government is consistent with the values of western civilization, which stress the dignity and the worth of the individual. Even if it is shown that non-democratic or totalitarian governments provide the same health care, or the same educational programs, or the same welfare benefits to their citizens, this fact should not reflect adversely on the moral quality of a democratic political system. We do not have to prove that democracy or participation or competition or equality produce "good" welfare programs or educational systems or health care in order to affirm our belief in these political values.

Summary

Policy analysis *is* political science. To argue otherwise is to simply spend one's time on parts of problems or processes which inevitably must relate to policy in order to be meaningful. Furthermore, policy analysis must be the product of empirical descriptive research or we can offer no more significant contribution than we as a field have in the past. Polemic, prescription, and intuition are no substitute for real research and as a result real understanding.

Thus, our graduate programs and research should be concentrated on the training of empirical skills and interdisciplinary expansion *vis-à-vis* policy analysis. Spadaro's point that our present subdisciplinary areas are self-limiting boundaries is well taken. And Golembiewski's and Stedman's arguments in their essays further illustrate their areas' limitations to developing policy scientists. Of course, not all here in this book agree with me that political science and policy analysis are indeed coterminous, which is all the more reason why we need more of this type of developmental dialogue. We all agree that we as political scientists need undertake an increased commitment to policy analysis; thus we disagree in the extent of that commitment and not in kind.

Our present models and theories are not totally adequate for descriptive policy analysis and operationalization let alone prescriptive or predictive findings. Therefore, perhaps Spadaro's Quantum Dynamics policy model offers at least as much utility and a potential "bridge" between descriptive and prescriptive research *only*, as far as I am concerned, if "values" are indeed approached empirically (which Zeigler also illustrates in the final chapter). Our immediate attention must be to generate more data and empirical bases and allow "post behavioralism" to remain post.

More and more we live in a world where traditional political boundaries and foci of interest are becoming obsolete. There is a "policy gap" in the real world, and in the academic world which we have helped to create. Eventually, we may find political "science" obsolete.

Notes

1. For an introduction to the literature in political science dealing with policy analysis, see Thomas R. Dye, *Understanding Public Policy* (Englewood Cliffs, N.J.: Prentice-Hall, 1972); Ira Sharkansky (ed.), *Policy Analysis in Political Science* (Chicago: Markham, 1970).

2. V.O. Key, Jr., *American State Politics* (New York: Knopf, 1956); Duane Lockard, *The Politics of State and Local Government* (New York: Macmillan, 1963); John H. Fenton, *People and Parties in Politics* (Glenview: Scott, Foresman, 1966).

3. Solomon Fabricant, *The Trend of Government Activity in the United States Since 1900* (New York: National Bureau of Economic Research, 1950).

4. Glenn W. Fisher, "Interstate Variation in State and Local Government Expenditures," *National Tax Journal* 17 (March 1964):57-74.

5. Seymour Sachs and Robert Harris, "The Determinants of State and Local Government Expenditures and Intergovernmental Flow of Funds," *National Tax Journal* 17 (March 1974):78-85.

6. Austin Ranney and Wilmoore Kendall, "The American Party System," *American Political Science Review* 48 (March 1954):477-485; V.O. Key, Jr., *American State Politics* (New York: Knopf, 1956), p. 99; Joseph A. Schlesinger, "A Two-Dimensional Scheme for Classifying States According to the Degree of Inter-Party Competition," *American Political Science Review* 49 (1955):1120-28; Robert T. Golembiewski, "A Taxonomic Approach to State Political Party Strength," *Western Political Quarterly* 11(1958):494-513.

7. Richard E. Dawson and James A. Robinson, "Inter-Party Competition, Economic Variables, and Welfare Policies in the American States," *Journal of Politics* 25 (May 1963):265-89.

8. Thomas R. Dye, *Politics, Economics, and the Public* (Chicago: Rand McNally, 1966).

9. The early works include Richard E. Dawson and James A. Robinson, "Interparty Competition, Economic Variables and Welfare Politics in the American States," *Journal of Politics* 25 (May 1963):265-289; Richard Hofferbert, "The Relation between Public Policy and Some Structural and Environmental Variables in the American States," *American Political Science Review* 60 (March 1966):73-82; Thomas R. Dye, "Malapportionment and Public Policy in the States," *Journal of Politics* 27 (February 1965):586-601; Herbert Jacob, "The Consequences of Malapportionment: A Note of Caution," *Social Forces* 48 (1964):261.

10. Ira Sharkansky and Richard Hofferbert, "Dimensions of State Politics, Economics and Public Policy," *American Political Science Review* 63 (September 1969):867-879; and Thomas R. Dye, "Income Inequality and American State Politics," *American Political Science Review* 63 (March 1969):157-162.

11. Charles F. Cnudde and Donald J. McCrone, "Party Competition and Welfare Policies in the American States," *American Political Science Review* 63 (September 1969):858-866.

12. Ira Sharkansky, "Agency Requests Gubernatorial Support and Budget in State Legislatures," *American Political Science Review* 62 (December 1968):1220-1231; and Thomas R. Dye, "Executive Power and Public Policy in the States," *Western Political Quarterly* 22 (December 1969):926-939.

13. Bryan R. Fry and Richard Winters, "The Politics of Redistribution," *American Political Science Review* 64 (June 1970); Jack Walker, "The Diffusion of Innovations among the American States," *American Political Science Review* 63 (September 1969):867-879; and Thomas R. Dye, "Inequality and Civil Rights Policy in the States," *Journal of Politics* 31 (November 1969):1080-1097.

14. Richard Hofferbert, "Ecological Development and Policy Change," *Midwest Journal of Political Science* 10 (November 1966):464-483.

15. Sharkansky and Hofferbert, "Dimensions of State Politics"; and Cnudde and McCrone, "Party Competition."

16. Ira Sharkansky, "Environment, Policy, Output and Input: Problems of Theory and Method in the Analysis of Public Policy," in Ira Sharkansky (ed.), *Policy Analysis in Political Science* (Chicago: Markham, 1970).

17. Lewis A. Froman, Jr., "An Analysis of Public Policies in Cities," *Journal of Politics* 29 (February 1967); Robert L. Lineberry and Edmund P. Fowler, "Reformism and Public Policy in Cities," *American Political Science Review* 61 (September 1967):701-716; Heinz Eulau and Robert Eyestone, "Policy Maps of City Councils and Policy Outcomes," *American Political Science Review* 62 (March 1968):124-143; and Thomas R. Dye, "Governmental Structure, Urban Environment, and Educational Policy," *Midwest Journal of Political Science* 11 (August 1967):353-380.

18. Of course, not all of this literature has been good. See, for example, John Crittenden, "Dimensions of Modernization in the American States," *American Political Science Review* 61 (December 1967):892-1002; Alan G. Pulsipher and James L. Weatherby, "Malapportionment, Party Competition, and the Functional Distribution of Government Expenditures," *American Political Science Review* 62 (December 1968):1207-1220.

19. Guenther F. Schaefer and Stuart Rakoff, "Politics, Policy, and Political Science," *Politics and Society* 1 (November 1970):52.

20. Richard Hofferbert, "Socio-economic Dimensions of the American States, 1890-1960," *Midwest Journal of Political Science* 2 (August 1968):401-418; Richard Hofferbert, "Ecological Development and Policy Change," *Midwest Journal of Political Science* 10 (November 1966):464-483.

21. Cnudde and McCrone, "Party Competition"; Sharkansky and Hofferbert, "Dimensions of State Politics."

22. See Thomas R. Dye, *Understanding Public Policy* (Englewood Cliffs, N.J.: Prentice-Hall, 1972), pp. 251-254.

23. Bryan R. Fry and Richard Winters, "The Politics of Redistribution," *American Political Science Review* 64 (June 1970):508-522.

24. John L. Sullivan, "A Note on Redistributive Politics," *American Political Science Review* 66 (December 1972):1301-1305.

25. Sharkansky, "The Political Scientist and Policy Analysis," *Policy Analysis in Political Science*, p. 8; and Ira Sharkansky, "Dimensions of State Policy," in Herbert Jacob and Kenneth Vines (eds.), *Politics in the American States*, 2d ed. (Boston: Little, Brown, 1971), p. 320.

26. Charles Lindbloom, "The Science of Muddling Through," *Public Administration Review* 19 (Spring 1959):79-88, and *The Intelligence of Democracy* (New York: Free Press, 1966).

27. Lindbloom, *Public Administration Review*; Aaron Wildavsky, *Politics of the Budgetary Process* (Boston: Little, Brown, 1964); and Ira Sharkansky, *Spending in the American States* (Chicago: Rand McNally, 1968).

28. Sharkansky, *Spending in the American States*, and "Economic and Political Correlates of State Government Expenditures," *Midwest Journal of Political Science* 11 (May 1967):173-192.

29. Sharkansky, "Some More Thoughts About the Determinants of Government Expenditures," *National Tax Journal* (June 1967):179.

30. Robert L. Harlow, "Sharkansky on State Expenditures: A Comment," *National Tax Journal* 21 (June 1968):215-216.

31. Brett W. Hawkins, *Politics and Urban Policy* (Columbus: Bobbs-Merrill, 1971), p. 55.

32. Robert R. Alford and Harry M. Scoble, "Political and Socioeconomic Characteristics of American Cities," *Municipal Yearbook* (Chicago: International City Managers Association, 1965), p. 83.

33. Hawkins, *Politics and Urban Policy*, p. 83.

34. Chester B. Rogers, "Environment, System, and Output," *Social Forces* (September 1969):86.

35. Robert L. Lineberry and Edmund P. Fowler, "Reformism and Public Policies in American Cities," *American Political Science Review* 61 (September 1967):701-716.

36. Heinz Eulau and Robert Eyestone, "Policy Maps of City Councils and Policy Outcomes," *American Political Science Review* 62 (March 1968):124-143.

37. Hawkins, *Politics and Urban Policy*, p. 87.

38. Phillips Cutwright, "Political Structure, Economic Development, and National Social Security Programs," *American Journal of Sociology* 70 (March 1965):537-550.

39. Ibid., p. 550.

40. Frederic L. Pryor, *Public Expenditures in Communist and Capitalist Nations* (Homewood, Ill.: Richard D. Irwin, 1968).

41. Ibid., p. 226.

42. Ibid., pp. 310-311.

43. Arnold J. Heidenheimer, "The Politics of Public Education, Health, and Welfare in the USA and Western Europe," *British Journal of Political Science* 3 (1973):315-340.

44. Larry L. Wade, *The Elements of Public Policy* (Columbus: Charles E. Merrill, 1972), pp. 33-41.

**General Reference to
Urban Literature**

Advisory Council on Intergovernmental Relations. *Factors Affecting Voter Reactions to Governmental Reorganization in Metropolitan Areas.* Washington: Government Printing Office, 1962.

Alford, Robert R., and Eugene C. Lee. "Voting Turnout in American Cities." *American Political Science Review* (September 1968):796:813.

Alford, Robert R., and Harry M. Scoble. "Political and Socio-economic Characteristics of American Cities." *Municipal Yearbook.* Chicago: International City Managers Association, 1965, pp. 82-97.

Booms, Bernard H. "City Governmental Form and Public Expenditure Levels." *National Tax Journal* (June 1966):187-199.

Brazer, Harvey. *City Expenditures in the United States.* New York: National Bureau of Economic Research, 1959.

Clarke, James W. "Environment, Process, and Policy." *American Political Science Review* (December 1969).

Clark, Terry M. "Community Structure, Decision-making, Budget Expenditures, and Urban Renewal in 51 American Communities." *American Sociological Review* (August 1968).

Cutright, Phillips. "Nonpartisan Electoral Systems in American Cities." *Comparative Studies in Society and History* (January 1963).

Derthick, Martha. "Incity Differences Administration of Public Assistance Programs." In James Q. Wilson (ed.), *City Politics and Public Policy.* New York: Wiley, 1968.

Downes, Bryan T. "Municipal Social Rank and Characteristics of Local Political Leaders." *Midwest Journal of Political Science* (November 1968).

Dye, Thomas R. "Urban School Segregation: A Comparative Analysis." *Urban Affairs Quarterly* (December 1968):141-165.

Dye, Thomas R. "Governmental Structure, Urban Environment, and Educational Policy." *Midwest Journal of Political Science* (August 1967):353-380.

Dye, Thomas R. "Urban Political Integration: Conditions Associated with Annexation in American Cities." *Midwest Journal of Political Science* (November 1964):435-446.

Eulau, Heinz, and Robert Eyestone. "Policy Maps of City Councils and Policy Outcomes." *American Political Science Review* (March 1968):124-143.

Froman, Louis A. "The Analysis of Public Policies in Cities." *Journal of Politics* (February 1967):94-108.

Gilbert, Claire W. "Some Trends in Community Politics." *Social Science Quarterly* (December 1967):373-381.

Gordon, Daniel N. "Immigrants and Urban Government Form, 1933-1960." *American Journal of Sociology* (September 1968):158-171.

Hawkins, Brett W., and Thomas R. Dye. "Metropolitan Fragmentation." *Midwest Review of Public Administration* (February 1970):17-24.

Hawkins, Brett W. "Life Style, Demographic Distance, and Voter Support of City-County Consolidation." *Social Science Quarterly* (December 1967): 325-337.

Hawley, Amos H. "Community Power and Urban Renewal Success." *American Journal of Sociology* (January 1963):422-431.

Kessel, John H. "Governmental Structure and Political Environment." *American Political Science Review* (September 1962):615-620.

Lineberry, Robert L., and Edmund P. Fowler. "Reformism and Public Policies in American Cities." *American Political Science Review* (September 1967).

Lineberry, Robert L. "Community Structure and Planning Commitment." *Social Science Quarterly* (December 1969).

Pinard, Maurice. "Structural Attachments and Political Support in Urban Politics: The Case of Fluoridation Referendums." *American Journal of Sociology* (March 1963):513-526.

Rogers, Chester B. "Environment, System, and Output: A Model." *Social Forces* (September 1969):72-87.

Schnore, Leo F., and Robert R. Alford. "Forms of Government and Socio-economic Characteristics of Suburbs." *Administrative Science Quarterly* (June 1963).

Sherbenov, Edgar L. "Class, Participation, and the Council-Manager Plan." *Public Administration Review* (Summer 1961):131-135.

Walton, John. "Substance and Artifact: The Current Status of Research in Community Power Structure." *American Journal of Sociology* (January 1966):430-438.

Williams, Oliver P., Charles S. Liebman, Harold Herman, and Thomas R. Dye. *Suburban Differences and Metropolitan Policies.* Philadelphia: University of Pennsylvania Press, 1965.

Wilson, James Q., and Edward C. Banfield. "Public-Regardingness as a Value Premise in Voting Behavior." *American Political Science Review* (December 1964):876-887.

Wolfinger, Raymond E., and John O. Field. "Political Ethos and the Structure of City Government." *American Political Science Review* (June 1966):306-320.

3

Public Administration and Public Policy: An Analysis of Developmental Phases

Robert T. Golembiewski

If scholars live or die in terms of the images they create, students of public administration are in trouble. This conclusion will be supported by emphasis on four developmental phases which have constituted the field's guiding images or concepts. Awareness of these developmental phases is important, perhaps even critical, for two reasons. Thus valuable perspective on where the field is can be gained from tracing how it got that way. Moreover, getting where you want to go is easier, if you are clear on where you have been and are.

The goals of this chapter can be stated more concretely. Especially in the last decade, public administration has come to emphasize a "public policy" concept of its scope and methods. How this came to be is a matter of substantial intellectual and practical interest, in its own right. Moreover, the "public policy" approach at once is little analyzed and also has significant implications concerning which scholars do what work in which ways. This combination provides substantial motivation for this chapter. The approach has certain unintended and largely unanticipated consequences which deserve explicit analysis, even if they will not prove to have the doomsday quality for public administration sometimes attributed to them. Finally, the relationships of public administration and public policy are basic to the total policy environment as indicated in Chapter 1.

Two substantial limitations of this effort require early owning. First, this chapter does not pretend to provide a resolution of the contemporary concern about public administration as a field. Rather it sketches how the field got where it is today, its relationship to public policy, and suggests some guidelines for its future development. Second, it unabashedly generalizes about the character and relative dominance of four concepts of a complex field, and hopes to compensate for the inevitable loss of nuance and qualification by emphasis on an important set of intellectual dynamics underlying public administration.

The first two revised sections of this chapter appear substantially as here in the *Georgia Political Science Association Journal* 2 (Spring 1974). Reprinted with permission.

I am pleased to acknowledge the reactions and counsel of my colleagues Nicholas Henry and Frank Thompson.

Précis of a Predicament:
Two Contrasting Images

Two opposed trends serve tolerably well to characterize the public administration of yesterday and today. Thus the field's early history is studded with symbols testifying to its rich destiny and performance. Not only were all problems ultimately administrative problems, for example, but the very existence of our civilizations depended upon the success with which we learned to cope with the administrative ultimates. Woodrow Wilson put the matter directly some eighty years ago. "It is getting harder to *run* a constitution," he noted, "than to frame one."[1] Wilson stressed the need to augment legal-institutional analysis with the panoply of science and art required to manage complex organizations of men and machines.

Public administration seldom was seen as wholly able to guarantee the safety of our civilizations, but major components of that challenge were considered manageable. "If those who are concerned scientifically with the phenomena of getting things done through cooperative human effort will proceed along these lines," read the Foreword to the monumental 1937 *Papers On The Science of Administration*, "we may expect in time to construct a valid and accepted theory of administration."[2] The measured confidence of these words had a firm basis. For public administration then was at the top of the heap of analytical competence in dealing with matters administrative, by common consensus.

More recently, observers have tended toward greater pessimism. "For a variety of reasons," Frederick Mosher concluded, "public administration stands in danger of . . . senescence."[3] Similarly, Martin Landau expressed a deep concern. Public administration, "that lusty young giant of a decade ago," in Landau's words, "may now 'evaporate' as a field."[4] The core difficulty is widely perceived as the lack of an organizing focus. For want of such a focus, research loses coherence and lacks cumulative relevance. The danger is particularly great today, given the manifold approaches to public administration that are both possible and necessary. As Mosher emphasized:

More is now known about public administration than was the case twenty years ago. But there is a great deal more to know. There are more depths to probe than were then visualized, and more different perspectives from which to start the probing. This field need bow to no other in respect to its sophistication about its subject matter. But such sophistication can senesce into mere dilettantism unless it is grounded in premises and hypotheses that are in some degree ordered and tested and that are continuously refreshed with new data and experience.[5]

Dwight Waldo brought such considerations to a conclusion that has had wide currency. If a healthy discipline "has a solid center as well as an active circumference," he articulated the common underlying theme, the state of public administration was disturbing. "I have a nagging work of late," Waldo confessed, "a fear that all is not as healthy as it should be at the center of the discipline."[6] Some few years later, matters had only worsened appreciably for Waldo, to judge from his reference to a "crisis of identity for public administration."[7]

Assigning dates to historical events is always hazardous, but the relative disadvantage of public administration became patent after World War II. There were many signs of this disadvantage, but the most public measure was the comparative postwar scrutiny in business schools and in public administration. The business school effort was long-run, well-financed, comprehensive, as well as searching and even searing. Two hefty volumes resulted,[8] which became required reading in business schools and motivated major changes in curriculum, staffing, and teaching methods. That self-review took a decade, more or less. The comparable effort of relevance to public administration[9] was lilliputian, and generated a single, less-distinguished and tamer volume. That volume inspired only very faint praise, as in the comment that "the very triteness and superficiality of the volume made it important."[10]

Whatever one's preference for richness or ashes, this seems an inopportune time to lose heart. The flurry of reorganizations, new programs, the search for efficiency/economy because of the growing need to justify each dollar of expenditures, the rapid obsolescing and/or impending retirement of the bulk of our top-level civil servants, and the growing competition for tax resources—these are among the factors that have contributed to the swinging back of the pendulum of attention toward administration. Many observers see a new dawn for public administration just around a developmental corner.[11]

How the Predicament Came to Be:
Four Developmental Phases

Whether one is optimistic or pessimistic about the future, however, public administration today faces a basic predicament. This section outlines the dimensions of that predicament through describing four phases in the development of public administration. From one perspective, to preview the argument, the conceptual development of public administration leaves some of its adherents faint-hearted when they should be bold, and concerned about their legitimacy when they should be striding confidently toward the demanding research and training objectives that recently have sprung into prominence. From an alternative perspective that conceptual development leaves other specialists buoyantly expecting too much, and consequently vulnerable to major disappointment, if not something worse. This is one hell of a predicament, in sum, which early sections will try to understand and with which later sections will seek to cope, however incompletely.

A 2 x 2 Matrix

There are many ways of schematizing the development of public administration, and the choice here is convenient and revealing. Essentially, the conceptual development of public administration is viewed here as being encompassed by the four cells of a 2 x 2 matrix relating two combinations of "locus" and "focus." "Focus" refers to the analytical targets of public administration, the "what" of concern for specialists. "Locus" refers directly to the "where," to the contexts that are conceived to yield the phenomena of interest. Both focus and locus are crudely distinguished here as "relatively specified" and "relatively unspecified."

This simple 2 x 2 paradigm accounts for much of the historical variation in the conceptual development of public administration. Roughly, that is, the contemporary condition of the field is the result of passing through four major stages or phases of conceptual development which differ both in locus and focus, and sometimes radically so. They are:

I. the *analytic* distinction of "politics" from "administration," interpreted as ideal categories or functions of governance, which functions are performed in different institutional loci in various degrees;

II. the *concrete* distinction of "politics" from "administration," with the former conceived as having a real locus in the interaction between legislatures and high-level members of the executive, and the latter as having a real locus in the bulk of the public bureaucracy;

III. *a science of management*, which emphasizes the isolation and analysis of administrative processes, dynamics, activities, or "principles," that are seen as universal or at least as having applicability in many organizations; and

	SPECIFIED	FOCUS	UNSPECIFIED
SPECIFIED	Stage III		Stage II
LOCUS			
UNSPECIFIED	Stage I		Stage IV

Figure 3-1.

IV. the pervasive *orientation toward "public policy,"* in which "politics" and "administration" commingle and which has an unspecified locus that encompasses the total set of public and private institutions and processes that are policy-relevant.

The basic argument here is that public administration was significantly influenced by these four major concepts of the scope of the field. Movement from one phase to another was not based on some kind of sudden and collective decision among scholars at a specific point in time. Each concept did peak at a different time, but major proponents of each remained after dominant emphasis had shifted toward the succeeding concept. Moreover, some students still reflect aspects of several phases, either as stages in their own development or as eclectic combinations of approaches.

*Properties and Problems of the
Four Phases*

To provide detail for the 2 x 2 matrix in Figure 3-1 is to sketch more of significance in the development of public administration. At the most general level, the dual choice of locus/focus helped determine the kind of work done in the field and who did it. To provide some sense of the overall developmental trend in who did what, at first the field moved toward a sharper definition of a distinct "vital center." In Phase IV, the concept of the field was broadened radically. Hence the contemporary concern that public administration does not have a distinctive vital center and active periphery at just the time when concerted research and applied effort are vital. Much detail about each of the conceptual phases is necessary to support this broad conclusion.

Phase I: Analytic Politics/Administration. Frank Goodnow's *Politics and Administration* provides the essential content for Phase I. The analytical focus of public administration is reasonably precise in that volume, as a first approximation, but the real locus of the appropriate phenomena is not specified.

Basically, Goodnow conceptually distinguishes "two distinct functions of government," which he designates politics and administration. "Politics has to do with policies or expressions of the state will," Goodnow explains. "Administration has to do with the execution of these policies." The heart of his distinction lies in the classic separation of powers, which prescribes the desirability of entrusting "in large measure" the expression or formulation of the "will of the sovereign" to "a different organ" than is charged with executing that will.[12]

Goodnow's basic distinction is not as crude as many have implied. For example, that distinction is not monolithic, either in locus or focus. Thus the two functions are *not* performed in different loci. "More or less differentiated organs" of government are established to perform the two functions, Goodnow notes, but no such organ is "confined exclusively to the discharge of one of these functions." Complexity does not permit such tidiness. For Goodnow, that is, students of public administration would seek out their phenomena and cope with them: in the executive or legislative or judicial branches; at state or local or federal levels; in matters both great and small. Not that all real loci were equally likely to produce phenomena of politics and administration. Goodnow's obscure terminology sometimes gets in the way of his argument on the matter of locus. But if we give him the benefit of an inept usage or so, he consistently conceives of the three branches of federal government as having different loadings of politics and administration. The legislative branch qua concrete locus is mostly politics, for example; and the lower bureaucratic levels are largely administration. Whatever the loading in a real locus, however, public administration is concerned with the administration component wherever it appears.

Relatedly, administration for Goodnow is neither homogeneous nor sealed off from politics. Thus administration includes the "function of executing the law," as well as "semi-scientific, quasi-judicial and quasi-business or commercial" functions. The latter functions are "a large part of administration" that is "unconnected with politics" and consequently should "be relieved very largely, if not altogether, from the control of political bodies." As for the "executive function," Goodnow notes oppositely, there can be no question about subjecting it to the "body entrusted ultimately with the expression of the state will."

Goodnow's conceptual concern with the analytical focus but not the locus of public administration may be brought to a summary conclusion. Wherever they occur, Goodnow argues, the target phenomena in public administration are defined as those activities of governance that possess "internal" criteria of correctness, which includes "semi-scientific, quasi-judicial and quasi-business or commercial activity." Moreover, the target phenomena include activities that have "little if any influence on the (political) expression of the true state will," and consequently require little if any "external" control, as by legislatures. "External" or political control is appropriate only when no "internal" criteria of success exist, or when some measure of broadly political consensus about the degree of correctness must suffice or is desirable, as in the case of the "executive function" component of administration.

Goodnow's basic approach had a major attractive feature, which is too little noted. Essentially, he contributed to the superficially-easy differentiation of the provinces of public administration and political science, and yet provided a stout umbilical. In terms of central tendencies, Goodnow's politics/administration (in Landau's words) each "referred to a different class of behavior and each presented a different set of problems." However, the total operations of government cannot be assigned completely to different agencies of government. Landau put the matter in these terms: "... the empirical processes of politics were far too complex to be discharged by any single governmental body and, similarly, administrative functions could not be deemed exclusive to any specific agency."[13] Differences in central tendencies, in short, coexisted with major conceptual overlap.

Goodnow's analytical distinction is a difficult one with which to live, and the magnitude of these difficulties may be indicated economically. For example, Goodnow provides only general leads for isolating the central phenomena within the analytical province of administration. This unspecificity is compounded by the fact that Goodnow urged upon public administration a cosmopolitan orientation as to its real locus. Oppositely, most fields in political science were and are uni-locus, despite some strong contemporary intentions to become "truly comparative." Goodnow's concept, consequently, would require that students of public administration confront legislative specialists (for example) with dibs on the latter's real locus. An analytical distinction is no match for a distinction based on concrete locus, however. This was particularly the case in Goodnow's time. Thus no substantial body of knowledge about "administration" then existed for whose broad applicability in various loci one could make a strong case.

Such perceived difficulties, by hypothesis, motivated search for another guiding concept. To preview the following description of three such conceptual stages, that movement did not stop until the field was defined so as to encompass virtually the whole of political science. Of course, this did not happen in one fell-swoop. But it happened quickly. The eyes of students of public administration were bigger than their stomachs; and those were bullish days indeed. This characterization helps us understand important components of the history of public administration, which we will summarize in thumbnail fashion: why ambitions were so expansive; why the pace of pushing forward the scope of the discipline was so rapid; and why a kind of dyspepsia resulted when, and persisted after, scholars forced their concept of public administration to attempt to swallow too much too quickly.

Phase II: Concrete Politics/Administration. Phase II in the search for public administration's boundaries had a long-lived impact on the field, and can be described briefly. Phase II proposed a sharp and concrete separation between "politics" and "administration." Basically, it is definite about the locus of relevant phenomena and vague about its focus.[14] As such, Phase II disingenuously caricatures Goodnow's basic distinction. "Politics" is the province of the legislators, as well as of elected chief executives and their senior political appointees. The locus of public administration is restricted to the governmental bureaucracy, but within that locus the field knows no analytical limits. Everything is its meat. Administrative case-law and administrative behavior, for example, are put cheek-by-jowl at a common trough in Phase II. In contrast, Phase I has a sharper analytical focus, but its locus is relatively unspecified.

The difficulties with Phase II are significant, both practically and conceptually. First, a real locus was given to the analytical distinction between politics and administration. This left proponents of Phase II with no defense against the correct charge—and it was leveled time after time—that "things are not that way" within the executive and its bureaucracy. The way things really are became a datum to be interminably discovered. Second, Phase II encouraged neglect of relevant phenomena in other loci, especially in business. The lessening—but still very real—isolation of business administration from public administration stands as perhaps the most unfortunate by-product of Phase II's defining the discipline in terms of a specific locus. This left many scholars out of intimate touch with the revolutionary developments that have taken place very recently in many schools of business. Third, in its very emphasis upon locus rather than focus, Phase II assumed that where phenomena occur is more significant than what the phenomena are. This seems a procrustean basis for differentiation.

In any case, Phase II significantly shaped the development of public administration. "For a half-century or so while political science was developing as a distinct discipline," Appleby concluded in 1949 about the academic staying-power of Phase II, "much of its literature tended to accept as substantially real a separation of powers which excluded from administration any—or at least important—policy-making functions." The distinction was consequential. "Under such a theory of separation," Appleby observed, "a civil service system was justified, accepted, and probably to a small extent over-sold."[15] Similarly, Phase II also encouraged two major emphases: the "neutral specialist" as the answer to the world's administrative problems;[16] and the bureau movement which assumed that hyperfactualism was the simple road to the good administrative state.[17] Like all ideas that gain currency, these two had a valid central theme. Given the revelations of the muckrakers, for example, pleas for more data and more trained personnel in public management were reasonable. Like most ideas that gain wide currency, however, that valid central theme was overextended by the conceptually careless and naive. Only slight exaggeration or conceptual carelessness about reliance on experts and on facts were required, that is, to pair the separation of politics/administration with an equally sharp separation between value/fact. Many observers provided that exaggeration and carelessness. Needless to say, fact/value for two decades was perhaps *the* dominant issue in public administration.

Phase III. A Science of Management. Expansionist tendencies in definitions of the boundaries of public administration also were manifest in Phase III, in two opposite ways. From one perspective, Phase III argued for a deepening of the analytical focus of the field. But another kind of expansionism was still the order-of-the-discipline, for Phase III was rejected, generally and early.

The history of Phase III may be phrased in bold terms without sacrificing essential accuracy. The concept had a short reign as king-of-the-mountain, even if its fling was glorious while it lasted. Moreover, Phase III did not capture public administration as did naive politics/administration, although it had many powerful proponents, and still retains some of them. Essentially, Phase III today gets its strongest support in business schools and in various academic units teaching "generic management."

Both the briefness and the brilliance of the ascendancy of Phase III in public administration have similar roots. Roughly, Phase III may be characterized as concerned with managerial phenomena, that is, with the administration component of Phase I. Phase III was variously restricted, but in an imperialistic sort of way. To sample facets of the paradox: Phase III often was expressed in terms of a concrete working locus at lower levels of organization; it proposed to deal with specific but diverse phenomena within that locus; and yet Phase III urged that its results applied to all or many organizations and not only to public ones.

Providing details about Phase III is complicated by the variety of forms in which it appeared, as well as by the fact that some of its forms are still evolving. Broadly, the Phase III spirit is reflected early in the "principles" literature. Somewhat later, that spirit got forceful expression in the decision-making schema of Herbert Simon, which sought to encompass a central and generic managerial process from mathematical/statistical and also behavioral perspectives.[18] And the Phase III spirit also is clear in contemporary work on organization change and renewal,[19] which stresses behavioral learning designs that lead to changes in interaction as well as in policies, procedures, and structures.

Such complicating factors notwithstanding, Phase III's status as the guiding concept for public administration was determined by reactions to three major technologies/orientations as they existed in the 1930s and 1940s. They are:

1. Scientific Management, as typified by time-and-motion studies;
2. early work in Human Relations, largely in sociological studies which emphasized the limitations of Weber's bureaucratic model and stressed "informal organization"; and
3. the focus on Generic Management.

Consider several significant commonalities of these major early expressions of Phase III. Paramountly, all three varieties are based on faith that a science of administration is both desirable and possible. Moreover, all three share the view that "administration is administration," wherever it is found. Proponents of Phase III did not place exclusive or even great stress on public *or* business contexts.

The three major expressions of Phase III also reflect an incredible diversity, both as between the three types as well as between several proponents of the same orientation. Scientific management, for example, shared a low-level bias—both conceptually and in level of the hierarchy stressed—with early work in human relations. Both of these Phase III varieties also treated values similarly, and unsatisfactorily. Thus garden-variety approaches to scientific management obscured the role of values in carelessly arguing that there is a "one-best way" to organize work that inheres in specific situations. Similarly, early human relations work—often called "cow sociology"—typically reflected the implicit goal of molding humans to more or less hostile but inviolate technological requirements. Technological values simply overshadowed the values of man, in crude but useful summary; and men adapted to the technology—whether willingly, or kicking and screaming, or somewhere in-between. At the same time, work in the early human relations tradition was largely a reaction against the mechanistic bias of scientific management. So great was this reaction, indeed, that work in the human relations tradition has only recently given major attention to the technological contexts within which behavior at work occurs.[20]

Generic management presented the most marked contrast with the other two varieties of Phase III work. It focused on processes and activities—leadership or planning or whatever—that were considered common to many or even all realms of the management of men, which processes and regularities might appear at many or all levels of any organization. Moreover, generic management also was seen as integrating the behavioral, the mechanical-procedural, and the substantive as they interact at work.[21]

In a simplified but meaningful contrast, generic management is to scientific management more or less as "Fayolism" is to "Taylorism."[22] Thus Taylor's scientific management emphasizes mechanical or technical features at low levels of industrial organizations, and generally excludes all but a narrow range of values centering on economy. On balance, in contrast, Fayol was concerned with processes such as leadership that are level-universal, that encompass mechanical/ technical but also behavioral aspects, that exist at all levels of all human organizations, and that patently must treat issues of value as well as empirical questions. At the same time, both Fayolism and Taylorism were motivated by the common goal of a science of management.

No doubt the key difference between generic management and scientific management or human relations lies in the treatment of values. Much long-standing work in the tradition of generic management made clear provisions for disciplining the use of empirical knowledge by suitable values. Basically, analysis and application were seen as posing different issues concerning values. Thus only a very narrow range of values was relevant for *analysis*, that is, for work leading to the development of an *empirical theory* of what conceptual entities co-vary in organizations. Consistently, Urwick announced in the major *Papers on the Science of Administration* that:

... there are principles which can be arrived at inductively from the study of human experience of organization which should govern arrangements for human association of any kind. These principles can be studied as a technical question, irrespective of the purpose of the enterprise, the personnel comprising it, or any constitutional, political or social theory underlying its creation.[23]

The key words are: *can be studied.* At the same time, values were seen as crucial in the *application* of any results of study. That is, values were crucial in developing *goal-based, empirical theories* of how Organization Man must go about getting what it is that he values based on empirical knowledge of what covaries with what. The key words at this second level are: *can be applied.*

Given that there is no simple description of generic management, then, it is characterized by a marked deepening or analysis following the model of Phase I. Generic management did emphasize the "internal" aspects of administration, "the carrying out of official policies and programs." However, that emphasis was no monomania, being a pragmatic judgment about where continued effort was most likely to generate early results of broad applicability. The judgment often was confirmed, as in the development of "group dynamics" with its development of major theoretical networks as well as applied technologies for organizational and personal change. Moreover, generic management packed great conceptual content into this narrowed focus, and sought near-universal generality. That is to say, Phase III proponents saw themselves as handling matters that were practically and theoretically formidable. With varying justice, a charge of trifling could be made against scientific management and early work in human relations, two other varieties of Phase III work.

The impact of Phase III, in whatever form, can only be evaluated in terms of polarities. When Gulick under the impetus of Phase III derived the famous term POSDCORB from the first letters of purported administrative functions, public administration was by general consensus at the top of the heap in terms of competence in comprehending large-scale organizations.[24] A rash of published and unpublished work spanning the period between the Great Depression and World War II established this superiority definitely over what was going on in business administration.

But early Phase III was more faith than good works. It was stronger on preaching about general "management principles" than in discovering specific ones. Moreover, the early work on human relations and the fantastic interest in scientific management had two features—a low-level bias as well as a markedly manipulative and unilateral character—that implied a wide range of difficulties for students of public administration whose professional socialization emphasized a normative ethos built around representative democracy.

Polarities are not necessary in evaluating the fate of Phase III as the dominant concept for public administration, however. The early successes under Phase III proved no match for the allures of a broader definition of the scope of public administrative. Less moderately, both proponents and opponents inclined toward the view that the three varieties of Phase III work were all more or less undifferentiated and inadequate. Martin can be relied on to describe the doomed character of Phase III, which he dated as having "approached full fruition" with the 1927 publication of W.F. Willoughby's *Principles of Public Administration*, and as having "achieved its pinnacle" with the 1937 *Papers on the Science of Administration*. Martin at once accurately illustrates the common lack of differentiation of Phase III efforts, and also contributes to it by his use of the blanket term "scientific management" to encompass all Phase III work. Martin notes:

As applied to public administration, the credo of scientific management came in time to be characterized by attention to administration without much stress on the *public* part of the term, by faith in "principles," by emphasis on science in administration, and by divorce of administration and values. . . .

In the atmosphere provided by scientific management, a mechanistic concept of public administration came to prevail widely and in important circles. Administration was separated from the legislative . . . "Politics" was anathema— not the politics practiced by administrators, but the politics of the "politicians". . . . Champions of the new order wrote and spoke . . . as though man were nothing more than "administrative man," eager to spring to his place in the organization table and fall to on his appointed segment of POSDCORB.[25]

Later Phase III varieties in public administration—especially Simon's decision-making schema—had to swim against the substantial and general tide of opinion represented here by Martin. Simon's *Administrative Behavior* was published just as the mass of specialists in public administration were gathering momentum for their rush into Phase IV, which will be discussed in detail later. Simon left no doubt as to his hunches about what was happening around him. He opted for Phase III, as specifically defined in terms of his decision-making schema, and he recognized its ties to Phase I.

These summary statements may be supported economically. Thus Simon predicted that the public policy redefinition of the scope of public administration implied the end of the golden days of Phase III, whose fuller flowering he correctly perceived as being just around the analytical corner.[a] Unfortunately for Simon, at least, he was a little too far ahead of the research that would substantiate his hopes. As it was, his argument was an easy target. And he also warned that the public policy orientation would set scholars in flight after multiple analytical will-o'-the-wisps, thereby destroying that "center" so vital to a healthy discipline. Simon held out little promise for the success of the effort, but he thought he knew what success in public-policy terms required: ". . . nor can it stop when it has swallowed the whole of political science; it must attempt to absorb economics and sociology, as well."[26] The maw of the public policy approach, that is, was cavernous for Simon, as it may be for others now.

Simon not only pointed with alarm, however. He provided an alternative definition of the scope of public administration in terms of focus. As Landau observed, Simon's contribution was ". . . all the more significant in the face of the general disorganization which had occurred. Simon was trying to redefine public administration so as to give it a 'solid center', a standard of relevance, a set of operating concepts—to make it, in short, a 'field' of inquiry. This was the function of the decision-making schema."[27]

---

[a]That fuller flowering occurred in the late 1950s and 1960s, basically in schools of business, industrial administration, or generic management.

Simon's decision-making schema may be described briefly, and this toward dual ends. The description will sketch the Phase III variant of the scope of public administration he proposed as an alternative to the public-policy orientation and that description will outline the senses in which Simon attempted to sharpen Goodnow's analytical distinction between politics and administration. Simon saw "deciding" rather than "doing" as the heart of administration, and focused generally on the "premise of decision" rather than on "decision." The distinction was deliberate and consequential, for it reveals Simon's analytic or synthetic interest, as opposed to an empiric one rooted in specific decisions. To develop his position, decision-making involves both factual and ethical elements. "Facts" and "values" differ fundamentally (see Chapter 1). Thus the former may be validated by empirical tests; and the latter are imperatives beyond empirical proof or disproof *per se*. In Simon's terms, "different criteria of 'correctness' ... must be applied to the ethical and factual elements in a decision."[28]

The basic distinction between factual and ethical elements is analytic or synthetic, as Simon recognizes. Reality does not always divide so neatly. Given that behavior in organizations is intendedly purposive at multiple levels, an "end" in some immediate means-end linkage may be a "means" in a more distant means-end linkage. Simon's decision rule for applying his analytical distinction is this: As far as decisions lead to the selection of "final goals," they are considered to be "value judgments" beyond empirical validation. When decisions implement any final goals, they are "factual judgments" (see Chapter 1).[29]

Major parallels were drawn by Simon between his schema and Goodnow's analytical distinction of politics and administration. Remember, Goodnow had proposed that politics and administration be distinguished analytically in terms of different criteria of correctness. Administrative issues are beyond politics in that they "do not require external control because they possess an internal criterion of correctness," embracing as administrative issues do the "fields of semi-scientific, quasi-judicial, quasi-business or commercial activity" which all have "little if any influence on the expression of the state will." Political issues, in contrast, are value-loaded and beyond scientific standards. Simon sees a transparent parallel here with his decision-making schema. "The epistemological position of [*Administrative Behavior*] leads us to identify [Goodnow's] internal criterion of factual correctness," he spelled-out the matter, "and the group of decisions possessing this criterion with those that are factual in nature."[30] "If it is desired to retain the terms 'politics' and 'administration'," Simon concluded, "they can best be applied to a division of the decisional functions that follows these suggested lines. While not identical with the separation of 'value' from 'fact', such a division would clearly be dependent upon the fundamental distinction."[31] Significantly, Simon is also careful to discourage the reader from interpreting his analytical distinction as one of locus, as a latter-day concrete separation of politics/administration based on value/fact differences. The point is patent in his discussion of democratic institutions, which he notes "find their

principal justification as a procedure for the validation of value judgments."
Simon continues:

If the factual elements in decision could be strictly separated, in practice, from
the ethical, the proper roles of representative and expert in a democratic
decision-making process would be simple. For two reasons, this is not possible.
First, as has already been noted, most value judgments are made in terms of
intermediate values, which themselves involve factual questions. Second, if
factual decisions are entrusted to the experts, sanctions must be available to
guarantee that the experts, will conform, in good faith, to the value judgments
that have been democratically formulated.[32]

Only conjectural explanations are possible about why a common grave was
generally dug for the three early varieties of work in Phase III, as well as for later
varieties such as Simon's decision-making schema. But communal grave-digging it
was, and at least six reinforcing factors seem both probable and significant in its
short reign. In large part, first, the demise of Phase III seems a result of
intellectual leadership from political science, which all but unanimously took to
the public policy track of Phase IV. Keeping up with the respected scholarly
Joneses no doubt was a potent factor, given public administration's subordinate
status within political science, and given the organizational ties common
between the two areas.

Second, the demise of Phase III seems due to a common feeling among
students that they had gone about as far as they could go with it.[33] The
fascination with the mnemonic POSDCORB, to exaggerate the point somewhat,
suggested to some that there was nothing really new in public administration.
This was reasonable enough a reaction, in the early flush of discovery and in the
absence of tools for intensive behavioral and mathematical/statistical analysis.
The manifold senses in which a Phase III concept could support theoretically
and practically significant work became manifest only in the late 1950s and
early 1960s, and by then most students identified with public administration
had long been on another track. In the interim, guardianship of Phase III had
passed essentially into the hands of researchers in our numerous schools of
business and departments of industrial administration, where fantastic advances
were made in mathematical and behavioral extensions of administration as
viewed internally. Public administration—which started it all—quickly became
largely a bastard child at a family outing featuring a feast of managerial research.
An increasing number of students trained in political science but having
particular interests in administration did the reasonable but difficult thing,
beginning especially in the 1950s. They sought, or were seduced into, employ-
ment in schools of business or "generic administration."

Third, the eclipse of Phase III can be attributed to the general unavailability
in public administration of the enhanced analytical skills required by the
concept, but for which no real groundwork had been laid. "For the man who

wishes to explore the pure science of administration," Simon described the training required to exploit generic management, "it will dictate at least a thorough grounding in social psychology."[34] But few students of public administration (or of political science) could boast such a background. More significantly, little motivation and less opportunity existed before World War II to develop such competencies. With few exceptions, moreover, the usefulness of social psychology in public administration was little explored in specifics.

This condition had two prime consequences. Primarily, Phase III was vulnerable to "put up, or shut up" challenges. Hence Wallace S. Sayre in 1958 dismissed Phase III "prophets" as having offered "a new administrative science" which was not widely accepted because of the patent failure of the concept to produce new and useful results.[35] In addition, and far more critically, the providing of appropriate skills and training for Phase III was left essentially to the other social sciences, and to business schools, whose adherents got an enormous head start in the behavioral and mathematical analysis of organizations. This head start led to increasingly active poaching on the disciplinary turf of public administration, which of late has encouraged public administration specialists in smallish numbers to develop some of that "thorough grounding" which Simon correctly perceived as necessary some two decades ago.

Fourth, Phase III had a short run because it was perceived as sharply narrowing the scope of public administration. Values were neglected in much work in Phase III, for example, particularly in scientific management and in early human relations. This neglect was unacceptable to many students of public administration, especially those steeped in the normative ethos of political science.[36] The deep concern felt by many capable students did not encourage the drawing of fine distinctions and, as typically happens, popularizers of the basic issues exaggerated the real points of difference. The deep concern of value-conscious scholars tended to be expressed in sharp denunciation, consequently, which was extended more or less uniformly to all three early varieties of Phase III work, as well as to later varieties such as Simon's decision-making approach.

Fifth, Phase III in many respects seemed a bad bargain, as a brief catalog of particulars implies. Perhaps primarily, Phase III had some patent parallels with the naive separation of politics and administration proposed by Phase II. These parallels include the common emphasis on internal administrative processes, as well as the common avoidance of value issues reflected in much of Phase II. The analytic guns being leveled against Phase II during the period around World War II thus often hit Phase III targets, even if they were sometimes innocent ones. Relatedly, Herbert Simon—a major Phase III proponent—tied his early work to Goodnow's *analytical* distinction between politics and administration.[37] Only a little overexuberance was required to conclude—as many did—that Simon was merely resurrecting the *concrete* distinction between politics and administration of Phase II, which political scientists were zestfully attacking even as Simon wrote.

Some observers also saw Phase III as more of a scholarly suicide pact more than an analytical promised land. To sample only: Phase III required commitment to "science" but did not furnish specific directions for attaining it; the several varieties of Phase III work required new competencies which either were being handled well by other specialists, or whose contribution to the study of public administration was unclear; all varieties of Phase III were seen as cutting off public administration from vast areas of traditional concern; and Phase III offered science as a colorless substitute for the rich prescriptive and normative concern that is so vital a part of the heritage of American political science and public administration.

Sixth, Phase III advocates hardly presented a unified front. For example, one advocate of a science of administration—Herbert Simon—delivered the most powerful indictment against the very "principles" that were long accepted by earlier preachers of the gospel of administrative science.[38] Such an indictment could be interpreted in two ways: as reflecting the logic by which science progresses; or as reflecting the improbability or impossibility of an administrative science.

The latter interpretation it tended to be, and neither proponent nor opponent was much given to generosity or forebearance. Oppositely, indeed, nuances had a way of becoming mammoth differences of principle. For example, Simon argued for his "pure science of administration" in terms that commonly were interpreted as intended to sever public administration from the consideration of values, as well as from broad areas of political science. However, Simon's major thrust was not always as sweeping as his interpreters claimed. At least part of the time, that is, Simon was clearly concerned only with establishing that there were at least two major kinds of work to be done in public administration, and that these two types of work must be distinguished. In addition, Simon did not see the two types of work as mutually exclusive. Indeed, they might be mutually stimulating. Thus Simon in 1947 saw two groups of students in public administration. One group sought after the "pure science of administration," which required "at least a thorough grounding in social psychology." The other, and far larger, group were deeply concerned with a broad range of values and eager about "prescribing for public policy." The latter ambition for Simon implied an enormous analytical range that "cannot stop when it was swallowed up the whole of political science; it must attempt to absorb economics and sociology as well." Simon saw the real danger of a loss of identity for public administration in the latter approach, but he did not see the matter in win/lose terms. "If my analysis is correct," he explained, "there does not appear to be any reason why these two developments in the field of public administration should not go on side by side, for they in no way conflict or contradict. But the workers in this field must keep clearly in mind in which area, at any given time, they propose to work."[39]

Could a massive and monolithic interest have encouraged the general lumping together of the conceptual good and bad of Phase III, and could that interest have discouraged the kind of living together of the two orientations to public administration held out by Simon? Speculate about a narrowly-political issue that had an unknown but probably significant impact. Directly, many observers came to the conclusion that a Phase III concept probably was "the single greatest threat to the continuing dominion of political science over public administration."[40] These may seem surprising words, but consider that in Phases I and II public administration was tied to political science via two major conceptual linkages: the two areas of scholarly activity focused on more or less overlapping stages of the formulation/implementation of the same public policies or programs. Phase III threatened both these linkages. As formulation of policy and its implementation were differentiated, that is, so also would be weakened the conceptual ties between the two areas of study. And if "administration is administration," this would challenge the basic tie of political science and public administration through common programs. Relatedly, also, separate schools and strong relations with business schools would become more appropriate for public administration. The threat was plain to many observers,[41] who were also concerned about the appearance of schools of generic management which were less vulnerable to a charge of being "business-dominated."

Preserving the "dominion of political science over public administration" was a great concern during the period after World War II, that much is clear. And Phase III won few admirers among those who saw it as a threat to the linkages of political science and public administration. Why the dominion of political science was of such concern after World War II can only be speculated about, but the speculations have a compelling quality. Clearly, political science had come upon hard days immediately after World War II.[42] Professionally, as by the National Science Foundation, the discipline was considered a distinctly-junior member of the social sciences. Organizationally, specialists in at least public administration and international relations were generating some real steam for secession. Financially, also, the American Political Science Association was experiencing a significant and prolonged challenge to its healthy existence. In sum, the Phase III concept of public administration would have had to offer tremendous advantages to gain wide acceptance at any time, and particularly so after World War II. The advantages of Phase III, however, were anything but clear at that time.

Phase III could not win for losing, in fact. It was widely seen as sharing a number of features with Phase II, such as the separation of politics/administration. Such sharing—sometimes real, sometimes not—encouraged censure. At the same time, where Phase III work differed fundamentally from Phase II, that also was considered censurable. That is, Phase III emphasized the universality of administration, which distinguished it sharply from Phase II's territorial definition of *public* administration. Moreover, all Phase III work often was perceived (and sometimes misperceived) as neglecting vast phenomenal areas of interests of students of public affairs, while it urged commitment to a science whose efficacy was then questionable. This uncomfortable duality invited rejection.

In sum, then, Phase III threatened long-standing identifications, at an inopportune time and with an approach whose potential could be challenged.

Phase IV: Public Policy Approach. Whatever the full catalog of reasons, many students moved toward a Phase IV concept of the boundaries of public administration, toward what is generally called the "public-policy approach." The emphasis can be dated accurately enough as a post-World War II phenomenon, and it was led by the most prestigious scholars from public administration and political science.[43] Phase IV was built upon two basic themes: the interpenetration of politics and administration at all or many levels (or "sets")[44] and the programmatic character of all administration.[45] In sum, these themes directed attention in public administration toward *political* or *policy-making* processes, as well as toward specific *public* programs.

Phase IV is definitely not monolithic. Two varieties of the genus require early distinguishing; and four varieties of "public policy" will be distinguished later. For present purposes, note only that the immediate discussion focuses on a gentle concept of "public policy," a kind of comfortable metaphor for a broad community of interest that many students share. Some later attention is also given to public policy as a focus for scientific inquiry, for many purposes a different notion altogether.

Whatever its specific variations, Phase IV had multiple attractions. Conceptually, that is, Phase IV reasserted the ties between political science and public administration in two ways: via emphasis on a common locus through the programmatic aspects of administration, and via stress on the interpenetration of politics/administration. Such an emphasis consequently highlighted the role of values in public administration, an emphasis congenial to almost all political scientists. At the same time, the emphasis also patently was not "mechanical" like scientific management, so often criticized by political scientists and such a major brand of Phase III work. In addition, in effect, Phase IV undercut the rationale for the pairing of public administration with business administration, both in substance and in spirit. Administration was not administration, in sum.

Other attractions of Phase IV became clearer over time, and especially in the late 1950s and early 1960s. Perhaps two factors contributed most to such a growing appreciation of the attractiveness. Thus both political science and public administration had moved into a "post-behavioral era,"[46] after two or three decades of preoccupation with "behavioralism." For present purposes, more or less, behavioralism in political science can be roughly characterized as:

1. *descriptive* in its approach to political policies, processes, and institutions, which encouraged an emphasis on what exists, or equilibrium
2. *interdisciplinary* in the sense that it "was widely felt that the study of

political behavior required that a political scientist must first be a psychologist or sociologist"[47] and master *their* research methods and technologies
3. *value-free* in the sense that only a narrow range of "scientific values"[48] was to be admitted to analysis
4. often[49] associated with a philosophically *"liberal" position* with an emphasis on "freedom, equality, and the dignity of man," typically expressed as an *ethical relativism* which defines the "good political life" as a resultant of the pushes and pulls of various groups or interests.

These characteristics of behavioralism ill-suited *the* issue of the 1960s and 1970s: "...in all the stress and disequilibrium, governments had failed to perform as fully and predictably as we had grown to expect."[50] The effects were dramatic. From one perspective, Lowi reports, "government in all its complexity became a series of variables rather than one undifferentiated constant" as it more or less was for the preceding thirty years. Moreover, to rely on Lowi again: "Suddenly there were thousands of students who were screaming against current political science courses and in favor of 'relevance'. Political science was, justifiably, accused of defending establishments."[51]

One scrambling first-approximation of the post-behavioral era was essentially a counter-manifesto. Thus substantial avant-garde attention in both political science and public administration was given in the 1960s to developing an approach that was:

1. *prescriptive* as to the content of political policies, processes, and institutions, which implies the need to re-raise and answer such traditional questions: What is the just state?
2. *intradisciplinary* in the sense that it redirected attention back to what Lowi calls macro-politics: "the nature, composition, and functioning of the political system" with emphasis on "political theory, public law, institutional economics, and old-fashioned political institutions"[52]
3. *value-loaded* in pervasive senses, in that values are explicitly admitted at all or many stages of analysis, even encouraged
4. *philosophically non-parochial*, as in admitting: *radical* values aimed at destroying the existing order as a prelude to building some new political order; as well as *conservative values* seeking the reformation of the existing order

The "policy orientation" well-suited these evolving emphases. The goodness-of-fit had at least four components. First, and no doubt primarily, the focus on policy had the effect on both political science and public administration of emphasizing their common and distinctive "political" content. As Kelley noted: "Most generally, the dispute of politics concern matters of policy, not grand ethical principles."[53] Greater relevance for both disciplines, then, would result from addressing the burning questions of the 1960s and 1970s, in this view, which also were the ultimate questions of justice, equity, and the good civic life which had been major preoccupations of the pre-behavioral political science.[54] For Lowi, the most important questions were:

- What is the policy as a policy, defined not as an isolated individual decision but as part of a "long line of intention" of government?
- What is the policy as a law, that is to say, what is the specific type of coercion behind any policy?
- What is the impact of the policy on the political system?
    - —e.g., How will different kinds of policy and coercion affect the long-run capacity to govern?
    - —e.g., How do current policies affect the access of all publics to the political system?
    - —e.g., How and to what degree do current policies and types of coercion provide defenses against bad policies?[55]

And Lowi advises asking these questions, as is, no matter how imprecise the tools of analysis. Better tools are to be worked toward, to be sure. But the central questions cannot be postponed until those tools become available.

Second, the emphasis on public policy would reduce the time and effort devoted to mastering interdisciplinary technologies and knowledge, and hence permit increased attention to unique disciplinary concerns, especially for beginning students. The underlying motivation can be diverse. Thus some are concerned that many or all students of political science or public administration can do no more than dabble in other disciplines, and induce paternalistic forebearance among real specialists. Moreover, some observers are at least dubious that interdisciplinary linkages can be developed in the proximate future, especially given the macro character of the central concerns in political science and the micro emphasis in much of sociology, psychology, and economics. More narrowly protectionist sentiments also may apply.

Third, political scientists had long maintained that "theirs is *the* policy science." Some observers were pleased to see political scientists now doing something to deserve that claim;[56] and others announced that "it may turn out that the sister disciplines have more to learn from political science than the other way around."[57]

Fourth, as Dye put it so straightforwardly, the emphasis on policy analysis is the "thinking man's response to demands for relevance." As was true in many disciplines, to provide brief background, both political science and public administration were rocked by forms of the political activism so prevalent in the late 1960s, whose major thrust was that professional relevance required drastic reshaping of how scholars approached their work and obligations. Commonly, this reshaping threatened academic values about objectivity, dispassionate analysis, the nature and use of "truth," and so on. Dye and others saw policy analysis as slipping between the horns of the dilemma, of permitting greater relevance while preserving academic values. He explains:

... that political science can be 'relevant' ... without abandoning its commitment to scientific inquiry; that social relevance does not require us to reject systematic analysis in favor of rhetoric, polemics, or activism; that knowledge about the forces shaping public policy and the consequences of policy decisions is socially relevant.[58]

Both concerning politics/administration and behavioralism, to conclude, the postwar support for Phase IV implied valid claims, but moderation was not the order of the day. For example, while Lasswell urged empirical science in the service of democratic values in his Phase IV definition, many others took the stress on values or policy to be rather more of a dancing on the grave of Phase III administrative science.[59] Moreover, leading Phase IV definitions—somewhat on the order of Phase I—argued the unreality of naive politics/administration. However, the general run of interpretations stampeded beyond such reasonableness.

Also expansively, Phase IV attempts to establish the linkages between political science and public administration often turned into exercises that conceptually implied the congruence of the two areas of study. Quite expansively, that is, the public-policy approach of Phase IV builds around variations on this theme: "... as a study, public administration examines every aspect of government's efforts to discharge the laws and to give effect to public policy...."[60] There is no mistaking the change, certainly. In surveying concepts of the scope of the field of public administration, for example, Landau sees the sharpest differences between the definitions of the 1930s and those of the 1950s. Indeed, except for transdisciplinary ambitions, Phase IV is the end-of-the-line. Landau put the point sharply: "The field of public administration is left with an imprecise and shifting base, indistinguishable from political science. [In Phase IV], public administration is neither a subfield of political science, nor does it comprehend it; it simply becomes a synonym."[61] That conclusion need not be tentative. Thus Waldo cites the "current view" that "a theory of public administration means in our time a theory of politics also."[62]

These considerations permit a general conclusion, and require an introduction to a more specific analysis. Overall, many students of public administration opted for Phase IV, consistent with their common training and identification with political science. Perhaps, in addition, some students were merely running scared. Political science was in delicate financial and professional condition following World War II, and it also was rocked by threats of secession. A public policy definition of public administration clearly served to reinforce ties-in-jeopardy. Such a surmise helps explain the swift and widespread acceptance of Phase IV, which essentially rolled-back some four or five decades of history which to a degree had differentiated political science and public administration. In this sense, then, Phase IV may have constituted something of a conceptual re-action.

To introduce a more specific level of analysis, four varieties of "public policy" must be considered to support two summary conclusions. First, all limits of real locus and analytical focus tended to be swept aside by some Phase IV definitions of the scope of the public administration. Second, more limited "public policy" concepts have added much richness to the analysis of governmental activities.

Four Varieties of "Public Policy": From Guiding Metaphor to Encompassing Paradigm

There is no way to tell whether "public policy" is the conceptual end-of-the-road for public administration. Indeed, only four points seem beyond any reasonable dispute. That is, the tide for public policy is running full and strong. As Dye notes: "today the focus of political science is shifting to public policy—to the description and explanation of the causes and consequences of government activity."[6 3] Consequently, a critical perspective is difficult to sustain while maintaining credibility. Moreover, the wide adoption of a Phase IV concept raises many issues of locus and focus. Finally, there are several more-or-less distinct public policy approaches, and these have characteristics and probable consequences that differ profoundly.

The approach here is to distinguish three major varieties of the "public policy" concept, and to speculate about their several impacts on public administration. Thus "public policy" has been conceived as:

1. a guiding metaphor that expresses a broad and diffuse scholarly community of interest
2. "descriptive policy analysis," after the fashion popularized in political science
3. "prescriptive policy analysis," after the pattern of an applied blend of the social sciences with technologies for choice and decision-making

Public Policy as Guiding Metaphor

Public policy as a guiding metaphor for a broad scholarly community of interest has long been with us, and usefully so, but only up to a point. To put the matter in the boldest terms, the public policy orientation was initially offered as an integrative concept reinforcing ties between political science and public administration. But only some varieties of the concept provide such integration. That is, Phase IV also contributes to fragmentation between political science and public administration, as well as to confusion within public administration. It is also likely that things will get worse.

The summary conclusions above will be developed in terms of three developmental themes in the history of public policy as a guiding metaphor. In turn, emphasis will be given to:

1. early public policy usage, which emphasized case studies;
2. frameworks for structuring the rigorous analysis of public policy-making and policies; and
3. public policy as defining the field of inquiry for public administration and political science.

By way of introduction, the first two themes imply a gentle reliance on public policy as a guiding metaphor, whose products often were useful aids to analysis and discussion of governmental activities. The third theme is seen as less benign, as more mischievous.

Early Usage and Case Studies. Case studies reflect an early reliance on public policy in their focus on the formulation and implementation of specific public policies. The case study approach—whose use has been common in policy research in political science generally—received its biggest boost in the seminal volume edited by the late Harold Stein. Its title—*Public Administration and Policy Development*—left little to the imagination about where it stood with respect to Phase II and early varieties of work in Phase III. The volume looked at case studies as both *process* and as *politics*. The former has basic reference "only to the internal functioning of a public agency," as in the act of bringing "to bear on a decision all the relevant intellectual resources" by using hierarchy to integrate appropriate specialties. "Politics" basically refers to an administrator's "understanding and pursuit of his objectives and his relations with the social environment outside his agency. . . ." To be sure, "politics" in this sense exists to a degree in all organizations, as when businesses give conscious thought to their several constituencies. But "politics" is at least in degree more prevalent in public administration, and it is "politics" that Stein emphasizes when he has a choice. He explains that "public administrators" generally stand apart from "private administrators" in one crucial particular: they are "far more deeply affected . . . by large, complex, often vaguely defined, social objectives and by need for adjusting effectively to a highly complex environment composed of many forces, frequently conflicting—individuals, private associations and the government itself."[64] The sources of these centrifugal pressures are diverse and deeply set, in the "Constitution, our customs and traditions, the size and complexity of our land and our society." Consequently, Stein notes that:

Every executive agency, and many of its top administrators, have responsibilities to or toward the President, to a variety of control agencies either only partially or not at all under the President's discretionary supervision, ordinarily to at least four congressional committees, to Congress more generally, and to an indeterminate number of individual Congressmen and Senators; to the organized and unorganized constituencies of the agency; to pressure groups, public and private, local and national, powerful or merely persistent; frequently to the courts, and occasionally to a political party.[65]

"It is in this atmosphere," Stein concludes, "that the administrator makes his decisions."

Beyond such general emphases, case studies can be characterized as often-massive chronicles that seek to "tell it like it was." They are careful historical accounts, told from the standpoint of the more-or-less neutral observer who assiduously seeks to develop a narrative after exhausting available documents and sources. The historical sequence of events in time normally provides the structure for organizing the case narrative. Beyond that critical assumption, early case studies eschew explicit theory or interpretation.[66]

The associated public policy concept was a general one, fittingly. Note that Stein does not even attempt to define policy, even though it is prominent in his volume's title. Policy is more illustrated than it is defined, in sum. Stein was in good company in this regard. For example, Appleby—who is by any measure the father of "public policy"—uses the term hundreds of times without being concerned with more than a general specification of the concept. Hence, to Appleby:

1. policy-making is . . . the exercise of discretion"
2. the matter involved "value-judgment, hence policy-making"
3. At every level, the answer to the question 'What is my judgment about this which I have to decide, or about this on which I need to have a judgment?' is a policy question.[67]

Beyond such general definitions, the acceptance of public policy as a broad metaphor is also implicit in other early conceptual fuzziness. To illustrate, administration for Appleby is one of the eight political processes, which may be said to be coextensive with "government." Although "all administration is political," in Dunsire's words, "some [administration] is more political than other."[68] Moreover, Appleby also proposes two "scales for distinguishing between kinds of administration": one runs from "more political" to "less political"; and the second distinguishes the kind of administration which involves more policy-making from the kind which requires less. Throughout, however, the terms "politics" and "policy" are only vaguely distinguished, and are all but equated.

The total sense is that of a very broad and amorphous concept, with a strong integrative thrust. Practically, that is, I surmise the concept was imprecisely drawn so as to provide an acceptable definition of mission-and-role for many scholars and practitioners. Conceptually, also, the looseness seems appropriate to the magnitude of the task of the policy orientation. Notice the integrative challenge in Jones' contrast of a "policy approach" with an "institutional approach." Jones explains that the latter emphasizes developing generalizations about a single institution. He notes: "Questions to be answered include the following: What is the function of this institution (e.g., Congress) in the overall political process? How is this function achieved: How does the behavior of specific actors contribute to the function of the instituion?" In contrast, the bias of leading questions necessary to ask about substantive public problems is pervasively integrative. As Jones explains: "This emphasis forces the student to consider cross-institutional relationships since it asks simply: How is this problem acted on in government? To respond intelligently, you must see where the problem takes you rather than limit yourself to one institution in government."[69]

The case study approach to the interpenetrations of politics/administration held center stage for a decade or so, and its net result was to strongly reinforce ties between political science and public administration. Thus interfaces between interest groups, legislatures, and administrative agencies were highlighted; the fact/value mix was inescapably illustrated, as in tethering concern with "public interest" to specific administrative ways of seeking the good civic life; the subtle interplay of policy development and implementation were dramatized; and various conceptual out-reaches were encouraged, as via explorations of the usefulness of such interdisciplinary empirical research as that on groups.[70] The overall picture is one of a complex comingling/separateness of various specialties in political science and public administration. Operating only somewhat in an opposite direction, some varieties of "public interest" formulations were unrelievedly prescriptive and subject to the charge that they were false to the real world, as perceived by politicians and working administrators.

Structured Analysis of Public Policies. More recently, a variety of attempts have been made to structure the analysis of specific public policies, again often using case studies. The goals of such "structuring" of analysis are direct. They seek to:

● emphasize description of what exists, as contrasted with prescription of what should exist

● engage in a rigorous search for the causes and consequences of public policies

● develop and test general propositions about these causes and consequences, whose accumulating product will be research findings of general relevance.[71]

These goals are tethered in one sense, and expansive in another. Thus the emphasis on accumulating descriptive propositions is rooted in paucity. "Social scientists," Dye advises in italics, "simply do not know enough about individual and group behavior to be able to give reliable advice to policy makers."[72] But that emphasis on description is also challenged by a broad vision of what needs doing, which only begins with a description of the content of public policy. Beyond that, public policy can be seen as a kind of dependent variable, which varies with environmental forces, institutional arrangements, and political processes. And beyond that, public policy also can be viewed as an independent variable (a point Spadaro, Dye, and Stedman also raise here). Thus policy can impact on the political system as well as on social and economic activities, in expected or unexpected ways.[73]

In short, the four goals for structured analysis of public policy refer to a vast analytic domain. This domain is detailed most conveniently within two categories, which are variably exclusive but usefully distinguished nonetheless.

Impact Analysis. Of the two categories of structuring the analysis of public policy, the more narrowly bounded seeks to focus on their impact. Following Dye,[74] "impact" is understood in the sense of multidimensional effects or consequences on:

1. some specific target situation or group, such as users of hard drugs;
2. "spillover effects" on situations or groups other than the target, such as young people riding in a curtained van who are not drug users but who some authorities might suspect;
3. future as well as immediate conditions, such as long-run "respect for law" as well as impact on present usage;
4. direct costs, as in resources devoted to programs consistent with policy goals, including police, informers, trained dogs, etc.;
5. indirect costs, including forfeiting other things that might be done with the resources.

The basic notion of impact analysis is straightforward, but the detailed working-through of uneven, apparently simple cases often contains major surprises. The focus is on policy as an independent variable: Does the implementation of a specific policy yield what is intended? With what unexpected consequences? Why? Consider the wide use of DDT in Asia after World War II. The realized and intended consequences included the alleviation of much human suffering by almost eliminating malaria. But the balance of humankind and nature is seldom trifled with. In this case, DDT usage had a major and largely unexpected impact on population growth. More recently famines in parts of the world can be traced in some degree to the well-intentioned efforts after World War II by organizations such as the UN's World Health Organization.

Although narrowly bounded in one sense, impact analysis of even a very specific policy can spiral out to overwhelming complexity. For example, analyses of the impact of our recent selective service policies required poking in the very guts of our social and educational institutions.[75] Similarly, efforts to assess the impact of such programs as Head Start soon had analysts wrestling with the child-rearing practices and cultural mores in the home and immediate neighborhood.

Hence little evidence exists about systematic learning from policy experience. As Dror concludes: "Very few evaluations of the real outcome of complex issues are made, and there are even fewer on which improvements of future policymaking can be based."[76] To put it otherwise, even determined analysts lack major parts of the puzzle of estimating policy impact. Specifically:

1. the major objectives may not be defined precisely, or they may be conflicting or even contradictory;
2. the principal outputs may not be subject to gross estimation, let alone precise measurement, due to their complexity;
3. it may be impossible to identify the inputs of required resources—especially "indirect" and social costs—so that they can be estimated and aggregated;
4. it may be difficult to compare alternative combinations of inputs and outputs;
5. it may be practically difficult and politically impossible to compare programs for alternative uses of the same resources.

More Ambitious Analysis. Whereas impact analysis is particularistic and is tied to specific policies, the following four varieties of analytic effort emphasize broad comparisons leading to generalizations. Moreover, these four varieties aspire to greater rigor in testing for associations and relationships. Some would call these varieties of policy analysis more scientific than impact analysis. They patently are more ambitious.

First, some students have sought to differentiate kinds or types of policies, so much the better to search for generalizations about differences between types. These can include differences in: where different classes of policies get support or opposition; what roles are played in various phases of policy-making by diverse elites or segments of the population; of how various types of policies come to be enacted or rejected; etc. For example, Mitchell and Mitchell distinguish six kinds of problems which have social or political significance, as mentioned previously.

- resource mobilization
- distribution of benefits
- allocation of costs
- controls
- adaptability and stabilization
- division of labor and role allocation.[77]

Substantial literatures have developed around such classificatory efforts, with the goal of a kind of fine-tuning for analyses of public policy. There are major problems of method and substance with these literatures when approached rigorously,[78] to be sure. But the purpose is straightforward: to provide subclasses of "policy" which can, however preliminarily, help structure the search for similarities or differences between classes.

Second, and relatedly, numerous attempts have been made to structure analysis by detailing the steps in, or the functions of, the generic process of policy-making. For example, Jones suggests ten "functional activities in the policy process," while urging the reader to understand that they are "tentative and undogmatic." He identifies:

1. perception
2. definition
3. aggregation/organization
4. representation
5. formulation
6. legitimation
7. application/administration
8. reaction
9. evaluation/appraisal
10. resolution/termination[79]

Illustratively, such lists can help in both the description and evaluation of policy-making. Descriptively, they encourage attention to the fullness of activities involved in policy-making, patently, and consequently underscore the need for integrative analysis (see the use of sets in Chapter 1). Thus the perception of an issue, referring to the list of policy-making functions, might be basically in an interest group or trade association; the formulation and legitimation of a policy response often would be accomplished in various congressional and executive offices; application and administration of that policy might be delegated far down the hierarchy in some public agency; etc. Moreover, evaluatively, such lists also can help in judging the adequacy of particular policy-making sequences. For example, evaluation and appraisal have long been neglected aspects of policy-making processes, even if they are critical ones. Lists like the one above highlight such neglect, and can remind both the formulators and analysts of public policy to go all the way.

Third, other students have attempted more elaborate efforts to structure the analysis of public policy. Thus one set of scholars have used various theoretical or interpretive frameworks to describe or discuss individual policy-making sequences. For example, Crane Brinton's[80] broad theory of social revolutions has been used as a conceptual framework for describing administrative reorganizations. And Graham T. Allison applies three conceptual models to the same single event: the blockade of Cuba by American forces during the missile crisis during the Kennedy administration.[81] Similarly, other scholars have attempted to use case studies or analysis of policy areas in novel ways. Thus Sundquist attempts to explain the cyclical character of our political and governmental systems, to add perspective on why periods of intense activity and relative quiet seem to alternate.[82] He makes liberal use of mini-case studies. Moreover, Mosher has sought to analyze a batch of case studies to help determine, among other aims, the degree of direct applicability in large organizations of the sociological and psychological research with concepts like "participation."[83] The latter research was often rigorous, but it then dealt basically with small groups. Mosher's goal, then, was to assess the applicability of a kind of micro-analysis in much larger organizations.

Significantly, these structuring perspectives or models need not be direct importations, as it were. Thus Dye illustrates the usefulness in analyzing public policy of six models that had variously gained significant attention in political science and public administration. These models include:

1. systems model
2. elite-mass model
3. group model
4. rational model
5. incremental model
6. institutional model.[84]

In permitting such illustrations of the simultaneous applicability of observational or interpretive perspectives that already had gained some currency, of course, policy analysis serves to build on the past, as well as to suggest higher-order integrations possible in the future.

Fourth, other scholars have sought to do wide-ranging analyses of broad policy areas, such as water resource development,[85] or the environment,[86] or whatever. The approach has one prime consequence. It avoids the particularism of individual case studies or, to say much the same thing, roots the analysis in an evolving context of law, precedent, and the working resolution of major issues-in-contention over time. The analysis of broad policy areas in this fourth sense, that is to say, helps emphasize the full sense of the "political" in political science.[87]

These four major kinds of approaches to structuring the description or discussion of policy-making processes have several common features that fill important needs. Thus they all direct attention to the kind and quality of the policy products that are being generated by our governmental institutions and processes. Any derivative insight is most helpful, given the widespread concern if not disillusionment with public policies today. Relatedly, such multiple efforts to structure reality can be revealing because they provide reinforcing perspectives. As we all know, where one sits determines what one sees. The application of various kinds of interpretive or analytical structures for viewing the policy-making process thus can enrich understanding and control. Finally, such structuring devices are oriented toward systematic analysis of public policy. This orientation is often seen as a good in itself, as developing an "increased concern for social relevance of potential study," and also as helping focus attention on the possibility of informed and meaningful choice, both for policymakers as well as for citizens. As Jones explains:

Why not . . . attempt to analyze in such a way that teachers, students, and policy makers can determine the social value of what is being learned? This is not to say that you or I should become advisers to those who are governing, though some of us shall. It is rather to suggest that students of politics should begin to employ their increasingly sophisticated tools of analysis so as to contribute more directly to social action.[88]

Public Policy as Defining the Field of Inquiry. Another class of interpretations has a less benign potential. Examples will be relied on heavily to illustrate the referent here, which is global in extent but elusive in content. That is, the focus is on interpretations of public policy as a broad conceptual umbrella for encompassing fields of study, as contrasted with defining or differentiating them. Only two points will be dealt with here specifically, by way of suggesting how the concept can contribute to a fragmentation between political science and public administration, as well as to confusion within the latter.

Consider a significant if delicate point, to begin. It is but a small step from arguing that, if specific public programs or policies are so central, the reasonable thing to do is to begin organizationally spinning-off an array of "administrations" that have so far made more or less strong claims for attention. These include: development administration, comparative administration, criminal justice administration, ecological administration, environmental administration, urban administration, transportation administration, welfare administration, *inter alia*. There is fragmenting potential aplenty in such a possibility.

Care is appropriate on this point, in the sense of affirming and denying. To affirm: such policy-oriented efforts as that of Price on science,[89] or Caldwell on the environment,[90] are patently central in public administration. That is to say, "public policy" can clearly and properly be *one* of the several secondary or tertiary organizing foci for public administration. To deny: having made such an affirmation, the position here rejects the capacity of any policy-orientation to provide the stable primary organizing focus. To the contrary, if anything, such an orientation is perhaps inherently fragmenting as a primary organizing focus, unless two conditions hold:

1. that students of public administration are willing to settle for relatively superficial acquaintance with a number of policy areas, as a concession to the complex historical, institutional, procedural, and personality detail involved in relative mastery of any one policy area; or

2. that students of public administration are able to develop detailed acquaintance with several policy areas, despite the complex historical, institutional,
procedural, and personality detail involved in relative mastery of any one
policy area.

The first condition is undesirable; and the second is unlikely. Their common
probable consequence is an unproductive discharge of energy spent in pursuit of
the undesirable and/or the unlikely.[91]

The probable effect of reliance on public policy as a primary organizing
focus, then, is to spin-off a variety of "administrations." My own view is that
such fragmentation is not practical now in public administration, given our
existing resources and knowledge, and given that a very substantial "critical
mass" of both is necessary to trigger concerted effort in any single "discipline"
or "field," however it is defined. In any case, public policy poorly serves those
interested in defining mission-and-role for public administration to the degree
that its basic thrust is to induce numerous mini-administrations.

A second way of illustrating the awkward effects of reliance on public policy
as the primary organizing focus is more robust. Even if the fragmenting potential
discussed above is effectively checked, that is, disciplinary exuberance re Phase
IV qua gentle metaphor has its clear costs. Paramountly, many phase variations
are so general as to be elusive and perhaps even dangerous. For example, Landau
stresses that the definition of the scope of public administration in terms of
public policy metaphor "challenges the integrity of the 'field'." The "rigidities
of the politics-administration dichotomy" need correction, he observed, but the
public policyers provided the correction only be defining away the problem. A
Phase IV concept, Landau continued, is "so extensive as to provide little
meaning." Indeed, he notes, the public policyers "make it virtually impossible to
specify an area of [governmental] activity that cannot be considered within
[their] scope." The Phase IV definition of the field, that is, often fails two
primary tests: it does not designate clearly the phenomenal field of interest; and
its locus is as wide as all political science. Landau pushes the point even farther.
"In the effort to define the field," he concludes, "the field evaporates."[92]

Recent disciplinary history provides support for Landau's position, given a
scattering of notable exceptions that seek to define scope and method for public
administration.[93] Two kinds of examples support the point. To begin, consider
Mosher's response to this central question: Is public administration a discipline?
He concludes:

Public administration cannot debark any subcontinent as its exclusive province—
unless it consists of such mundane matters as classifying budget expenditures,
drawing organization charts, and mapping procedures. In fact, it would appear
that any definition of this field would be either so encompassing as to call forth
the wrath or ridicule of others, or so limiting as to stultify its own discipline.
Perhaps it is best that it not be defined. It is more an area of interest than a
discipline, more a focus than a separate science.[94]

This response implies significant costs for public administration as a distinct area of inquiry. Rather than being a proud area of specialization, public administration must somehow find its "chief satisfaction in providing a way of looking at government." Waldo expressed one logical conclusion of this perspective: "What I propose," he noted, "is that we try to act as a profession without actually being one and perhaps even without the hope or intention of becoming one in any strict sense." This offers only a vague opportunity, if it is not a death-rattle. Waldo himself observes: "Frankly, it took some courage to say that, as it is patently open to ridicule."[95]

Some scholars go even further on the theme that "public administration cannot debark any subcontinent as its own." For example, a recent text comes close to defining public administration as a kind of derivative or resultant category. The volume's "principal roots are in political science," the reader is told, "and it seeks to bring together that information about administration that is most relevant to an understanding of the larger political process. Of necessity, much of this information concerns *public* administration."[96]

"Descriptive Policy Analysis"

Not all public policy variants rely on a global concept; nor do they all propose to redefine the boundaries of public administration. Beginning in the 1960s, that is, a number of political scientists began pioneering in the discrete analysis of quantified aspects of public policies, relying on newly-available electronic data-processing equipment to manipulate large batches of data according to well-established statistical conventions, within the broad framework of "systems theory."[97] In this approach, to quote Thomas Dye: "Public policy is viewed as an output of a political system which is acting in response to environmental forces and in which outputs themselves are viewed as having an independent feedback effect upon the environment in the political system."[98] Such work is here labeled "descriptive policy analysis," respecting the distinction suggested by Yehezkel Dror without employing his terminology.[99]

Descriptive policy analysis is straightforward in concept, but single studies can deal with a hundred variables and hence often are complicated. Essentially, the focus is on individual public policies—or more precisely, on narrow indicators of some characteristics or outcomes of the implementation of public decisions in selected issue-areas—both as dependent variables and independent variables. The analyst then searches for differences among units at the same or similar level of government—often states, but not necessarily so—that covary with differences in quantifiable aspects of similar policies. For example, in a historically-significant study Dye analyzed the interaction between some "system characteristics" of our several states and differences in aspects of their public policies. His research design is schematized in Figure 3-2. Contrary to the

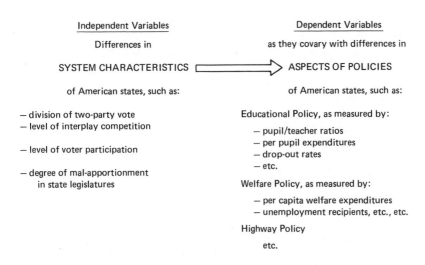

Figure 3-2. A Characteristic Research Design for Descriptive Policy Analysis. Source: Based on Thomas R. Dye, *Politics, Economics, and the Public: Policy Outcomes in the American States* (Chicago: Rand McNally, 1966).

common wisdom, Dye reports that system characteristics have little impact on public policy outcomes. He concluded:

... partial correlation analysis reveals that these system characteristics have relatively little *independent* effect on policy outcomes in the states. Economic development shapes both political systems and policy outcomes, and most of the association that occurs between system characteristics and policy outcomes can be attributed to the influence of economic development. Differences in the policy choices of states with different types of political systems turn out to be largely a product of differing socioeconomic levels rather than a direct product of political variables.[100]

Explanatory policy analysis patently constitutes an important area of inquiry but, for a variety of reasons, it does not provide a viable mission-and-role for public administration. Moreover, it is possible that the approach also implies major conceptual problems for political science.

Four points support these conclusions. First, explanatory policy analysis gets double-barrelled reproof for what it is as well as for what some of its adherents maintain it should become. The approach has been criticized because it fixates only on those narrow aspects of policy that have been quantified, which to some observers leaves something to be desired. Thus Jones hopes in print: "Perhaps Dye's analysis will be extended to consider the major determinants of policy outcomes that are less easily quantified—perhaps more significant to the polity."[101] If the approach is too narrow for some, however, it also causes problems because some adherents argue that an adequate descriptive policy analysis in the longer-run requires a profound redefinition of disciplinary territory. Thus for Dye there "is no doubt" that the evolution of explanatory policy analysis "requires an expansion of the traditional boundaries of political science well beyond any previous definition of those boundaries." He argues:

If public policy is to be the dependent variable in our research, we must be prepared to search for policy determinants among economic, social, cultural, historical, technological factors, as well as political forces. If public policy is to be the independent variable, we must be prepared to search for policy consequences which are economic, social, cultural, historical, and technological, as well as political.[102]

Second, some commentators have been concerned to emphasize the critical differences between "descriptive" and "prescriptive" approaches to policy analysis. The following section attempts to describe the evolution of the latter approach. For present purposes, the prescriptive approach seeks to bridge several related gulfs: that between "study" and "practice," as well as that between a "pure science" and an "applied science." The thrust toward application does not characterize descriptive policy analysis, which is steadfastly oriented toward analysis or study only. This simplification implies major analytical advantages. But that simplification also constitutes a major limitation as far as public administration is concerned, which in essence is devoted to bridging the gap between thought or research and action.

Several methodological concerns exacerbate this significant limitation. For one thing, the most common statistical procedures in descriptive policy analysis—various forms of correlation analysis—are competent only to establish covariation, as distinguished from causality or interrelationship.[103] So it is necessary to be careful in interpreting such descriptions of what exists as those Dye offers, so as to respect the limitations of the statistical technology. Hence the results of the typical piece of descriptive policy analysis can only be used cautiously, if at all, in formulating answers to key questions with which policymakers must deal. Such a key question is: "If we vary X in a specific case, what will happen to variable Y?" At its best, descriptive policy analysis is better suited for making only tentative statements of this form: "If you look at variable X in a number of justifications—like states, or cities—we may find some non-random distribution of differences of variable Y." This is useful information, but it must be interpreted narrowly. Larry L. Wade expresses the point elegantly:[104]

... as Morss has pointed out, these studies in no way *explain* the manner in which community decisions get made; at most they enable one, within a more or less known margin of error, to predict what state expenditures will be, given knowledge of the variables (nonpolitical) which are related to expenditures.[105]

This is clear enough. However, if prediction is what is sought, the wrong variables have been analyzed since the best predictor of a state's expenditures is probably the state's revenues. Another excellent predictor would be last year's expenditure, modified by whatever growth factor, if any, appears to be roughly constant.[106] Of course, neither revenues nor past expenditures, although very highly correlated with current expenditures, explain anything at all. They are aids to prediction, however, and are important for that reason.

Moreover, the phenomenon of "spurious correlations" implies potentially significant questions about the real meaning of any such distribution of scores of Y and X.[107]

These methodological concerns may be expressed economically. Any description of the covariates of policy—as dependent or independent variable—should be tentatively interpreted as long as non-experimental research designs are employed. And this will be a very long time indeed, in the general case, given the enormous problems of formulating experimental designs that are policy-relevant.[108] Time-series designs—observing the interaction of any variables X and Y over a long period of time—sometimes can help in this regard. But the passage of time typically sees major changes in environmental, cultural, legal, or demographic characteristics that complicate or even confound analysis.

Third, the units of analysis in descriptive policy analysis—typically states, or cities, or regions that coincide with state boundaries—may be more convenient than they are realistic wholes that deserve to be treated as entities. The issues are fiendishly complicated, and for now only two points are clear. Thus data-gathering would be enormously more complicated if, for example, Sharkansky had not chosen to define regions as having boundaries coterminous with state lines, as he realizes.[109] Convenient compilations typically classify data in terms of some legal jurisdiction, such as a state, of course. Moreover, it is not clear whether convenience distorts reality, in this case, or just delightfully simplifies the task of analysis.[110]

Fourth, despite its substantial impact on research[111] and on contemporary leading ideas,[112] the literature of descriptive policy analysis has generated some important second thoughts. Relevant revisionary themes relate to both broad concept as well as to interpretations of specific results. At the conceptual level, for example, Sharkansky and Hofferbert conclude that: "We have been too simple-minded in our measurement of 'politics' and 'policy'." Moreover, they note: "There is no single answer to the question: 'Is it politics or economics that has the greatest impact on public policy?'"[113] Wade adds important qualification relevant to common interpretations of descriptive policy analysis as constituting a world-view of the determinants of policy. He notes:

What we may undoubtedly observe is that *some* political factors are not closely or even remotely associated with the determinants of public policy, but this is a far cry from asserting that policy is produced largely or even principally by socioeconomic factors in all, even most cases. [The] views which hold politics to be insignificant to policy choices [are exaggerated].[114]

Such ferment is encouraging from a scientific perspective, of course, but it also implies caution. Descriptive policy analysis does provide a model for research with a self-correcting potential. But the work with correlates of aspects of policies is controversial in its implication of an economic determinism; and that work does raise methodological questions. Hence the area clearly can support scientific inquiry, and indeed requires it. Judgments about the adequacy of the world-view implicit in much existing research are best delayed, however.

"Prescriptive Policy Analysis"

Other proponents—and without doubt, *the* presently most influential proponents—of a public policy concept make Dye's expansionism look puny in comparison. These proponents argue for an emerging field of policy sciences, which is here called "prescriptive policy analysis." Policy sciences do not define the scope of public administration, except to provide for its inclusion in a broad supra-discipline, one version of which was described by Bunker in these terms:

The creation in 1968 at the State University of New York at Buffalo of a new Doctoral Program in Policy Sciences recognized both the growing body of significant scientific work bearing upon an understanding of policy processes and the need to work toward its integration and its utilization in the improvement of practice. The Buffalo program is concerned with the development of the policy sciences as an interdisciplinary field bridging the social and decision sciences, and with the preparation of hybrid research-scientists/practitioners who can make the fruits of this new interdiscipline accessible to policy-making and social guidance elements in our society.[115]

There is no simple way to introduce the policy sciences, and probably no really satisfactory brief way. But we can try. At the broadest level, Harold Lasswell provides useful guidance. "The policy sciences may be conceived," he notes, "as knowledge *of* the policy process and of the relevance of knowledge *in* the process."[116] This takes a very critical step beyond "descriptive policy analysis," in short, which focuses on knowledge of the policy process only. That step is both significant and difficult to attempt. As Bernstein notes, social science research has been "disappointing" in furnishing guidance for policymakers, and governments have therefore had to make policy decisions on the basis of scanty information about their probable effects. The policy sciences seek to fill this critical void. As Bernstein continues:

Policy analysis is the attempt on the part of social scientists to remedy this informational vacuum by studying the problems of society through systematic frameworks which include the means for gauging changes in society's condition through various policy interventions taking the form of either allocation or regulation.[117]

Lasswell argued for the same step in 1951, to be sure, but developments since then add the force of major increases in technical sophistication to his argument. For one thing, the intervening years have witnessed the evolution of and experience with what Dye calls "public choice models." They include operations research, cost/benefit analysis, and so on, and commonly "emphasize concepts of rationality and focus on the relation between values achieved and values sacrificed in public policy alternatives."[118]

The application of such models was given major impetus in the 1960s by a pressing need to decide between alternative courses of public action, given new and often unreconcilable demands for greater shares in public goods. At first, the need for policy analysis was most recognized in national security affairs, where "policy sciences first got named and flourished." When domestic problems were first considered, in Lewis' words, they "were largely macro-economic and were themselves associated with our emerging world role: Could we 'afford' our foreign policy?" Then came the 1960s. Then Lewis reminds us: "What is now termed the urban crisis was blasted into the forefront of public attention by the events of Watts, Hough, Detroit, Newark and on and on, [and] actions were set in train which might ultimately cause substantial reallocation of resources to the internal problems of the nation that show their symptoms most dramatically in our cities."[119]

This combination of technology and experience in national security, and of urgent domestic need, has emboldened many to urge development of the policy science. Consider the visionary words of Dror:

Establishment of policy sciences as a new supradiscipline involves a scientific revolution, requiring fargoing innovations in basic paradigms. Particularly essential are: (1) integration between various disciplines, and especially of social sciences with analytical decision approaches; (2) bridging of the "pure" vs. "applied" dichotomy; (3) acceptance of tacit knowledge as a scientific resource; (4) changes in interface between science and values; (5) broad time perspectives; (6) focus on metapolicies; (7) commitment to policymaking improvement; and (8) concern with extrarational and irrational processes, such as creativity.[120]

Without wishing to rain on anyone's parade, but risking that consequence nonetheless, two conclusions seem patent. The policy sciences clearly do not provide an immediate conceptual or practical solution to the problem of defining mission-and-role for public administration. That is particularly the case for those who find it strategic or politic to maintain strong ties with political science.

These two broad conclusions cannot be proved in any vigorous sense, but two perspectives on such a proof can be shared conveniently. It is necessary to be harshly selective, but the two perspectives should serve to make the present point. One of these perspectives is conceptual, the other is practical.

A cluster of major conceptual concerns with "prescriptive policy analysis" may be distinguished. Essentially, granted that this may only be a temporary condition, it is fair enough to characterize the policy sciences as resting on optimistic assertions that they can or usually should avoid the inadequacies or awkward assumptions of predecessors, primarily "systems analysis" and "systems engineering." This negative and hopeful mode of establishing the policy sciences as a new supra-discipline is reflected, for example, in Dror's list of "required innovations" detailed above. Consider one commonly-cited "unrealistic assumption" of the decision and analytic technologies associated with systems analysis, such as operations research. That is, they admit only variables that can be quantified. To improve on such an inadequacy, Dror prescribes that the policy sciences should and perhaps can admit a far broader range of data dealing with institutional or political factors, or even with what Dror calls "tacit knowledge." Similarly, if many systems analysts accept "unrealistic assumptions" about "economic rationality," Dror prescribes that the policy sciences should and perhaps can provide satisfactory inclusion of "extrarational and irrational processes."

This negative and optimistic mode of establishing the policy sciences raises substantial concerns. Basically, at a minimum, the should/can gap can be an enormous one. To emphasize how a new supra-discipline should surpass its predecessor may motivate needed exploratory commitment and effort. But such emphasis can also: fail to recognize valuable lessons in the experiences of those predecessors; it may have to rediscover objective dilemmas that remain as recalcitrant as they were when the predecessors failed to resolve them; and the boosterism may be ungenerous and induce counterproductive competition. Hence Radnor's plea "for unity in place of competition"[121] in efforts that seek to establish the role of the policy sciences vis-à-vis the "management sciences" or "systems analysis." Hence also Radnor's caution about the present developmental stage of the policy sciences, and his conviction about what progress will inevitably mean:

> ... Policy Sciences if it does develop, in trying to become operational, [will develop] its own set of "unrealistic assumptions," in many applications. We should also adopt a large measure of suspicion for any science and technology which purports to be *the* science or technology which eliminates once and for all the unrealistic assumptions and models of its predecessors. It is the very essence of systematic and scientific approaches that we endeavor, as best we can, to model and approximate the systems that we wish to analyze. There are no sciences without models, there are just sciences with better or poorer models. The development of useful and operational models will be a critical testing point for Policy Sciences.[122]

Among some political scientists, at least, the emphasis on prescriptive policy analysis is suspect in this regard in a special sense. That is, some observers see policy sciences as simply providing a new front or legitimation for the very micro-analytic methods and technologies whose use was earlier inspired by the behavioral era in political science and public administration. Such observers question, or deny, the applicability of micro-phenomena relevant to policy analysis.[123] Or such observers may question or deny the applicability of the assumptions of the technologies of other disciplines. For example, Adams questions whether two assumptions of economics drawn from the private sector—the production model and evaluation by return on investment—make sense in the analysis of public policy.[124]

Moreover, it may even be that the should/can gap is simply insurmountable in a more basic sense. Hence Rittel and Webber argue that the "search for scientific bases for confronting problems of social policy is bound to fail," the best intentions and efforts of researchers notwithstanding. The reason lies in the "wicked" nature of the problems of social policy. They explain:

Policy problems cannot be definitively described. Moreover, in a pluralistic society there is nothing like the undisputable public good; there is no objective definition of equity; policies that respond to social problems cannot be meaningfully correct or false; and it makes no sense to talk about "optimal" solutions to social problems unless severe qualifications are imposed first. Even worse, there are no "solutions" in the sense of definitive and objective answers.[125]

In contrast, the problems with which science has successfully coped are "tame," they are analytical pussycats by comparison. One observer made that comparison in an interesting way. Electrons are easier to study, he noted, if only because they cannot read tomorrow's newspaper describing their behavior, and because they cannot opt to change that behavior on the basis of their reading.

It is probably premature to judge whether Rittel and Webber are correct. It is certainly not too early to agree that the problems of public policy are truly wicked ones, and well beyond our present power to deal with scientifically.

Conceptual issues aside, a cluster of practical concerns must be faced if prescriptive policy analysis is to provide conceptual guidance for public adminis-tration, and especially so for those who desire strong interfaces with political science. Paramountly, the policy sciences are proposed as a supra-discipline and—although all versions are developmental and no pattern can yet be called prototypical—their common organizational form is an interdisciplinary program or school.

Even this early evolutionary form implies several practical concerns. Primar-ily, at least in the short-run, the interdisciplinary thrust raises the hoary issue of the complex relationships between individual scholars and practitioners, their several subject-matter disciplines, and the matrix organization. In this sense, the policy-sciences approach does not resolve the issue of mission-and-role for public administration or political science. Rather, it relocates the issue, and brings to bear on it a new set of constraints/opportunities, which probably will differ widely from case to case. Bunker implies relocation vs. resolution in his discussion of "prescriptive policy analysis" as "an applied social science approach," while acknowledging that "the task of bridging between the form and content of the social sciences and policy problems is still far from complete." He sees social science as heuristic, as enriching "frames of appreciation," but as essentially a failure in helping decisionmakers deal with the problems they confront. Bunker acknowledges only a "partial exception to this indictment" in some areas of applied welfare economics. He concludes:

Part of this strain between scientific and applied concerns derives from the fact that while scientific work tends toward specialization and the divergence of disciplines, policy problems don't present themselves as convenient packages suited to the prevailing styles of disciplinary research. There are many other facets of this problem. . . . It is enough for us to say here that our commitment, contrary to prevailing fashions in the social sciences, is toward interdisciplinary and problem-oriented approaches. This applies to both the research and practice aspects of the roles for which we prepare our graduates.[126]

Even given this indeterminancy, however, it is safe to say that a viable partnership for political science or public administration in any policy science supra-discipline will practically require that many, and perhaps most, adherents of those two disciplines who somehow join will bring with them substantial skills in the several relevant behavioral and analytical technologies. Bunker implies this need in his description of the Buffalo doctoral program, which rests on four basic orienting perspectives: (1) general systems theory with special attention to open systems; (2) the central concepts and propositions of welfare economics; (3) contemporary organization theory; and (4) the insights into human information processing provided by cognitive psychology. He explains:

Each of these fields has its penumbra within which each of the others fall, yet each provides an essential and unique framework. General systems theory provides an intellectual stance that aids the perception of function and the ordering of complexity; welfare economics, a theory of choice and a framework for comparison of alternatives; cognitive psychology, a reminder that ideas are not given in nature and that varieties of percepts and images are infinite, lawfully determined, and extremely influential in policy transactions; and organization theory, a sense of the concrete setting of relationships, roles, and purposive assumptions, and normative judgments in which policy issues are embedded.[127]

Bunker notes that not all students are required to develop a working competence in operations research, or quantitative systems analysis, or whatever. But those students are required to become familiar "with the major applications and limitations of these methods, an acquaintance with the logic and intuitive mathematics underlying their use, and an ability to communicate and collaborate with quantitative analysts in project situations."[128]

There are substantial reasons to believe such a partnership will be a difficult one to achieve, if only for three reasons. Practically, although exceptions certainly exist, neither political science[129] nor public administration[130] have provided a particularly congenial humus for the growth of such skills. In a power sense, moreover, Foss argues that political science "has the lowest professional status of any of the social sciences," which implies some obvious difficulties. For Foss, himself a political scientist, the low status has a solid existential base. He notes: ". . . political scientists really do not identify with the profession and our professional organizations have done little to serve their members or enhance the status of the profession; [and] political scientists have little knowledge and few skills that are of interest or value to anyone except other political scientists."[131] Finally, reflections of the concerns above are not always subtle. Consider the reaction of Lowi to learning that the prevailing outlook of political scientists was not even included in the original plan for a symposium on "interdisciplinary approaches to policy study." He explains:

This implied two things. It implied that an interdisciplinary approach to public policy had little to learn from political science. More significantly, it implied that if political scientists were now to interest themselves in policy studies, their primary obligation would be to learn how policy analysis is done from all the social science disciplines *except* political science. There is much we would need to know and are afraid to ask. In effect a political scientist who would be a policy analyst must also be a sociologist, or an economist, or a physical scientist, or an anthropologist, or a geographer, or some combination of these. And the members of those sister disciplines would not have to feel any obligation to become political scientists.[132]

To Lowi, this meant only a regression to the 1950s and the biases of its behavioral era which he hoped had been left behind.

On the whole, then, policy science programs may imply some major political issues for those seeking viable reflections of the interests and concerns central to political science or public administration. Some sense of the kind and quality of those issues is highlighted by this reaction of Vernon Van Dyke to the prospect of participation by students of political science and public administration in a "prescriptive policy analysis" concept. These students, he warned,

. . . might soon find themselves shoulder to shoulder with professors and researchers of almost all other disciplines, trying to solve all kinds of problems . . . An all-out policy orientation would help take political scientists fully into the realm of normative problems and social engineering. The prospect is appalling. . . .[133]

Other observers are less appalled than they are impressed by a kind of "mandarin delusion" underlying the desire to "get into the action"[134] that pervades prescriptive policy analysis, but he is concerned that the desire is more or less doomed to frustration. The heart of it for Horowitz is that: "Social scientists engaged in governmental work are committed to an advocacy model defined by politicians. For the most part, they do not *establish* or even *verify* policy—only legitimize policy."[135] That is, Horowitz concludes that the usual heroic scenario of the policy sciences is substantially a myth. That usual scenario takes some such form:

1. public officials become aware of a "need to know,"
2. but since existing knowledge is inadequate,
3. public officials arrange grants or contracts so as to get appropriate aid from "outside knowledge factories,"
4. and the resulting increase in knowledge then becomes the basis for some action by the originating public officials.

Horowitz proposes an alternative scenario, which he sees as "more nearly empirically verifiable." It begins with policies being decided, somewhere in government. The goals are some real or assumed need of a non-governmental elite or a mass constituency, spurred along by some ambitious public administrators or legislators seeking "to define their uniqueness in the political heavens." Only then, Horowitz notes, is there generated "a frantic search for precedent in the past, justification in the present, and rationalization in the future." And it is only then, he adds, that "social scientists are called to do 'feasibility studies', 'demonstration effects', and 'simulation analyses', which prove beyond a shadow of a doubt the legitimacy of the course of decision-making accomplished [without] any reference to the empirical world."[136]

*Public Policy as Stimulating
a New Paradigm*

The emphasis on public policy at once nourishes and feeds upon a massive reevaluation of this age's leading ideas. That reevaluation takes many forms. At the broadest social level, this generation's writer-of-songs caught the essential spirit in a few words: "The times they are a-changin'." More specifically, political scientists have directed attention to a new and still-emerging *weltanschauung*, a new orientation to the world of scholarly inquiry. And students of public administration, relatedly, have heralded the coming of a new paradigm, a different way of conceiving and structuring their priorities for concern and analysis.

This section develops multilevel attention to these several reevaluations of leading ideas, beginning with major concerns at the frontiers of today's political science. These concerns center around an apparent change in disciplinary focus which may imply a new weltanschauung, or world view, a replacement for the leading ideas that have defined the leading edge of political science over the last two or three decades.[137] Van Dyke distinguishes the two analytic world views at the level of first approximation.[138] The first is concerned with the *form*, or *processes*, of public policy and shares much conceptual ground with the behavioral approach introduced earlier. The second analytic world view stresses the *content* of public policy, and it is consistent with major emphases in the post-behavioral approach also sketched above. Table 3-1 attempts to add substance to Van Dyke's basic distinction, at the risk of overdrawing the differing emphases.

The times during which old world views are challenged or toppled are, almost by definition, exciting and frightening in variable degrees. Hence balance and perspective are likely to be in short supply. So note here that any guiding concept is only a tether, no more and no less; and that is its strength and its weakness. At different times, the balance of benefits over costs will vary. At its best, one world view can provide researchers with a valuable map to significant analytic territory. At its worst, that same weltanschauung may enmesh researchers in a set of sentiments which its subscribers sense only dimly or not at all, a "metaphysical pathos of ideas," even as it misdirects their attention from the relevant to the comfortable and accepted. As Gouldner develops the point:

Table 3-1
Two Alternative World Views for Political Science

Old weltanschauung: form or processes	New weltanschauung: content
1 emphasis on developing general knowledge, theory, and science	1 emphasis on promoting human welfare
2 emphasis on value-free findings	2 emphasis on values, goals, moral judgments
3 emphasis on overall patterns of activity and behavior, on general and enduring features of governmental processes	3 emphasis on specific even if transient features of the content of public policies or issues
4 emphasis on those processes considered presently susceptible to scientific analysis	4 emphasis on structure, dynamics, or policies that are considered relevant to public welfare, their susceptibility to specific analysis being a lesser concern
5 emphasis on large groups, institutions, aggregates	5 emphasis on feelings, attitudes, and motivations of individuals
6 emphasis on the individual as a type, an aggregate statistic, a role-player subject to massive determinative forces that are (largely) uncontrollable	6 emphasis on the individual as a valuing, deciding, and choosing organism who can and should define his environment in significant ways
7 emphasis on non-rational and irrational behavior and upon the situational factors inducing them	7 emphasis on purposive behavior by individuals who reason or act in support/ opposition to specific policies
8 tendency to be action-distant, not of direct relevance to the policy-maker	8 desire to be action-proximate, of direct relevance to the policy-maker

Source: Jean A. La Ponce and Paul Smoker (eds.), *Experimentation and Simulation in Political Science* (Toronto, Canada: University of Toronto Press, 1972), p. 371.

. . . commitment to a theory often occurs by a process other than the one which its proponents believe and it is usually more consequential than they realize. A commitment to a theory may be made because the theory is congruent with the mood or deep-lying sentiments of its adherents, rather than merely because it has been cerebrally inspected and found valid. This is as true for the rigorous prose of social science as it is for the more lucid metaphor of creative literature, for each has its own silent appeal and its own metaphysical pathos.[139]

This writer sees himself as having a foot in both camps represented in Table 3-1. Most of his own work is consistent with the new weltanschauung in major particulars; and yet there are significant reasons to restrain exuberrance. Basically, the emphases of the new world view in Table 3-1 are necessary reactions against extreme extensions of its predecessor. However, history urges caution in such cases. At an extreme, for example, the new world view might encourage a neglect of a man's collective experiences and needs. Indeed, it might even curtail the development of an expanding science. At the very least, lack of caution might exacerbate an inherent potential for conflict. If nothing else, for example, win-lose competition concerning world views can engage powerful forces, including the bittersweet succession of one scholarly generation by another, the related testing of concepts of personal self-worth and of professional standing, and so on. Such competition would be regrettable since, at least in today's political science and public administration, the two world views contain notions of complementary value that should not be sacrificed. The task is more to integrate the two world views, and rather less to displace one by the other.

The evolution of world views in public administration is usefully detailed in terms of three more specific "paradigms."[140] Following Thomas S. Kuhn, the term paradigm is used here to refer to an "essential characteristic of normal science," a general and often implicit agreement about the:

basic concepts [that] establish the essential elements of analysis; and relational postulates and axioms [that] specify the essential rules of reason. These rules of reason enable members of an intellectual community to pursue a structure of inferential reasoning where the work of one can be added to the work of others. Frontiers of knowledge can be extended with reference to the understanding shared by all members of the community.[141]

Scientific understanding also can occur when a paradigm proves inadequate and is replaced by a more comprehensive and applicable one. The period of transition is typically unsettling, as comfortable ideas come unhinged and successor paradigms are proposed and evaluated.

More or less, public administration has experienced the development of three paradigms defining its boundaries. Each of these paradigms will be sketched below in a separate table, and briefly discussed. The paradigms did not somehow explicitly succeed and eliminate one another, please note. Although dominant attention did shift from one to another, over time, the paradigms are best seen as variably-powerful conditioning influences on the work of individual scholars and practitioners.

Traditional Paradigm. Observers agree that the early history of public administration was based on a set of leading ideas like those in Table 3-2.[142] This agreement exists despite some dispute about the intellectual pedigree of that paradigm. Thus most scholars essentially see in Table 3-2 the imprint of the German theoretician Max Weber, who was the major contributor to what has come to be known as the "theory of bureaucracy."[143] Others see the Traditional Paradigm as more of a product of the ideas of Woodrow Wilson and his followers,[144] one of whose papers is universally acknowledged to be a kind of birth certificate for public administration.[145]

The sense of Table 3-2 should be patent. So we need not pause, except to establish how this introduction to public administration paradigms complements the earlier analysis of phases of conceptual development. The traditional paradigm clearly underlays the work characterized above as Phases I and II. But it also provides the world view for some Phase III work, such as that in scientific management. However, the bulk of Phase III work is responsive to the set of leading ideas to be described immediately below. Such multiple and partial overlaps make the history of ideas in public administration a subtle enterprise.

Social-Psychological Paradigm. Beginning with the World War II period, more or less, a new paradigm began to significantly influence the literature of public administration. Conveniently, this new set of leading ideas is here called the Social-Psychological Paradigm, and is detailed in Table 3-3.

"New" here has at least three meanings, which in effect help specify how the Social-Psychological Paradigm differed from the Traditional. First newer paradigm emphasized description, on definite balance, while the earlier one was essentially prescriptive. Consequently, the thrust of much work in the Social-Psychological Paradigm can be characterized in these terms:

- such work often establishes that the conditions prescribed by the Traditional Paradigm do not in fact exist; and/or
- such work sometimes establishes that, even when the conditions prescribed by the Traditional Paradigm do in fact exist, the predicted consequences do not occur in many or most cases.[148]

There is both advantage and disadvantage in this persistent bias of work reflecting the Social-Psychological Paradigm. Illustratively, such work at its best provides a picture of what administrative reality is; and it can also generate a growing awareness of the conditions associated with desirable existential states. However, such work at its worst also can encourage some convenient but dangerous assumptions. These assumptions include two central ones: that what

Table 3-2
Traditional Paradigm

Guiding Political Philosophy	centralized model: power is more responsible and responsive to the degree that it is unified and directed from a single center
Focal Unit of Analysis	formal or legal structuring of individual jobs[146] and their aggregation into complex authority/responsibility networks for accomplishing broad purposes, with jobs being viewed as "building blocks" of larger and static organizational structures[147]
Central Emphasis	emphasis on *a* collectivity that magnifies the impact of separate individuals, permitting several to accomplish what not even the most skillful or powerful individual can do.
Central Concepts	legitimate authority and responsibility
Implied Metaphor of "Organization"	a "trickle down" metaphor: in which there is a single dominant center of power, with absolute or substantial sovereignty and legitimate authority, whose members have little or no control or influence over it.
Guiding Principle	perfection in hierarchical ordering so as to achieve economy and efficiency
Central Focus	prescriptively intra-organizational: on how authority and responsibility in organizations should be structured so as to be internally efficient, effective, and even orderly, reinforced by sharp distinctions between "politics" and "administration"
	the focus is on developing processes and structures for internal control in organizations, with the goal of heightening efficiency and production
Model for Motivating/ Controlling Behavior	within public agencies: command-obey model, a vertical linkage of organizational superiors to subordinates
	between agency and its clients: basically through the ballot box, which impacts on elected officials and, through them, on high-level political appointees
	this pairing of representative democracy in "political" life with autocracy in "administrative" life may seem anomalous or even contradictory, but the pairing reflected the intended superiority of political mandates and also implied the complementary concept of administration as technical, as narrow implementation, and as value-neutral
Dominant Role for Officials	the responsible technocrat, whose tenure and competence are protected by public employ in exchange for political and equal service to all policies and to all administrative superiors

Note: This paradigm borrows several emphases from Vincent Ostrom, *The Intellectual Crisis in American Public Administration* (University, Ala.: University of Alabama Press, 1973), esp. 28-29.

is, also should be; or that any differences are of no concern in the scientific study of management.

Second, relatedly both paradigms focus on the single organization, but the newer paradigm is behavior-oriented, on balance, while the Traditional Paradigm emphasizes legitimacy, structure, and authority relationships. Crudely, in the

Table 3-3
Social-Psychological Paradigm

Guiding Political Philosophy	pluralist model: power is more responsible and responsive to the degree that it is exerted by multiple collectivities, both large[149] and small[150]
Focal Unit of Analysis	"informal" collectivities such as the small group are seen as key elements in large productive or social organizations; indeed, the abreaction to the formal or legalistic approach is so complete that much derivative work can be characterized as focusing on "people without organizations"[151]
Central Emphasis	emphasis on several collectivities or "reference groups," in whose incomplete congruence individuals variously find freedom and fear, security and anomie, emotional support and oppressive conformity[152]
Central Concepts	cohesiveness, group climate or atmosphere, leadership, etc.
Implied Metaphor of "Organization"	a "percolate up" metaphor: in which authority and sovereignty are seen at least as two-way streets, with some formulations like that of Barnard even arguing that: "Authority is the character of a communication (order) in a formal organization by virtue of which it is accepted by a contributor to or 'members' of the organization as governing the action he contributes. . . . Therefore under this definition the decision as to whether an order has authority or not lies with the persons to whom it is addressed, and does not reside in 'persons of authority' or those who issue these orders."[153]
Guiding Principle	increasing the congruence between: the demands of formal organizations; the personality needs of organization members; and the characteristics of the reference groups of members[154]
Central Focus	descriptively intra-organizational: on how organizations and their members actually behave, especially as contrasted with formal prescriptions, with two themes being dominant: —that formal authority is not adequate to describe or prescribe relationships in effective organizations;[155] —that "politics" and "administration" are not sharply differentiated[156] moreover, such descriptive work increasingly begins to generate prescriptions about how to increase the integration of organizations and their employees, with the goals of heightening production *and* employee satisfaction:[157] —in part, these prescriptions are technique-oriented, and deal with decentralized delegation, greater employee participation, etc. —in larger part, these prescriptions are ends-oriented[158] and thus argue for the replacement of the Traditional Paradigm with models of man that rest on such formulations as Theory Y, on Maslow's self-actualizing man, on Argyris' dimensions for individual growth, or Herzberg's concept of motivators vs. satisfiers, etc.[159]
Model for Motivating/ Controlling Behavior	within public agencies: emphasis on how employee participation and group decision-making can complement and to a degree supplement the command-obey model[160] between agency and its clients: emphasis on describing how the control of "politics" over "administration" is limited,[161] as by:

Table 3-3 (cont.)

	—short tenure and inexperience of top-level political appointees; —the identifications of career employees with specific programs or policies, with respect to which they are not neutral even while they might be neutral toward specific political parties or candidates; and —the impact of interest groups on the development and implementation of public policy
Dominant Role for Officials	the representative civil servant who variously influences policy in its development or implementation, and who often identifies with a specific public program and hence is not neutral,[162] but who—because of lateral entrance and the open character of our public personnel systems—reflects the needs and aspirations of the broader citizenry.[163]

latter paradigm, the organization comes first, and people must adapt to it. In the Social-Psychological Paradigm, in contrast, the priorities accorded to organization/individual are certainly not reversed, but their relative weights clearly shift in major ways. Illustratively, the essence of the two themes of "participation" and "group decision-making" is that people and their needs matter, even in organizations, and perhaps especially in organizations. These two themes, of course, are major interpretive derivations from the descriptive research encouraged by the Social-Psychological Paradigm.

Third, the Traditional Paradigm is rooted somewhere "up there" or "out there," as in authority figures and legitimacy. The Social-Psychological Paradigm has a more existentialist and even popular bias, in the behavior of members of an organization. This bias is reflected most dramatically in the definition of authority as in fact residing not in those who issue orders, but in those who are the targets of these orders. To be sure, not all observers were willing to go as far as Simon certainly did go, or as far as Barnard may have gone, in this critical matter of definition. But the Social-Psychological Paradigm clearly provides encouragement for assigning real importance to the receivers of orders. The Traditional Paradigm emphasized the order-giver, in contrast, and encouraged a view of order-receivers as "the hands," a most revealing measure of their worth.

Most Phase III work reflects the impact of the Social-Psychological Paradigm. Note however, that some later varieties of derivative behavioral work in the Phase III tradition—such as the recent attention to organization development—in effect share aspects of the paradigm described above as well as of the one to be introduced immediately below. Much the same may be said of some recent work with rational or formal models of mathematical and statistical analysis. They often reflect aspects of the Traditional Paradigm while they also contribute to this evolving third paradigm.

Humanist/Systemic Paradigm. The very designation of this third paradigm implies the magnitude of the intellectual dilemmas for which it seeks resolution. The goal is nothing less than to integrate that which commonly stands in contraposition, if not stark opposition. Thus the third paradigm is referred to as "humanist" because it places far stronger emphasis on the sovereign individual as needful than does the Social-Psychological model which, however, did much to start that conceptual ball rolling. And the third paradigm is called "systemic" because it proposes to utilize tools and models for analysis that are oriented toward maximizing some sort of broad social utility from the most rigorous analysis of the most comprehensive possible set of social priorities and objectives. This second component of the Humanist/Systemic Paradigm shares significant common ground with "prescriptive policy analysis" described above, as well as with the Traditional Paradigm. The Humanist/Systemic Paradigm, then, is one huge conceptual suture seeking to graft together much that has been disparate, if not separate.

Table 3-4 details this third paradigm, which derives from a large number of sources. The major explicit expressions consistent with this paradigm, however, are in the literature of the "new public administration"[164] and in the recent integrative effort of Vincent Ostrom.[165]

Several major characteristics of the Humanist/Systemic Paradigm deserve discussion. First, like the Traditional Paradigm, the third paradigm is strongly prescriptive. The point is perhaps most easily made in terms of the role demands on public managers that have been derived from the general world view of the third paradigm. Ross Clayton and Ron Gilbert provide an especially comprehensive and artful example of this genre,[170] which is abstracted in Table 3-5. That table takes some liberties with their presentation, but these are minor. Clayton and Gilbert, in effect, prescribe in some detail two ideals: how the public manager should view self; and how the public manager should view the recipients of public services. These "ideal views" contrast sharply, depending upon whether the public manager operates within the framework of the Traditional Paradigm or that of the Humanist-Systemic Paradigm.

Second, one useful way to look at the third paradigm is that it seeks to overcome the limitations of its predecessors by assimilating them. That is, its systemic component owes much to the Traditional Paradigm; and the humanist component derives from the research and thought in the Social-Psychological Paradigm. The third paradigm is very attractive from this point of view, for there are compelling theoretical and practical reasons for attempting such an integration.[171]

Third, and relatedly, the Humanist-Systemic Paradigm rests on substantial development and extension of the theory and technology of its humanist and systemic components. That is:

1. on the humanist side,[172] the third paradigm rests on

Table 3-4

Humanist/Systemic Paradigm

Guiding Political Philosophy	market model: power is responsible and responsive to the degree that it is divided among multiple wielders who can and do limit and control one another
	this prescription is based on:
	—observations as to how large organizations, both public and business, tend to serve their own internal needs at the expense of the needs of their clients or customers, or how they tend to misread or neglect feedback from clients or customers[166]
	—observations as to how supposedly-countervailing organizations can in fact collude to submerge or distort the needs of common clients or customers, as in "sweetheart contracts" between "labor" and "management"
	—conclusions as to the ineffectiveness of *the* tool of popular control, voting in elections by itself, given new tools for inducing and managing public opinion
Focal Unit of Analysis	individuals as sovereign customers with market power, which power is enhanced by the deliberate fragmentation of authority within any one jurisdiction or organization, as well as between several of them
Central Emphasis	emphasis on unmediated response to needs and aspirations of individuals, which implies minimal control or interference by government or other large bureaucracies
Central Concepts	costs/benefits, congruence between social objectives and allocations of resources
Implied Metaphor of "Organization"	a systems metaphor: in which any organizational system is seen as one of a nest of systems of increasing comprehensiveness, with an ultimate system specifying the priorities or social objectives against which the processes and outputs of all less-comprehensive systems are to be judged[167]
Guiding Principle	equity in the service of social justice
Central Focus	prescriptively inter-systemic: the focus is on an organization and its multiple interfaces with clients as well as with other organizations in its total environment[168]
	for example, the emphasis is on the delivery of services which implies, at least, an interface between:
	—efficient internal agency processes;
	—employees who are highly motivated to be responsive to clients, and who are also willing and able to change as well as to integrate diverse specialties at the point-of-delivery; and
	—consumer demands as to when, where, and how agency services are desired
	consistently, distinctions between "politics" and "administration" are blurred or disappear; and determining what is internal to an organization and what is external becomes more come chancy and arbitrary

	the focus is on the kind and character of distribution/consumption, with the goal of heightening and balancing satisfaction both for users of an organization's goods/services, as well as for employees through the quality of the organizational life they experience
Model for Motivating/ Controlling Behavior	within an agency—as well as between an agency, its clients, and other competing/collaborating organizations—many models are potential alternatives to hierarchy, to the ballot box, and to various forms of employee participation: —bargaining —exchange —competition —non-violent demonstration and confrontation —and, perhaps, violent demonstration and confrontation
Dominant Role for Officials	the responsive administrator, a proficient advocate who can be a pleader for a cause dictated by social equity while applying technical or programmatic expertise to the pursuit of that cause any deviations from equity "always should be in the direction of providing more and better services to those in lower social, economic, and political circumstances"[162]

Note: This paradigm draws several emphases from Vincent Ostrom, *The Intellectual Crisis in American Public Administration* (University, Ala.: University of Alabama Press, 1973), esp. pp. 111-12.

—a model of man consistent with the several "growth psychologies," of the person as having relatively specific needs qua human, the satisfaction of which needs constitutes a kind of ontological goal for human development; and

—technologies for individual and organization change, such as those deriving from the "laboratory approach"

2. on the systemic side, the third paradigm rests on

—models for the comprehensive analysis of complex exchanges or input/output transactions, such as systems analysis; and

—technologies for quantitative analysis and decision-making, such as linear programming, queing theory, etc., whose use really began with World War II and has rapidly expanded since then

Fourth, the Humanist-Systemic Paradigm variously seeks to expand the field-of-vision of the two other paradigms. Thus the behavioral focus of the Social Psychological Paradigm often neglects systemic features; and the intraorganizational focus of the Traditional Paradigm encourages the neglect of relationships between organizations, which was also a weakness of the Social-Psychological Paradigm. The Humanist-Systemic Paradigm proposes to include the perspectives of the other two paradigms, and yet improve on them by stressing systemic interrelations.

Table 3-5
The Public Manager, Ideal Views of Self and of Recipients of Public Services, and Two Paradigms

Perceptions of public managers in relation to:	Ideal View of Self	
	In Traditional Paradigm	In Humanist-Systemic Paradigm
—projects	an administrator of	a champion of
—policy	a policy implementer	a policymaker
—perception of political authority	organizationally centered—vertical	community centered— horizontal
—effectiveness criteria	committed to economic and efficient government	committed to social and economic justice
—change	an adaptor who copes	an advocate who influences

Perceptions of public managers in relation to:	Ideal View of Recipients of Public Services	
	In Traditional Paradigm	In Humanist-Systemic Paradigm
—program design	targets to impact	consumers with choices
—political force field	electors of representatives	direct participators
—human needs	categorical	comprehensive
—resource allocation	units or cases	discrete individuals
—services	as a privilege	as a right

Source: Based on Ross Clayton and Ron Gilbert, "Perspectives of Public Managers: Their Implications for Public Service Delivery Systems," *Public Management* 53 (November 1971): esp. p. 10.

Given this expansive characterization—which implies an amalgam of can-do and hope-for—it is no wonder that the third paradigm implies problems as well as promise for guiding work in public administration. Four concerns are most prominent. First, the prescriptive quality of the paradigm raises momentous questions about whether the world can actually become enough like the paradigm requires that it should be. The point is not an obscure one. For the paradigm proposes at once that power be systematically dispersed enough so that consumers of public services have meaningful market power. Yet it also requires that power be concentrated enough to permit the development/enforcement of comprehensive social objectives and priorities. Both individual and comprehensive systemic needs are to be met in the process. The aim is certainly a commendable one; but the required balancing and fine-tuning pose at least a formidable challenge.

Two points, especially, exacerbate the present concern that the prescriptive vision of the Humanist/Systemic Paradigm may be so attractive as to discourage facing monumental practical problems. Thus neither a technology nor representational system yet exist capable of inducing the required paradigmatic blend of individual and systemic needs. Some relevant theory and experience exists with a technology having similar goals in small groups and even large organizations,[173] but no easy extrapolation to broad social systems seems possible. Indeed, that technology is only now beginning to raise the kind of ethical and practical questions that bear on its usefulness for inducing and maintaining appropriate social systems in relatively small units.[174]

Moreover, the history of unattainable prescriptive systems has been a bad one. Consider the excesses committed in behalf of the apocalyptic vision of Marxism, or of the missionary zeal to create "one world in Christ" by "bringing Christianity to the heathen." Specifically, if the ultimate vision seems attractive enough, it can tempt humans to very convenient judgments about the end justifying the means. The human capacity for tragic even if temporary delusion in this regard is a large one, indeed, to judge from our inglorious history.

Second, at a more practical level, the Humanist/Systemic Paradigm prescribes blending two broad technologies that tend to rest on different, even opposed, world views. Broadly, the paradigm proposes to unite these two approaches to administrative phenomena that have stubbornly resisted assimilation or integration:

1. the *rationalists* whose contributions to administrative thought and practice have tended to emphasize technical analysis and quantitative methods, as in
   —Scientific management, as manifested in time-and-methods work and micro-motion analysis
   —mathematical and statistical technologies for decision-making or problem-solving
   —systems analysis associated with PPBS, as in cost-benefit analysis, etc.
2. the *humanists* whose contributions to administrative thought and practice have tended to emphasize social integration and behavioral methods, as in
   —the organization behavior literature, which, in general, establishes the importance of meeting human developmental needs at work
   —the organization development literature, which, in general, proposes a set of learning designs to facilitate the development of organizational arrangements that will be growthful for humans by meeting their developmental needs.[175]

There is no easy and satisfactory way to explain the usual contraposition of the rationalists and humanists, but adherents of the two orientations find themselves on different sides of many fences. Sometimes, that explanation is easy enough. Thus at least some rationalist thought assumes the world view consistent with the Traditional Paradigm, a more-or-less unvarnished Theory X view of the world. And the humanist preoccupation is very likely to be with some variant of growth psychology, one relatively straightforward version of which is the Theory Y world view. A simplified contrast of the Theory X and Y world views is sketched in Table 3-6. They permit easy, and cheap, victories of the humanists over the rationalists. Thus the latter can be rightly accused of ignoring the motivational and emotive aspects of human behavior, and of building upon the shifting sands of assumptions that humans need be considered only as "rational man" or "economic man."

Such an easy explanation often does not apply, however, so the analyst has no alternative but to try harder. Perhaps more often, the rationalist orientation emphasizes administrative reality *as it should be*, given assumptions built into various mathematical/statistical models; and the humanist orientation emphasizes administrative reality *as it can be*, given the central concept of Man as a growth-oriented being whose full range of needs must be met at work to motivate an involved, committed, and even eager participant in increasingly complex and rapidly-changing productive systems. Both rationalists and humanists are likely to disparage work *as it is*. Rationalists are likely to see existing work as a jerry-built and inefficient set of non-systemic compromises; and humanists are likely to see existing work as built around assumptions that—if they are not in fact positively repressive of the human spirit—they at least do little or nothing to encourage the growthful experience at work that will result in more satisfied and productive organizations members.

Table 3-6
Two Sets of Organizationally-Relevant Assumptions and Beliefs

work is inherently distasteful to most people	most people can find work as natural as play
most people prefer to be directed and have little desire for responsibility in developing and maintaining a social system	most people prefer to be self-controlling in the pursuit of organization objectives, and can develop and maintain appropriate social systems;
most people have little capacity for creativity in work or in developing values or norms to guide behavior	most people can exercise significant creativity in organizational problem-solving and in developing values or norms to guide behaviour
motivation occurs only (or mostly) at an elemental stimulus-response level	motivation often occurs in response to opportunities for personal and group development, as well as in response to opportunities to control the work environment; and
therefore, people in organizations must be closely controlled and directed, and often coerced	therefore, most people can be allowed substantial initiative for self-control, self-direction, and self-motivation.

Note: The underlying assumptions and beliefs are based on Douglas McGregor, *The Human Side of Enterprise* (New York: McGraw-Hill, 1960), pp. 33-58.

This second perspective helps, but still leaves much to be explained about why adherents of rationalist and humanist orientations are often at odds. Another try accounts for more of this unexplained variance, perhaps much of it. Most often, perhaps, the difference between rationalists and humanists is a matter of degrees rather than high principle. Thus rationalists may provide for motivational and emotional materials, but they usually assign them a lesser importance than humanists are comfortable with. And humanists may give too little effective attention to rational or technical concerns, similarly, as rationalists perceive the situation.

Such differences in degree can become a polarity, when the chips are down. Specifically, adherents of the two persuasions are likely to differ in their orientations to action-taking. One wag caught much of the sense of this difference in observing that the issues between rationalists and humanists were differences between "pushers and shovers" and "touchers and feelers," at base, differences in degree that could easily escalate into polarities. Oversimply, perhaps, emphasis on individual needs can be seen as implying major difficulties for meeting systemic needs. Hence providing more room for the "touchers and feelers" can make life more untidy for the "pushers and shovers," and vice versa.

A good sense of this mutual potential for escalation is reflected in a discussion of the obvious point that all institutions are today experiencing the profound consequences of a major change in the patterns of needs and motives that individuals are increasingly expressing. Thus two observers note that: "Extrinsic rewards such as pay, job security, fringe benefits, and conditions of work are no longer so attractive. Younger people are demanding intrinsic job satisfactions as well. They are less likely to accept the notion of deferring gratifications in the interests of some distant career."[176] Changes in motives and needs seem to underlie such effects. "In most organizations today," these observers conclude, "the dominant motives of members are the higher-order ego and social motives—particularly those for personal gratification, independence, self-expression, power, and self-actualization. . . ." These newly-aroused motives can take a variety of forms, many of them already familiar. For example:

1. the emphasis on self-expression and self-determination, as in "doing your own thing"
2. the emphasis on growth and self-actualization, as in the "growth center" movement or in sensitivity training
3. the unleashing of power drives, as in revolutionary movements
4. the rejection of established values as repressive and exploitative, which sometimes involves rejection by revolution and is a combined effect of forces such as those above.

There is no easy management of such forces, once unleashed. The difficulty of fine-tuning is manifest, as in the observation that: "With the need for self-expression goes the ideology of the importance of spontaneity; of the wholeness of human experience; the reliance upon emotions; and the attack upon the fragmentation, the depersonalization, and the restrictions of the present social forms." Some observers see traces of these consequences in the anti-intellectualism variously characteristic of many social trends or movements of the late 1960s. These trends or movements include: the ferment among many college and high school students; some forms of the "encounter movement"; and so on. Rationality often comes to be regarded as rationalization in such trends or movements. Or, as in Wordsworth's romanticism, the intellect becomes "that false secondary power which multiplies delusions."[177]

This second point is a simple one, if its development has been longish and complex. The Humanist/Systemic Paradigm poses a real challenge in prescribing the integration of two approaches to administrative phenomena that often have been at sixes-and-sevens. A few notable exceptions permit some optimism that at least partially reconciliable needs are involved, however.[178] But the enormity of the challenge is unmistakable, and it is too little remarked by proponents of the third paradigm.

Third, given these formidable barriers to achieving the balance prescribed by the Humanist/Systemic Paradigm, an organizational equivalent of Gresham's law seems highly probable. In economics, Gresham's law holds that bad money drives out the good. The organizational equivalent maintains that, if both individual and systemic needs cannot be met, or do not seem attainable, preoccupation with systemic needs will be dominant. Even further, some argue that even for relatively small organizations, that is the way it will be *whether or not* it is possible to meet individual needs in any comprehensive way. That is to say, many observers find congenial Carl Rogers' argument that increased concern with human relationships is perhaps *the* prerequisite for managing our institutions. But even many of those observers are not very optimistic that such a "future is in the cards for us." Illustratively, one observer concludes from his experiences in urban settings: "Indeed, the old-fashioned concerns with power, prestige, money and profit so far outdistance the concerns for human warmth and love and concern that many people consider the latter extremely irrelevant in the basic decision making. Sadly, it is my feeling that they will continue to do so."[179]

Such tendencies, patently, do not suggest that success is probable in the delicate balancing of individual needs with the "old-fashioned concerns" a critical balance required by the third paradigm. And, of course, so much the worse for the Humanist/Systemic Paradigm.

Fourth, even granted there is too much bureaucratic bigness in government and business, it is almost certainly the case that even determined efforts at disaggregation will leave us with still-huge units of organization long after passing the point of a reasonably economic smallest-size of operations. For example, one can argue that the thirteen major American oil companies control a very large share of their market, and hence are too "big." But a single modern refinery still costs perhaps $100 million, or more. Consequently, the minimum size of an "oil company" would be "large" even if it were economic to limit each company to a single refinery, which it most definitely is not. Similarly, many public programs are inherently massive, as was (and is) the NASA space program.[180] Hence those who yearn for a return to some kind of gemeinschaft scale of things—as did Karl Marx and as do many contemporary social commentators—are likely to be very much disappointed, short of some total breakdown of life as we have come to know it.

Such facts constitute major objective dilemmas for the third paradigm, and imply major limitations on approaching its philosophical ideal.

Some Concluding Comments

There is no single satisfactory way to conclude this complex analysis, but seven concluding emphases serve to highlight the major thrusts of this argument. These emphases derive directly from the present argument, or are related to it.

First, this analysis is not intended as a King Canute commanding the waters of Phase IV to stop rising, or enjoining Phase II to remain at low ebb. If Phase IV is viable over the long run, for example, the analysis will little harm its development, and may even steer it some. If Phase IV is fated to pass, more powerful forces than this essay will have done the job.

At the same time, there are major practical and conceptual difficulties, ambiguities, and dilemmas with Phase IV variations, as well as with each of the three alternative paradigms that have been dominant in the developmental history of public administration. This analysis seeks to point up such problems, particularly in the context of insistent contemporary demands to settle on a *new* comprehensive paradigm for public administration, and soon.

That insistence on a comprehensive paradigm encourages a disregard of the difficulties, ambiguities, and dilemmas highlighted in this analysis; and that insistence urges early closure toward *a* comprehensive paradigm when it is not clear that public administration is remotely near a stage of development that warrants any serious pretension about any imminent movement toward *a* comprehensive paradigm.

I devote detailed attention to this central point elsewhere,[181] but present purposes can be served by a powerful suggestion of the broader proof underlying the conclusion. Consider the opinion of Kuhn, who is *the* central figure referred to by public administrationists intent on searching for *a* comprehensive paradigm, or a model for analysis "in which a community of scholars shares common theoretical assumptions, and a common language defining essential terms and relationships."[182] Despite the major effort in public administration, in which Kuhn is often cited as *the* authority, Kuhn is clearly not bullish about a comprehensive paradigm, on the order of the physical sciences. "It remains an open question," Kuhn observes flatly, "what parts of social science have yet required such paradigms at all."[183] This would seem to settle the issue for public administration, which has a shorter and less-advanced history of empirical inquiry than many of the "social sciences." Many public admistrationists, then, seem to be emphasizing an unproductive approach. Indeed, it is suggested here that the emphasis may be cruelly counterproductive.

Second, the preceding analysis should establish that each of the "public policy" variations has strengths and weaknesses. The latter are especially prominent in those variations that seek to prescribe mission-and-role for public administration. Those patent weaknesses should at least urge major caution about early reliance on any of the public policy variations—or on any one of the three paradigms described above, for that matter—as *the* comprehensive model for analysis in public administration.

In sharp contrast, in fact, I have elsewhere argued in detail that we should forget about *a* comprehensive paradigm as an early priority in public administration.[184] At best, fixation on that singular paradigm may only inhibit the development of the very analytic skills and traditions that are required to generate a comprehensive paradigm. Epigramatically, public administration shows every evidence of the desire to score a run without touching many of the bases. This exuberance is understandable, and even attractive. The overwhelming sense of the literature is that this exuberance has generally been counterproductive, however, as in the case of the new public administration.

Third, although the point does not get detailed treatment here, proponents of *a* paradigm in public administration usually stop far short of specifying the skills and technologies necessary to exploit it. This is clearly awkward, if the real goal is to move beyond the present stage of development.

This puts the point mildly, in all probability. Consider one sharper formulation of the present position. In the absence of a longish experience with appropriate skills and technologies, the choice of *a* paradigm will have to be political, broadly speaking. As useful and necessary as such a choice is for many purposes, it is not likely to facilitate empirical analysis. In fact, considerable mischief is likely. A prime derivative consequence in political science, for example, has been a kind of recycling of emphases that tend to negate one another.[185] The goal of scientific analysis, in contrast, is a cumulative building upon and extension of a succession of emphases. This cumulative ideal process has been popularly characterized as seeing farther by standing on the shoulders of conceptual giants. In totalitarian societies, political decisions about scientific issues can be far more unfortunate.[186]

Fourth, and relatedly, public administrationists often have generated commitments to Phase IV variants, or to the varieties of the Humanist/Systemic Paradigm without attention to some elemental questions. These neglected questions will only be sampled here:

1. Does the analytic model require skills/technologies that are presently in the kit of public administrationists, or which can be developed by them in some proximate future?
2. Do the skills/technologies imply major redefinitions of scholarly turf and, if so, are public administrationists willing to encourage and accept such redefinitions?
3. Is there any value in preserving "public administration" as a major identification and, if so, does any specific paradigm promise to enhance that identification?

The view here is that the developmental history detailed above constitutes a rich legacy which can and should be preserved. But the pursuit of *a* comprehensive paradigm is not ideally suited to encourage that preservation, and indeed may jeopardize it. The argument is a complex one, but its essence is that the fuss-and-feathers associated with choosing a paradigm—given the minimal experience and traditions in public administration with empirical analysis—probably will absorb energies that could be devoted to developing and testing skills and technologies useful for inquiry and application, whatever *the* paradigm will eventually come to be. A detailed attempt to build one "mini-paradigm" with its associated skills and technologies upon the rich developmental legacy of public administration has been completed,[187] and should be consulted by those interested in the full meaning of the present point.

Fifth, to continue the preceding emphasis, at least from where I sit, "public administration" deals with such a diversity of phenomena that I presently value several conceptual qualities above others. These include a certain acceptance of conceptual untidiness; a substantial tolerance for differences in approaches as well as for ambiguities; and a major commitment to hold things together in public administration, by an act of the will, if necessary, while major and diverse efforts are set in motion to generate the progress on which some future, meaningful and unifying conceptualizations can be based. The time-frame is reckoned in terms of decades, at least.

That is to say, any reasonable circumscription of what it is that public administrators actually do would include emphasis on at least:

1. the *internal processes* of any public administrative system, which encompass behavioral and rational-technical features;
2. *output measures*, as they relate to both employees and clients of any such system;
3. *transactions with other systems*, whether public or business or whatever; and
4. the *contextual envelope* within any public administrative system exists, with the "envelope" including such features as: specific public programs or policies; the character of the surrounding political, social, and economic institutions and values; the applicable laws, traditions, and cultures; etc.

5. value or normative criteria necessary to evaluate the four classes of emphases above

The implications of this bundle of emphases labeled "public administration" seem obvious enough against the background of the developmental history above. Illustratively, even Phase I or II concepts of public administration are not impossibly troublesome if the focus is on internal processes. Oppositely, however, such a limited perspective would be false to the fuller world of public administration. Similarly, the Social-Psychological Paradigm is both a reasonable and necessary guide for an emphasis on internal processes. But aspects of the Humanist/Systemic Paradigm are patently useful when the focus broadens to include other features in any reasonable circumscription of public administration as a discipline.

Alternatively, a more or less exclusive commitment to any one phase or paradigm implies the underemphasis or even neglect of critical perspectives or targets highlighted by other phases or paradigms. The potential costs are especially onerous in that no one phase or paradigm is defined with enough specificity to permit a meaningful choice, today, except perhaps the choice to reject Phase II.

A major conclusion also inheres in this bundle of emphases necessary to provide meaningful content to "public administration." That is: a clarity about one's analytical target *and* about one's dominant motivating phase or paradigm at any point are required, as opposed to an exclusive choice of one such phase or paradigm. Simply, there is too much work necessary to develop the content of each of the emphases above to run the risks inherent in the premature choice of *a* focus for inquiry.

Sixth, exacerbating the choice of a focus for public administration is the fact that any reasonable definition of the field must encompass inquiry and also application. Much of the developmental history above does not come to grips with this troublesome but necessary blending, a kind of interactive duality. Paramountly, the need to emphasize application inescapably raises the central question: applications toward what goals or for which values? This involves a complexity that inquiry can avoid at least in part, and especially in the physical and natural sciences. But such avoidance is not even remotely possible in any reasonable characterization of public administration.

The centrality of application and of values in public administration also argues against early closure as to *a* paradigm. Directly, the available phases and paradigms are value-loaded in some subtle ways, and have numerous value-relevant consequences, few of which can be said today to be obvious and beyond doubt or substantial qualification. This is clearly the case for the Traditional Paradigm, for example, which not only implies a desirable social order in organizations, but also tends to generate a family of consequences about which considerable is now known and whose consequences are morally consequential.

Commitment to a paradigm is chancy, consequently, especially under present conditions of our growing but still largely-incomplete knowledge about the empirical consequences of approaches consistent with each of the three paradigms sketched above. Far better than seeking *a* comprehensive paradigm, at *this* stage of the game, is to aggressively test increasingly-precise features of each paradigm, as has been done with such growing success in the case of the Traditional and the Social-Psychological paradigms.

Seventh, consequently, there are no definitive answers to what broad structuring concept is appropriate for providing balanced attention to the five phenomenal classes listed above. Or to put the same point in alternative terms, any presently-reasonable working solutions have a mixed-model character. At the University of Georgia, for example, our working approach to organizing curricula at both the doctoral and master's level is to organize around three perspectives on the public manager's job:

1. *Public Management Core*, which can be fulfilled by such courses: a broad public administration survey course; public personnel; organization theory and behavior; and public budgeting and finance
2. *Management Specialization*, which involves work in one of a wide range of functional activities; e.g., data-processing, finance, planning, personnel, etc.
3. *Policy Specialization*, which requires work in one of a wide range of substantive areas of greater or less specifity: the environment; neighborhood control; urban politics; housing and real estate; civil-military relations; inter-governmental relations; natural resources; social welfare; government regulation of business; international relations or politics; among many other potentials.

Roughly, this program is an intended amalgam of Phases III and IV, as described above: the framework attempts to meld the universal and scientific emphasis of Phase III with the programmatic and political thrusts of Phase IV. Looked at in another way, the broad degree design seeks to emphasize aspects of both the Social-Psychological and Humanist/Systemic paradigms, while avoiding a definitive choice between them. The core is relatively fixed; the two specializations can be widely variable. Practically, the range of alternatives available is a function of the range of course and faculty resources available, which means that the model above is suitable only for either:

1. a very large school of public administration or public affairs,
2. or a large university with a substantial public administration staff and fluid interdepartmental and interschool relationships.

These several concluding perspectives can be brought to a single overall point of view. In sum, the developmental history of public administration urges a kind of "medical school model" as a guide for its immediate progress, and perhaps even for a substantial period of time. Such a model stands in quite sharp contrast to the broad organizing bias more or less strictly patterned after some of the physical sciences at advanced stages of development, many public administrationists have accepted just such a model at a verbal level, as in the common emphasis on the need for a comprehensive new paradigm. Waldo well frames the essential contrast. He questions the common emphasis on the search for a "grand theory," or "unified theory," after the fashion of some of the physical and natural sciences. Waldo concludes: "The proper orienting analogy [for Public Administration] may not be ... astronomy ... but medicine, law and other professions. Schools of medicine, for example, use data and theory from dozens of fields, these data and theories change frequently and are never fully reconciled one to the other."[188]

Notes

1. Woodrow Wilson, published "The Study of Administration" in 1887. It is reprinted in *Political Science Quarterly* 56 (December 1941):486-506.

2. Luther Gulick and Lyndall Urwick (eds.), *Papers on the Science of Administration* (New York: Kelley, 1969), p. V. The volume was initially published in 1937 by the Institute of Public Administration.

3. Frederick C. Mosher, "Research in Public Administration," *Public Administration Review* 16 (Summer 1956):171.

4. Martin Landau, "The Concept of Decision-Making in the Field of Public Administration," in Sidney Mailick and Edward H. Van Ness (eds.), *Concepts and Issues in Administrative Behavior* (Englewood Cliffs, N.J.: Prentice-Hall, 1962), p. 2.

5. Mosher, "Research in Public Administration," p. 171.

6. Dwight Waldo, *Perspectives on Administration* (University, Ala.: University of Alabama Press, 1956).

7. Dwight Waldo, "Scope of the Theory of Public Administration," in James C. Charlesworth (ed.), *Theory and Practice of Public Administration* (Philadelphia, Penn.: American Academy of Political and Social Science, 1968), p. 5.

8. Robert Aaron Gordon and James E. Howell, *Higher Education for Business* (New York: Columbia University Press, 1959); and Frank Pierson, *The Education of American Businessmen* (New York: Carnegie Corporation, 1959).

9. Committee for the Advancement of Teaching, American Political Science Association, *Goals for Political Science* (New York: Sloane, 1951).

10. Albert Somit and Joseph Tanenhaus, *The Development of Political Science* (Boston: Allyn and Bacon, 1967), p. 188.

11. Paul Buchanan (ed.), *An Approach to Executive Development in Government* (Washington, D.C.: National Academy of Public Administration, 1973);

Frank Marini (ed.), *A New Public Administration: The Minnowbrook Perspective* (Scranton, Pa.: Chandler, 1971); and John M. Pfiffner and Robert V. Presthus, *Public Administration* (New York: Ronald Press, 1967), p. 5.

12. Frank Goodnow, *Politics and Administration* (New York: Macmillan, 1900), esp. pp. 10, 11, 18, and 85.

13. Landau, "Concept of Decision-Making," p. 17.

14. William F. Willoughby, *Government of Modern States* (New York: Appleton-Century, 1936), pp. 219-21.

15. Paul Appleby, *Policy and Administration* (University, Ala.: University of Alabama Press, 1949), p. 3.

16. Dwight Waldo, *The Administrative State* (New York: Ronald Press, 1948), pp. 32-33.

17. See Duane Lockard's reaction to a request by a young black official who advised that political scientists could make their greatest contribution to governing a large city by finding "some ways to break the civil service stranglehold." Lockard noted: "His request is not an ill-conceived one by any means. . . . It is worth remembering how large a role political scientists played in helping create the civil service system; perhaps more attention should now be paid to means for correcting the overdose." ("Value, Theory and Research in State and Local Politics." Paper presented at Annual Convention, American Political Science Association, Los Angeles, Calif., 1970.)

18. Herbert A. Simon introduced the schema in *Administrative Behavior* (New York: Macmillan, 1947), but specific derivative research products took more than a decade to develop. By that time, Phase III's fate had long been decided. Moreover, Simon's technology was beyond that of most public administration scholars, though it had a substantial audience in business schools, in generic management programs, and in industrial administration.

19. Robert T. Golembiewski, *Renewing Organizations* (Itasca, Ill.: F.E. Peacock, 1972).

20. For a useful introduction to technological contexts, see Charles Perrow, *Organizational Analysis: A Sociological View* (Belmont, Calif.: Wadsworth, 1970).

21. For a full development of the point, see Marshall E. Dimock, *A Philosophy of Administration* (New York: Harper & Bros., 1958).

22. This essential argument was made to a political science audience by Norman M. Person, who sought to describe the limits of "Taylorism" while arguing for the broader usefulness of a generic management variety of Phase III. See "Fayolism as a Necessary Complement to Taylorism," *American Political Science Review* 39 (February 1945):68-85.

Selecting examples of Phase III work must be arbitrary, but the following sources illustrate the broader family: Chester I. Barnard, *The Functions of the Executive* (Cambridge, Mass.: Harvard University Press, 1938); Simon, *Administrative Behavior*; Peter Drucker, *The Practice of Management* (New York: Harper

& Bros., 1954); Marshall E. Dimock, *Administrative Vitality* (New York: Harper & Bros., 1959); Robert T. Golembiewski, *Men, Management and Morality* (New York: McGraw-Hill, 1964); Herbert Kaufman, *The Limits of Organizational Change* (University of Ala.: University of Alabama Press, 1971); and Golembiewski, *Renewing Organizations.*

23. Lyndall Urwick, "Organization as A Technical Problem," in Gulick and Urwick, *Papers on Science of Administration*, p. 49.

24. This superiority of public administration is a dominant emphasis in such sources as Gordon and Howell, *Higher Education*, esp. pp. 379-93.

25. Roscoe Martin, "Political Science and Public Administration," *American Political Science Review* 46 (September 1952):667.

26. Simon, "A Comment on 'The Science of Public Administration'," *Public Administration Review* 7 (Summer 1947):202.

27. Landau, "Concept of Decision-Making," p. 15.

28. Herbert A. Simon, *Administrative Behavior*, 2nd ed. (New York: Macmillan, 1957), esp. pp. 45-50.

29. Ibid., pp. 4-5.

30. Ibid., p. 55.

31. Ibid., p. 58.

32. Ibid., pp. 56-57.

33. Consider the fascination with POSDCORB, for example. The mnemonic represents Planning, Organizing, Staffing, Directing, Coordinating, Reporting, and Budgeting, and long remained the essential skeletal structure for teaching and writing in public administration. Thus Luther Gulick, "Notes on A Theory of Organization," in Gulick and Urwick, *Papers on Science of Administration*, p. 13, asks: "What is the work of a chief executive? What does he do?" He replies: "The answer is POSDCORB."

34. Simon, "A Comment on 'The Science of Public Administration'," p. 202.

35. "Premises of Public Administration," *Public Administration Review* 17 (Spring 1958):194.

36. Somit and Tanenhaus, *Development of Political Science*, pp. 42-48.

Dwight Waldo confronted one major attitudinal consequence of this "humanistic ethos and a related conception of liberal education as concerned with 'higher things'." The PA specialist is assigned a derivative "second-class citizenship status" within political science, since he deals with the nuts-and-bolts of day-to-day public management rather than "the great and persistent problems of government." (Dwight Waldo, "Public Administration," p. 154, in Marion D. Irish, editor, *Political Science* [Englewood Cliffs, N.J.: Prentice-Hall, 1968].)

37. Simon, *Administrative Behavior*, 2nd edition, pp. 55-58.

38. Herbert A. Simon, "The Proverbs of Administration," *Public Administration Review* 6 (Winter 1946):53-67.

39. Simon, "A Comment on 'The Science of Public Administration'," p. 202. A similar distinction is made by Luther Gulick, "Science, Values and Public

Administration," in Gulick and Urwick, *Papers on Science of Administration*, esp. pp. 191-92.

40. Martin, op. cit., p. 665.

41. Martin, "Political Science and Public Administration," esp. pp. 665-66; and Mosher, "Research in Public Administration," pp. 175-76.

42. Somit and Tanenhaus, *Development of Political Science*, especially pp. 147-49; 153; and 167-170.

43. Phase IV may be roughly dated by Appleby's *Policy and Administration*, published in 1949. See also Daniel Lerner and Harold D. Lasswell (eds.), *The Policy Sciences* (Stanford University Press, 1951); and Austin Ranney (ed.), *Political Science and Public Policy* (Chicago: Markham, 1968).

44. Harold Stein, "Preparation of Case Studies," *American Political Science Review* 45 (June 1951):479-87.

45. For example, Martin, "Political Science and Public Administration," p. 669, argued that administration must have roots to have meaning, and these roots rest in the soil of specific programs. In contrast to the generic management emphasis of Phase III he urged that: "The administrator does not administer only: he administers *something*, and what he administers is of basic importance. . . ."

46. George J. Graham, Jr., and George W. Carey, *The Post-Behavioral Era: Perspectives on Political Science* (New York: McKay, 1972).

47. Theodore J. Lowi, "What Political Scientists Don't Need to Ask About Policy Analysis," *Policy Studies Journal* 2 (Autumn 1973):62.

48. The point caused some monumental and momentous conflict. In some approaches, as in some versions of logical positivism, values were variously defined as out-of-bounds. Other interpretations tried to distinguish types of theories as well as stages within a single type where value concerns were appropriate and necessary. On the latter approach, see Robert T. Golembiewski, *Behavior and Organization* (Chicago: Rand McNally, 1962), esp. pp. 48-60 and 69-79.

49. George V. Carey notes: ". . . by all outward evidences most behavioralists accept liberalism, and most liberals accept behavioralism." ("Beyond Parochialism in Political Science," in Graham and Carey, *Post-Behavioral Era*, p. 45.)

50. Lowi, "What Political Scientists Don't Need to Ask," p. 64.

51. Ibid., pp. 64-65.

52. Ibid., pp. 66 and 65.

53. E.W. Kelley, "Political Science as Science and Common Sense," in Graham and Carey, *Post-Behavioral Era*, p. 206.

54. Christian Bay, "Thoughts on the Purposes of Political Science Education," in Graham and Carey, *Post-Behavioral Era*, pp. 88-102.

55. Lowi, "What Political Scientists Don't Need to Ask," pp. 66-67.

56. Phillip O. Foss, "Policy Analysis and the Political Science Profession," *Policy Studies Journal* 2 (Autumn 1973):68.

57. Lowi, "What Political Scientists Don't Need to Ask," p. 62.

58. Thomas R. Dye, *Understanding Public Policy* (Englewood Cliffs, N.J.: Prentice-Hall, 1972), p. xi.

59. Compare Lerner and Lasswell, *Policy Sciences*, with Herbert Storing (ed.), *Essays on the Scientific Study of Politics* (New York: Holt, Rinehart and Winston, 1962), esp. pp. 65-116.

60. Marshall E. Dimock, Gladys O. Dimock, and Louis W. Koenig, *Public Administration* (New York: Rinehart, 1953), p. 12.

61. Landau, "Concept of Decision-Making," p. 9.

62. Dwight Waldo, "Scope of the Theory of Public Administration," in Charlesworth, *Theory and Practice of Public Administration*, p. 14, attributes the quote to John Gaus.

63. Dye, *Understanding Public Policy*, p. 3.

64. Harold Stein, *Public Administration and Policy Development* (New York: Harcourt, Brace, 1952), p. XV.

65. Ibid.

66. For statements re cases as they are and as they should be, see Edwin A. Bock (ed.), *Essays on the Case Method in Public Administration* (New York: Inter University Case Program, 1962).

Some critics trace a major liability of the case approach to this bias. Lowi takes such a position, and suggests an extrapolation. He notes: "Broad-gauged theories of politics are not related, perhaps not relatable, to observable cases." Theodore J. Lowi, "American Business, Public Policy, Case Studies, and Political Theory," *World Politics* 16 (July 1964):687.

67. Appleby, *Policy and Administration*, p. 156.

68. A. Dunsire, *Administration: The Word and the Science* (New York: Wiley, 1973), p. 156.

69. Charles O. Jones, *An Introduction to the Study of Public Policy* (Belmont, Calif.: Wadsworth, 1970), p. 4. Reprinted by permission of the publisher, Duxbury Press.

70. Direct linkages may be drawn between the "interest group" literature a la David B. Truman's *The Governmental Process* (New York: Knopf, 1951), and such efforts as Robert T. Golembiewski's *The Small Group* (Chicago: University of Chicago Press, 1962).

71. Dye, *Understanding Public Policy*, p. 6.

72. Ibid., p. 13.

73. Ibid., p. 3.

74. Ibid., p. 292.

75. James W. Davis, Jr., and Kenneth M. Dolbeare, *Little Groups of Neighbors* (Chicago: Markham, 1968); and Gary L. Wamsley, *Selective Service and a Changing America* (Columbus, Ohio: Merrill, 1969).

76. Yehezkel Dror, *Public Policymaking Reexamined* (San Francisco: Chandler, 1968), p. 275.

77. Joyce M. Mitchell and William C. Mitchell, *Political Analysis and Public Policy* (Chicago: Rand McNally, 1969), pp. 392ff.

78. For such an attempted analysis of "issue areas" and "community elites," see Robert T. Golembiewski, William Welsh, and William Crotty, *A Methodological Primer for Political Scientists* (Chicago: Rand McNally, 1967), pp. 149-90.

79. Jones, *An Introduction to Public Policy*, pp. 10-11.

80. Crane Brinton, *The Anatomy of Revolution* (New York: Holt, Rinehart and Winston, 1938).

81. Graham T. Allison, *Essence of Decision: Explaining the Cuban Missile Crisis* (Boston: Little, Brown, 1971). See also his "Conceptual Models and the Cuban Missile Crisis," *American Political Science Review* 63 (September 1969):689-718.

82. James L. Sundquist, *Politics and Policy* (Washington: The Brookings Institution, 1968).

83. Frederick C. Mosher (ed.), *Governmental Reorganizations: Cases and Comments* (Indianapolis, Ind.: Bobbs-Merrill, 1967).

84. Dye, *Understanding Public Policy*, esp. pp. 17-35.

85. The prototypical book is Arthus Maass' *Muddy Waters* (Cambridge, Mass.: Harvard University Press, 1951).

86. Lynton Keith Caldwell, *Environment* (New York: Natural History Press, 1970).

87. Kelley, "Political Science as Science."

88. Jones, *Introduction to Public Policy*, p. 5.

89. Don K. Price, *The Scientific Estate* (Cambridge, Mass.: Belknap Press, 1967).

90. Caldwell, *Environment*.

91. Unless I seriously misread between the lines, for example, I see signs of this tension in Don Allensworth, *Public Administration: The Execution of Public Policy* (Philadelphia: J.B. Lippincott, 1973).

92. Landau, "Concept of Decision-Making," p. 9. See also Vincent Ostrom, *The Intellectual Crisis in American Public Administration* (University, Ala.: University of Alabama Press, 1973).

93. For one exception, see Charlesworth, *Theory and Practice of Public Administration*.

94. Mosher, "Research in Public Administration," p. 177.

95. Dwight Waldo, "Scope of the Theory of Public Administration," in Charlesworth, *Theory and Practice of Public Administration*, p. 10.

96. Ira Sharkansky, *Public Administration: Policy-making in Government Agencies* (Chicago: Markham, 1970), esp. p. 9. For a similar but somewhat modified treatment, see John Rehfus, *Public Administration vs. Political Process* (New York: Scribner's, 1973).

97. David Easton, *A Framework for Political Analysis* (Englewood Cliffs, N.J.: Prentice-Hall, 1965).

98. Thomas R. Dye, "Policy Analysis and the Urban Crisis," mimeod., no date.

99. Yehezkel Dror, "Some Diverse Approaches to Policy Analysis," *Policy Studies Journal* 1 (Summer 1973):258-60.

100. Thomas R. Dye, *Politics, Economics, and the Public: Policy Outcomes in the American States* (Chicago: Rand McNally, 1966), p. 293. See also Richard I. Hofferbert, "The Relation Between Public Policy and Some Structural and Environmental Variables in the American States," *American Political Science Review* 60 (March 1966):73-82; and R. Dawson and James Robinson, "Inter-Party Competition, Economic Variables, and Welfare Policies in the American States," *Journal of Politics* 25 (May 1963):265-89.

101. Jones, *An Introduction to Public Policy*, p. 144.

102. Dye, "Policy Analysis and the Urban Crisis."

103. Donald T. Campbell, "From Description to Experimentation," in Chester W. Harris (ed.), *Problems in Measuring Charge* (Madison, Wisc.: University of Wisconsin Press, 1963), pp. 212-42.

104. Larry L. Wade, *The Elements of Public Policy* (Columbus, Ohio: Merrill, 1972), pp. 22-23.

105. Elliott Morss, "Some Thoughts on the Determination of State and Local Expenditures," *National Tax Journal* 19 (March 1966):95-103.

106. See Ira Sharkansky, *Spending in the American States* (Chicago: Rand McNally, 1968).

107. Keith R. Billingsley et al., "Spurious Correlation in Aggregate Data Analysis Using Index Variables," *Georgia Political Science Association Journal* 1 (Fall 1973):102-111.

108. Some policy choices have been the subject of experimental studies, of course, as in the case of the form of welfare payments in this country. See also Jean A. Le Ponce and Paul Smoker (eds.), *Experimentation and Simulation in Political Science* (Toronto, Canada: University of Toronto Press, 1972), pp. 94-105.

109. Sharkansky, *Regionalism in American Politics*, pp. 23-25.

110. For example, Daniel J. Elazar argues that more meaningful regions can be isolated if their borders are so defined that parts of some of the same states can be assigned to different regions, in contrast to Sharkansky's convention. See *American Federalism: A View from the States* (New York: Crowell, 1966).

111. John H. Fenton and Donald W. Chamberlayne, "The Literature Dealing with the Relationships Between Political Process, Socio-Economic Conditions, and Public Policies in the American States: A Bibliographical Essay," *Polity* 1 (Spring 1969):388-404.

112. Wade, *The Elements of Public Policy*, esp. pp. 21-41.

113. Ira Sharkansky and Richard I. Hofferbert, "Dimensions of State Politics, Economics, and Public Policy," *American Political Science Review* 63 (September 1969):867 and 878.

114. See also Dye, *Understanding Public Policy*, esp. pp. 254-61; Wade, *The Elements of Public Policy*, p. 25.

115. Douglas R. Bunker, "A Doctoral Program in the Policy Sciences," *Policy Sciences* 2 (1971):35.

116. Harold D. Lasswell, "The Emerging Conception of the Policy Sciences," *Policy Sciences* 1 (1970):3.

117. Samuel J. Bernstein, "Toward A General Paradigm for Policy Analysis," *Policy Studies Journal* 1 (Autumn 1972):49.

118. Dye, "Policy Analysis and the Urban Crisis."

119. Joseph H. Lewis, "Policy Sciences and the Market," *Policy Sciences* 2 (1971):291, 293, and 299.

120. Yehezkel Dror, "Prolegomena to Policy Sciences," *Policy Sciences*, 1 (1970):10.

121. Michael Radnor, "Management Sciences and the Policy Sciences," *Policy Sciences* 2 (1971):447. A revised version of this paper also appears in *Management and Policy Science in American Government* edited by Michael J. White, Michael Radnor, and David A. Tansik.

122. Ibid., p. 451.

123. Most prominently, see Lowi's "What Political Scientists Don't Need to Ask."

124. Harold W. Adams, "On Economic Values in Policy Analysis," *Policy Sciences* 1 (1970):207-215.

125. Horst W.J. Rittel and Melvin M. Webber, "Dilemmas in A General Theory of Planning," *Policy Sciences* 4 (1973):155-69.

126. Bunker, "A Doctoral Program," pp. 33-42.

127. Ibid., p. 36.

128. Ibid., pp. 39 and 39-40.

129. For detailed efforts in political science to apply economic concepts and methods, see Robert L. Curry and Larry L. Wade, *A Theory of Political Change: Economic Reasoning in Political Analysis* (Englewood Cliffs, N.J.: Prentice-Hall, 1968); and Wade and Curry, *A Logic of Public Policy* (Belmont, Calif.: Wadsworth, 1970).

130. Substantial progress has been made by students of public administration in mastering behavioral technologies. Illustratively, see the integration of such materials in the popular text by Felix and Lloyd Nigro, *Modern Public Administration* (New York: Harper & Row, 1973).

131. Foss, "Policy Analysis," p. 69.

132. Lowi, "What Political Scientists Don't Need to Ask," p. 62.

133. Quoted in Dye, "Policy Analysis and the Urban Crisis."

134. William Gorham hits this theme hard, and also specifies the necessary conditions for "Getting Into the Action," *Policy Sciences* 1 (1970):169-76.

135. Irving Louis Horowitz, "Social Science Mandarins: Policymaking as Political Formula," *Policy Sciences* 1 (1970):340.

136. Ibid., p. 340.

137. Somit and Tanenhaus, *The Development of Political Science*, esp. pp. 173-94.

138. Vernon Van Dyke, "Process and Policy as Focal Concepts in Political Research," in Austin Ranney (ed.), *Political Science and Public Policy* (Chicago: Markham, 1968), pp. 23-39.

139. Alvin W. Gouldner, "Metaphysical Pathos and the Theory of Bureaucracy," *American Political Science Review* 44 (December 1955):498.

140. Thomas S. Kuhn, *The Structure of Scientific Revolution* (Chicago: University of Chicago Press, 1962).

141. Vincent Ostrom, *The Intellectual Crisis in American Public Administration* (University, Ala.: University of Alabama Press, 1973), p. 13. © 1973 by The University of Alabama Press. Used by permission.

142. For a recent statement of this kind, see: Ibid.

143. See, for example, Dwight Waldo, *The Administrative State* (New York: Ronald, 1948), esp. pp. 47-64.

144. Ostrom, *Intellectual Crisis*, esp. pp. 23-29, 99.

145. Wilson, "The Study of Administration."

146. The formal treatment of jobs is exemplified by Frederick W. Taylor's work, as reported in *The Principles of Scientific Management* (New York: Harper, 1911).

147. Max Weber's treatment of bureaucracy is the classic statement of the formal or legal approach to structuring jobs in complex networks.

148. Fritz J. Roethlisberger and William J. Dickson, *Management and the Worker* (Cambridge, Mass.: Harvard University Press, 1939), provide the seminal study.

149. The classical macro-level statement of what is called "interest-group liberalism" is provided by John Kenneth Galbraith, *American Capitalism: The Concept of Countervailing Power* (Boston: Houghton Mifflin, 1952).

150. For an influential summary statement at the micro-level, see Edward A. Shils, "The Study of the Primary Group," in Daniel Lerner and Harold D. Lasswell (eds.), *The Policy Sciences* (Stanford, Cal.: Stanford University Press, 1951), pp. 44-69.

151. The characterization comes from Warren G. Bennis, "Leadership Theory and Administrative Behavior: The Problem of Authority," *Administrative Science Quarterly* 4 (December 1959):259-301.

Examples of the emphasis on "informal organization" or "groups" or "cliques" are everywhere in the literature. Witness Sayle's conclusion: "The individual's most immediate and meaningful experiences of work are obtained in the context of the work group and his work associates. The larger organization is experienced by indirection, but membership in the small group contributes directly to the shaping of attitudes and behavior toward the entire world of work." Leonard R. Sayles, "Work Group Behavior and the Larger Organization," in Joseph A. Litterer (ed.), *Organizations: Structure and Behavior* (New York: Wiley, 1963), p. 163.

This pervasive bias only recently has begun to motivate revisionist effort, as by Charles Perrow who seeks to redirect attention toward "the structural emphasis" and away from "people problems" and "leadership problems." *Organizational Analysis*, esp. pp. 1-2. For some empirical data as to the significance of the "formal organization," see William E. Reif, Robert M. Monczka, and John W. Newstrom, "Perceptions of the Formal and Informal Organizations," *Academy of Management Journal* 16 (September 1963):389-403.

152. For an early expression of this point of view, see Emile Durkheim's seminal *La Division du travail social.*

153. Chester I. Barnard, *The Functions of the Executive* (Cambridge, Mass.: Harvard University Press, 1964), p. 163.

154. Such an orientation has been reflected diversely, as in the interest in sociometry, in group dynamics, and most broadly in the "third force" or humanist approach in the behavioral sciences, and in psychology especially. See A.H. Maslow, *The Farther Reaches of Human Nature* (New York: Viking Press, 1971).

155. Illustratively, see Peter M. Blau, *Bureaucracy in Modern Society* (New York: Random House, 1959); or Michael Crozier, *The Bureaucratic Phenomenon* (Chicago: University of Chicago Press, 1964).

156. The theme was the dominant one in the post-World War II revisionist literature in public administration, as in Appleby, *Policy and Administration.*

157. Robert T. Golembiewski, *Behavior and Organization* (Chicago: Rand McNally, 1962), pp. 87-210, provides one such detailed approach to these two goals.

158. For a summary treatment, see Robert T. Golembiewski, *Men, Management, and Morality* (New York: McGraw-Hill, 1965).

159. For an introduction to these "growth psychology" models, see: Ibid., esp. pp. 161-202.

160. The classic demonstration is by Lester Coch and John R.P. French, Jr., "Overcoming Resistance to Change," *Human Relations* 1 (1948):512-32.

161. See Joseph Harris, *Congressional Control of Administration* (Washington, D.C.: Brookings Institution, 1964); and Dean E. Mann, "The Selection of Federal Political Executives," *American Political Science Review* 58 (March 1964):81-99.

162. "For it is in the crucible of administrative politics today that public policy is mainly hammered out, through bargaining, negotiation, and conflict among appointed rather than elected officials. The bureaucratization of the policy process is particularly pronounced in defense and foreign affairs, but it reaches into domestic politics as well." (Francis E. Rourke, *Bureaucracy, Politics, and Public Policy* [Boston: Little, Brown, 1969], p. vii.)

163. For a summary critique, see V. Subramanian, "Representative Bureaucracy: A Reassessment," *American Political Science Review* 59 (December 1967):101-109.

164. Marini (ed.), *New Public Administration.*

165. Ostrom, *The Intellectual Crisis in American Public Administration.*

166. As in Blau, *Bureaucracy in Modern Society*; or in Anthony Downs, *Inside Bureaucracy* (Boston: Little, Brown, 1967). The charge was a common one against monopolies and other forms of "giant business," as in our trust-busting era or in the muckraking literature. See Eric Goldman, *Rendezvous With Destiny* (New York: Knopf, 1952), esp. pp. 55-232. It is only recently that such a charge has been commonly directed against "big government," especially by liberals against the federal government. Illustratively, see the intellectual mini-history by Aaron Wildavsky, "The Empty-Head Blues: Black Rebellion and White Rebellion," *The Public Interest* No. 11 (Spring 1968):3-16. As one prominent indication of this major change, see Theodore J. Lowi, *The End of Liberalism* (New York: Norton, 1969), p. xiii. Lowi phrased the new guiding insight in revealing terms: "government itself is the problem."

167. PPBS is the most refined, if often the most maligned, expression of this point of view. For a telling critique, see Ida R. Hoos, *Systems Analysis in Public Policy* (Berkeley, Calif.: University of California Press, 1972).

168. The general neglect of environmental forces was characteristic of much research in both public administration and political science, in large part due to the dominant "behavioral" orientation in both fields. Dye explains in *Understanding Public Policy*, p. 23, that: "Political Science has been so preoccupied with describing political institutions, behaviors, and processes, that it has frequently overlooked the overriding importance of environmental forces in shaping public policy."

In the study of large productive organizations, a similar reorientation was expressed in such theoretical statements as that of S.E. Emery and E.L. Trist, "The Causal Texture of Organizational Environment," *Human Relations* 18 (February 1965):21-31.

The neglect of environmental differences also was highlighted by the inapplicability of "developing countries" of generalizations derived from the American experience. See Dunsire, *Administration*, esp. pp. 134-52.

169. H. George Frederickson, "Creating Tomorrow's Public Administration," *Public Management* 53 (November 1971): esp. pp. 2-3.

170. Ross Clayton and Ron Gilbert, "Perspectives of Public Managers: Their Implications for Public Service Delivery Systems," *Public Management* 53 (November 1971):9-12. Reprinted by special permission. © 1971 the International City Management Association.

171. In the U.S. Department of State, for example, proponents of a PPBS-like system perceived that adoption of that rational-technical system required broad organizational and personal change via a humanist ACORD. The effort had

mixed consequences, and its history is still being written. For some clues as to the logic that paired a humanist technology for change with a rational-technical system, see Frederick C. Mosher and John E. Haar, *Programming Systems and Foreign Affairs Leadership: An Attempted Innovation* (New York: Oxford University Press, 1970).

172. Stephen R. Chitwood and Michael M. Harmon, "New Public Administration, Humanism, and Organizational Behavior," *Public Management* 53 (November 1971):13-22.

173. See, for example, Golembiewski, *Renewing Organizations.*

174. As in Richard E. Walton, "Ethical Issues in the Practice of Organization Development," from *Action Research Program in Organizational Innovations* (Division of Research, Graduate School of Business Administration, Harvard University, 1973).

175. Illustratively, see the recent debate in *Public Administration Review*, featuring Chris Argyris and Herbert Simon. Consult Herbert A. Simon, "Organization Man: Rational or Self-Actualizing?" (July 1973):346-53; Chris Argyris, "Organization Man: Rational *and* Self-Actualizing?" *Public Administration Review* 4 (July 1973):354-57; and Simon's letter, *Public Administration Review* 4 (September 1973):484-85.

176. Daniel Katz and Basil S. Georgopoulous, "Organizations in a Changing World," *Journal of Applied Behavioral Science* 7 (May 1971):350. Reproduced by special permission.

177. Ibid., p. 351.

178. For the detailed development of one rationalist/humanist interface, see Arthur C. Beck, Jr., and Ellis D. Hillmar, *A Practical Approach to Organization Development Through MBO* (Reading, Mass.: Addision-Wesley, 1972).

179. Quoted in Warren G. Bennis, "A Funny Thing Happened on the Way to the Future," *American Psychologist* 25 (July 1970):601-602.

180. The point is discussed in detail in Paul R. Schulman, "Large Scale Public Policy," Ph.D. dissertation, Johns Hopkins University, 1973.

181. Robert T. Golembiewski, *Public Administration as a Developing Discipline* (New York: Marcel Dekker, Inc., in press).

182. Vincent Ostrom, *The Intellectual Crisis in American Public Administration* (University, Ala.: University of Alabama Press, 1973), p. 13.

183. Thomas S. Kuhn, *The Structure of Scientific Revolutions* (Chicago: University of Chicago Press, 1970), p. 15.

184. Golembiewski, *Public Administration as A Developing Discipline.*

185. G. David Garson, "On the Origins of Interest-Group Theory," *American Political Science Review* 68 (December 1974):1505-1519.

186. For the tendency run riot, see Zhores A. Medvedev, *The Rise and Fall of T.D. Lysenko* (New York: Columbia University Press, 1969); and David Joravsky, "The Lysenko Affair," *Scientific American* 207 (November 1963):41-49.

187. Golembiewski, *Public Administration as a Developing Discipline.*

188. Dwight Waldo, "The Administrative State Revisited," *Public Administration Review* 25 (March 1965):16-17.

4

Political Parties, Interest Groups, and Public Policy

Murray S. Stedman

Policy-Formulation in Theory and in Practice

The classical democratic theorists of the nineteenth century—in Britain, but also in France and the United States—took it for granted that political parties were supposed to and in fact did formulate public policy. In telescopic form, their model may be summarized as envisaging a fairly clear linear relationship between public opinion and public policy. Public opinion was held to be reflected in the choices the electorate made between rival parties. Acting as transmission belts, the parties took these choices into the legislature. It was then understood to be the responsibility of the legislature to translate public opinion (i.e., majority opinion) into public law, or, to use a more recent expression, public policy. Even when a political system did not always work in this precise fashion, this sequence of operations was considered to be the norm.

So widespread was the acceptance of this model that even such an anti-party theorist as Ostrogorski agreed with its premises. Others who suspected that parties might be more tyrannical than democratic—Mosca, Pareto, and Michels, for instance—also endorsed the general theorem that parties created public policy.

But in time there began to be doubts from several different sources that the assumption of rationality on which the model rested was entirely valid. If it could be shown that public opinion, i.e., the electorate, actually made choices on an irrational basis or unequal basis, then it followed that public law might be an output not of rational decision-making but of other factors.

Among those who questioned the rationality of public opinion, several were outstanding. A heavy blow against the assumptions of rationality in the democratic political process was struck by Karl Marx and his allies. If, as they contended, the state was little more than the "executive committee of the bourgeoisie"—that is, a front for the great industrialists and bankers and their associates, it was obviously ridiculous to take the electoral process seriously. Under this theory, political democracy was held to be mostly a sham, and the only hope of liberation lay in the overthrow of those regimes which combined a parliamentary government with a capitalist economy. The Marxists, of course, managed to convince a sizable number of persons that their negative view of political democracies was correct.

135

A very different kind of challenge came from the writings of Sigmund Freud. Beginning with him, and continuing until the present, the Freudians have stressed the irrational or "unconscious" in a person's behavior. Even psychoanalysts such as Fromm and Horney, who parted from some aspects of the original Freudian thesis, continued to point out that there is a great deal of irrationality in human behavior, including, of course, political behavior.

Illustrations of other kinds of criticism of the rationality position have come from Gustave LeBon, the famous French sociologist, who held that peoples rarely act in their own best interest; from the Englishman Graham Wallas and the Spaniard Ortega y Gasset, who developed the concept of the mass mind; and from Walter Lippmann, who put forth the idea in *Public Opinion* (1922) that most persons think in terms of stereotypes. By this he meant that most political judgments are not made on the basis of empirical fact but on preconceived and erroneous perceptions. From this it follows that public opinion is based mostly on myths, which may or may not be true, but which defy empirical refutation.

To make matters even worse, a more recent assault on rationality has come from cultural (in Britain, "social") anthropologists. The basic idea is that culture conditions our behavior and that much of what we consider to be in the realm of rational choice or of "free will" is in fact largely beyond our personal control. In this connection, one thinks of anthropologists such as Margaret Mead, Alexander Leighton, and Clyde Kluckhohn, all of whom have enjoyed a huge readership. In this general camp also belongs the noted psychologist B.F. Skinner, whose work *Beyond Freedom and Dignity* (1971), stressed the importance of social environment (culture) on all aspects of behavior.

In short, insofar as the classical model of democracy depended on an informed and rational electorate, the model was under severe attack.

Party Government

Nonetheless, the model continued to have a good deal of utility for historians and political scientists who sought to describe and to explain particular political systems. It remained in the background, for example, in the continuing debate over "party responsibility," which is to say government by a disciplined and program-oriented political party. Though the history of the debate in the United States is well known to specialists in political parties, it seems desirable to give a brief summary of the argumentation for the benefit of non-specialists.

In its modern form, the discussion began in earnest with the publication of two books of Woodrow Wilson. The books were written with an interval of twenty-four years, and during that time Wilson's position changed drastically. In the summer of 1884 Wilson completed his book *Congressional Government*. At that time he was a graduate student at Johns Hopkins University. In addition to his interest in American government, he remained throughout his life a keen and admiring observer of the British parliamentary political system.

The principal emphasis in *Congressional Government*, published in 1885, was on the differences between congressional and parliamentary government. In his Preface, Wilson states: "Congressional government is committee government; Parliamentary government is government by a responsible Cabinet Ministry."[1] Throughout the work, Wilson made light of government by congressional commitees and lavished high praise on the British form of parliamentary government under a strong cabinet. In his analysis, Wilson made a very strong case for what later came to be called the "party government" doctrine.

It is not entirely clear why, in *Congressional Government*, Wilson refrained from proposing cabinet government on the British model as the solution to the difficulties he saw in the United States. Only a year earlier, in an article, he had proposed exactly that. Even so, the thrust in Wilson's first book is clearly in the direction of cabinet government, and the preference is for a British type of party system (responsible, disciplined, centralized national parties) as against the American type (weak, decentralized, undisciplined national parties). To revert to our earlier discussion, Wilson preferred the British to the American type of national party because he believed that the former was superior as a formulator of public policy.

Over the years the views of the early Wilson toward responsible party government have been echoed—usually with some modifications—by latter commentators. Though a full listing of these commentators would serve no useful purpose, it is essential to recognize the contributions of E.E. Schattschneider to the debate. For the most successful modern exposition of the doctrine book place in 1942 with the publication of Schattschneider's *Party Government*. The thesis of the book is that ". . . party government (party centralization) is the most practicable and feasible solution of the problem of organizing American democracy."[2] It was Schattschneider's contention that a highly centralized, well financed, and disciplined national two-party system would deliver through Congress a public law output which would be consistent with electoral platforms. Furthermore, he saw this kind of party system as a unifying factor between Congress and the White House. In short, the key to reorganizing American democracy was to reshape the party system.

Schattschneider added judicious qualifications to his overall proposals, but no such inhibitions were in evidence in a brief report issued in 1950 entitled *Toward a More Responsible Two-Party System.*[3] The *Report* was the product of the Committee on Political Parties of the American Political Science Association. As was natural under the circumstances, Schattschneider served as chairman of the sixteen-member committee, and also served as a member, though not as chairman, of the five-member drafting committee.

The *Report* stirred up a considerable tempest, mostly in academic circles. It was poorly drafted and suffered from internal inconsistencies. Some of the recommendations were purely mechanical, such as extending the term of House members to four years. But some of the recommendations, at least in the eyes of the critics, showed an immature or even erroneous understanding of democratic political theory.

More than two decades have passed since the publication of the CPP *Report*, and it still is a useful jumping-off point for academic debate. Aside from this, the doctrine of party government has become moribund, since neither politicians nor the general public are aware of its existence.

The Presidential-Party Thesis

The rival thesis to the party government doctrine stresses the importance of presidential government. As was noted earlier, the modern version of the presidential-party doctrine also began with the publication of a book by Woodrow Wilson. In the years following 1885 Wilson had dramatically changed his views on the relationship between the president and Congress. The evolution of his thinking was made public in 1908 when he published a collection of carefully prepared lectures under the title *Constitutional Government in the United States.*[4]

The general position taken in this book is that the center of power in the national government had shifted from Congress to the president. This being the case, it was logical for Wilson to argue that the president should increase his authority in his own party. It seemed to him both reasonable and desirable that a president elected on a national program should have the machinery at his disposal to execute that program. Clearly, this meant the president would exert an increased authority over members of his own party in Congress.

During his eight years in office, Wilson tried, and with some success, to put into practice his concept of a strong party as a vehicle for presidential leadership. With the exception of Franklin D. Roosevelt, succeeding presidents have not endorsed the doctrine of strong presidential parties. There have been strong chief executives—Truman, Kennedy, Johnson, Nixon—but the key to their leadership was to be found outside the national presidential party.

In recent years, the strongest case for strengthening the presidential parties has been made not by a sitting president but by a leading political scientist, James MacGregor Burns. There is no need to summarize here the fine points in Burns' position, for his books are readily available. What is to be noted here is that Burns has continued and up-dated the thesis expressed by Woodrow Wilson in 1908.

Two Possible Kinds of Presidential Parties

In the absence of dramatic changes in the American constitutional system, the usual adversary relationship between the White House and Congress may be expected to endure. The national presidential party—called into existence every four years and then virtually dissolved—will have interests different from the more active congressional parties. But the fact remains that there will continue to be presidential "parties." The interesting analytical problem is to calculate whether they are in evolution and if so, in what direction.

Logically, there would appear to be two different kinds or types of presidential parties. The first is a personal or temporary presidential party, which is what we usually have. It has certain pronounced characteristics which are worth looking at. There is a very large degree of dependence on the president himself, varying with the personality of the office-holder at the time. The party is "jerry-built" for the express purpose of winning the presidential election. In 1972, for example, the Committee to Re-elect the President operated solely on behalf of President Nixon. It considered the Republican National Committee, and its allied organizations, to be more or less out of the presidential race. CREEP followed an independent path in raising funds, in committing acts of political sabotage and expionage, and in the ill-fated attempt to install electronic surveillance equipment in the Democratic National Committee headquarters in the Watergate complex. As the Watergate revelations gradually unfolded, old-line Republicans associated with the Republican National Committee exploded in fury. They were especially displeased to learn that CREEP had more money than it could possibly spend effectively for electoral purposes, while at the same time the Republican National Committee was suffering from economic undernourishment.

There are other characteristics to the temporary or personalized presidential party, and these may be seen especially clearly in the ranks of the losing presidential party. Its leadership is shifting and ill-defined. It is probably in debt. The party institutions are weak. There is even now a comparatively low degree of party discipline in Congress. There is little long-range planning, though some fraction of the party is usually calling for such planning, e.g., committees on energy resources.

It is logically possible to project another kind of presidential party—one which is institutionalized and permanent, one which has strong central machinery. Such a party would be far from a British party disguised in the American environment. The separation of powers would still institutionalize warfare between the presidential party and its counterpart in the Congress. Stalemate between the two branches would continue to be the general order of the day. But there would be these positive features, at least: the sharing of decision-making power between the president and other party leaders; a permanent leadership in the leading opposition party; the creation of permanent machinery to assist the presidential party; an emphasis on long-range planning by the party officials. It may be said that all of this would cost a good deal of money. But the objection misses the mark. The current presidential parties raise enormous sums for their candidates. What is desirable is that these sums be used for purposes over and beyond mere electioneering. There would be no dearth of suggestions as to how the surplus funds might be usefully expended.

The Varying Functions of
Party Systems

There is a good deal of confusion and contradiction in the vast literature about parties as to their relationship with public policy. The CCP *Report* was apparently premised on the assumption that an ideal party system would operate as that in Britain did in the general election of 1945. In that landmark election, the Conservatives were quite clear as to what they would do if they won control of Parliament: they would roll history back to the pre-1939 era and attempt to keep it in that framework. In contrast, the Labour party promised a complete program of nationalization of certain basic industries and a very extensive plan of socialized medical and health services. When, somewhat unexpectedly, Labour scored a smashing electoral victory, it promptly proceeded to enact into law every major commitment it had made to the electorate.

But, ironically, the 1945 British general election has proved to be unique. Subsequent elections have shown no such clear-cut divisions between the major parties. In fact, there has been a good deal of straddling on major issues, and some questions which formerly divided the parties—nationalized health services, for example—are now supported by both major parties as well as by the Liberals. In addition, once in office, the parties have not hesitated to adopt new policies which stood in contradiction to those exposed in the party manifestoes. For example, the Conservative party has a long record of keeping governmental intervention in the economy at a minimum. Despite this philosophy, the Heath government, confronted with severe economic crises, did not hesitate to impose stringent controls over the economy. The Nixon Administration in the United States also did a sharp about-face in its general economic outlook when it embarked upon a series of various "phases" to attempt to control an inflation that was obviously out of hand. In short, in both Britain and in the United States, pragmatism won out, in these instances, over party doctrine.

One of the reasons for the failure to determine the relationship between party and public policy stemmed from the inability of political scientists to establish a typlogy that would permit different party systems to be carefully compared. The Duverger breakdown of party systems into mass parties, cadre parties, militia, and cell parties is interesting but not especially relevant to considerations of public policy.[5]

In 1964, a significant advance in our understanding of party and policy relationships took place with the publication by Frank J. Sorauf of a volume entitled *Political Parties in the American System.*[6] Drawing on earlier studies as well as his own insight, Sorauf pointed out that there are four principal functions which party systems may fulfill. First, and most universally among the world's democracies, "is the mobilization of voters behind candidates for election."[7] This electoral function dominates the two major American parties, and the cycle of their activity depends almost completely upon the calendar of elections.

Second only to the electing function is the "party's role as a teacher—its function as a protaganist for political attitudes, ideas, and programs."[8] Usually, American parties have been weak in this role. They avoid espousing the broad world view such as that of European Socialist parties, and are normally content to be identified simply as parties in favor of peace or prosperity. American parties, as do all others, "also perform the even more general education role of political socialization."[9] To use a sociological term, the parties serve as "reference groups," and for their loyalists the parties offset the confusion of the political world by suggesting the "right" side of an issue or controversy. And for the sophisticated party followers, as Sorauf notes, the party relates a value or a set of values—liberalism, conservatism, racial equality, national pride, and so on—to the policy or candidate alternatives that exist. In the United States, of course, the organizing and directing of political perceptions is shared with the mass media and with the interest groups.

In the democracies, the parties also perform, in varying degrees, "the function of organizing the policy-making machinery of government."[10] To take an obvious example, in the United States Congress and in state legislatures the party caucus is the basic unit of organization. From the decisions of the caucus come the determinations as to who will be the presiding officers, the committee chairman, and the other leaders. But it is at this point that a principal difference between the American system and parliamentary systems becomes evident. The American parties campaign vigorously, even frantically, but after winning an election, they notably fail to seize and use the policy-making power. This failure on the part of the winning party to govern was at the heart of the "party responsibility" debate previously discussed.

Finally, political parties "seem to be involved in a series of "non-political functions."[11] European parties more often than their American counterparts sponsor scout troops, social clubs, adult-education classes, health and insurance programs. In extreme cases, such as the French Communist party, there is almost a closed society for the faithful: they can work, read, and spend their leisure almost entirely within a Communist-oriented environment.

In the light of the foregoing typology, it is clearly reasonable to agree with Sorauf's conclusion: "The emphasis a party places on one or two of these functions, and the style with which it carries them out, distinguishes it from its competitors and from the parties of other political systems."[12] Furthermore, successful performance in one area may be incompatible with successful performance in another. American parties have long contended that they would suffer electoral losses were they to stress the development of programs and ideologies. Such losses they are not, of course, prepared to accept. They therefore devote themselves almost entirely to the electoral function. In this respect, they differ not only from minor parties in the United States but from the large competitive parties of the other established democracies.

The Party System Viewed as
a Sub-System

Other chapters in this volume deal with the general problems which are raised when systems analysis is applied to the field of public policy. Here it is necessary only to take into account the impact of the systems approach on the understanding of the operations of the party system.

Developed originally for political science by writers in the field of comparative politics, the concept of a national government as a political system has now gained widespread acceptance. Attention is given to the scope of political activities within a society. Implied in the term "system" is both an interdependence of parts and a boundary between the system and its social environment. Since the system is interdependent, when the properties of one component change, the other components of the system are in one way or another affected.

In systems theory, there are usually considered to be three phases: input, conversion, and output. Inputs are described as demands (for example, for services or regulation on behalf of public safety) and supports (for example, payment of taxes, or participation by citizens in the form of voting or discussion).

Conversion has reference to the internal process of decision-making. This would include legislative statutes, executive orders, administrative regulations, and court decisions.

Outputs are closely related to inputs, and include a wide variety of considerations, for example, the impact of taxation, the regulation of behavior, and the allocation of certain goods and services.

Even though the systems approach is more of a framework than a true theory, it is evident its application may result in an altered view of political parties. Operationally, the party (along with interest groups) makes certain inputs in the form of demands and supports. In the legislature, the party may or not play a role in the decision-making associated with the conversion process. The policy output may, in turn, have a feedback which affects other aspects of the political system.

Another application of the systems approach is to view the party as a subsystem of the larger political system. From that perspective, what affects the larger political environment is almost certain to have some influence on the functions, structure, and attitudes of the party. Conversely, what happens in the smaller party subsystem would be expected to have some feedback effect on other components of the larger system.

But the most important effect of the systems approach is to destroy the illusion that the political parties are isolated and independent entities largely in control of their own destinies. On the contrary, the thrust of systems analysis is that changes will occur in the party system only or at least largely as a result of basic alternations in the total political environment; e.g., the "quantum dynamics" policy model developed earlier.

If this is so, Schattschneider was wrong, and the key to reorganizing American democracy is most emphatically not the political party. Rather the reverse is true: to change the functions, structures, and attitudes of the parties it is first necessary to change the political environment. Short of vast and even revolutionary convulsions in the total social environment, it is far from clear how the political environment can be changed in any rational way.

The net result of this kind of speculation cannot be gauged with any great degree of precision. It is clear that political scientists and citizens have begun to take the political parties far less seriously as formulators of public policy than the parties themselves do. There has probably been a correspondingly increased appreciation of the role of interest groups and movements as initiators of policy formulation, both in the United States and in Britain.

A decade ago, Sorauf foresaw the development of this kind of scholarly analysis. He noted on the subject of parties: "They cannot single-handedly reform the political system and political institutions, but that is not their job."[13] What, then, is their job? Sorauf continues: "Except to a small group of admirers who consider them as ends in themselves—and as esthetically pleasing political artifacts—they are means by which we promote and facilitate the systems of representation and decision making in a democracy."[14] These contributions, by themselves, attest to the value of the role played in the political system by the parties, and lend at least credence to Dye's arguments in Chapter 2.

The Public's View of the Party and Policy Relationship

We have innumerable scientific studies in the field of political behavior, but they throw little light on how the public views the relationship between party and policy. These studies examine how the voter perceives candidates and issues, how the voter makes up his mind for whom to vote for (or against), and the correlations between socioeconomic status and party preference. What they notably do not demonstrate is the voters' perception of party outside and beyond the electoral function.

Presumably by the use of public opinion polls some direct evidence on this question could be gathered and analyzed. But until that is done, we must rely on indirect evidence and inferences which are available. The most impressive single strand of evidence comes from the increasing disenchantment with the major parties, both in Britain and in the United States. During 1973 various polls were taken of the British electorate with the clear objective of measuring current party preferences. The results which emerged were consistent and startling: about a third of the respondents supported the Conservatives (who then controlled the government), another third supported Labour (the Opposition party), and fully another third endorsed the Liberals (who held only a handful of seats in Commons). It would be hard to find a better way of saying "a plague on both your houses," so far as the two major British parties were concerned. During the same year the Liberals did unexpectedly well in special elections to fill seats in Commons made vacant by death or resignation.

It seems clear that the mood of the American electorate, in the 70s, is somewhat similar particularly with the Watergate affair behind us. By whatever method one defines Independency, Independency is on the rise nearly every-where.[15] One illustration was the substantial third-party vote for Governor Wallace in the 1968 presidential election. Another was the landslide vote for Republican presidential candidate Richard Nixon in the 1972 election, combined with retention of both Houses of Congress by the Democrats. Similar phenomena have been noted in the state and municipal elections.

Nor has the status of politicians been notably high in Britain or in the United States. In the United States one serious poll asked respondents to list various professions in a descending order of confidence accorded each group. At the very bottom of the list were the used-car salesmen, but just above them came the politicians. It seems unlikely that the events of the second Nixon Administration have contributed to a reordering of popular assessment on this question.

What this obviously suggests is that the electorates in Britain and in the United States take the parties and politicians much less seriously than the parties and politicians take themselves. It also seems then to suggest that the parties are not especially thought of as innovators of policy.

Democratic Attempts at
Policy Formulation

Despite this overall view of parties and policies, there continues to be strong movement inside the Democratic party at its national levels to regard the party as at least a potential policy-formulator. This has been illustrated in Congress where various attempts have been made from time to time to set up "study groups," the real purpose of which is to formulate proposals for congressional consideration and, hopefully, approval. For several reasons, such groups have been relatively unsuccessful. They have usually represented only a minority of activist and liberally-oriented Democrats. Besides their minority status inside the Congress, these same Democrats have suffered the disadvantage of being program-minded in a legislative body that is primarily constituency-minded.

A different kind of illustration comes from the Democratic National Conventions of 1968 and 1972. Though the 1968 convention at Chicago did succeed in its principal assignment—the nomination of presidential and vice-presidential candidates—it did so in an atmosphere of unprecedented bitterness on the convention floor and unparalleled violence outside the convention hall. As a result of a complex set of charges, but especially one declaring that important segments of the traditional Democratic electorate were underrepresented in terms of delegates, the convention set up machinery intended to rewrite the rules governing the selection of delegates to future conventions.

When the election of 1968 had settled down into history, the machinery intended to create changes in convention selection and composition went into action. The most important agency was the McGovern Commission, named after its chairman, Senator George McGovern of South Dakota. The commission held hearings in different parts of the country, and received a good deal of advice from women's groups, civil rights groups, and black organizations, as well as from the usual politicians and academicians.

As a result, the rules were rewritten, and in this form were adopted by the Democratic National Committee. State legislators were urged to revise their laws in order that the new criteria designed to insure larger representation of women and of "minorities" could be met. (Otherwise, a state's delegation might not be accepted by the Credentials Committee at the 1972 convention.) Delegate selection was permitted in a variety of ways, but proportionate representation was the key concept in each case.

Finally, the Democratic Convention convened in Miami Beach. One of its first official acts was to expel the delegation from Cook County, headed by Chicago's Mayor Richard J. Daley. In its place the convention seated a rival delegation headed by the Rev. Jesse Jackson and his associates. An interesting aspect of the situation was that the Daley delegation had been chosen by the Democratic electorate through the process of winning contests in electoral districts in the usual fashion. While, on the other hand, the rival delegation had been self-appointed on the basis of small and informal caucuses totally outside the party organization.

From this point on, the convention was in obvious trouble, but that is not the principal concern here. What deserves underscoring is the failure of the McGovern Commission, and subsequently of the National Committee, to distinguish between two antagonistic and incompatible definitions of "democracy."

In operational terms, political democracy in the United States has been associated with the idea that whoever in a particular district receives more votes than any one else is declared the winner of the election. It is then the right and privilege of the winner to claim to represent the totality of his party's electorate in that district. This is the traditional system, and its key component is the idea of representation based on plurality (or usually in practice, majority) preference. One of the consequences of such a system is that sizable minorities may not be represented at all, or may be severely underrepresented, as happens in most elections for city councils. But it is based on actually winning an election.

In contrast, the idea that a certain percentage of seats must be reserved for persons other than those who have won elections—some kind of a quota arrangement or a plan for preferential and reserved status—flies straight in the face of traditional electoral practice. The emphasis is placed not on who wins a contest but on certain categorical qualities: sex, race, income, and age. The target is to guarantee that the delegates to a national convention will in some general way share the sexual, racial, income, and age make-up of the Democratic electorate. The emphasis is on *representativeness* of these characteristics, not on *representation* by persons who, regardless of sex, race, income, or age, have managed to win a real election in their districts.

Clearly, these two operational definitions of democratic procedure are incompatible. This became quite evident at the Miami Beach Democratic Convention, which ended in confusion. The confusion present at the convention was geometrically compounded as the Democratic campaign continued. The Democrats lost traditional constituency after constituency as the weeks rushed by toward Election Day. Richard M. Nixon, as it subsequently turned out, had need neither of the Watergate break-in nor of the White House "plumbers" to register one of the greatest electoral triumphs in presidential history.

Somewhat chastened by the magnitude of their defeat in the presidential election, the Democrats decided that further and more modest changes in rules governing the selection of delegates were needed. During 1973 various alternative actions were considered by a commission empowered to make recommendations to the National Committee, and plans were considered for a 1974 "conference," which, somewhat on the British model, would attempt to formulate a party position on important issues.[a]

What all this activity seems to indicate is that there still is a fairly substantial body of Democratic activists who would like to re-shape at least the presidential party (through the nominating and party platform process) so that it would become more program-oriented. It seems highly unlikely, however, that it will be easy for Democratic "reformers," old-line politicians, and the AFL-CIO chieftains (who temporarily deserted the Democrats in 1972 but returned in 1973) to agree on a program with any degree of specificity. In any event, specificity brings with it the probability of fragmentation, which is not how presidential elections are won.

The Initiation of Public Policy

From the preceding discussion it is apparent that the initiation and formulation of public policy are vastly more complex processes than democratic theorists of a century ago believed them to be. At the level of the national government in the

[a]Only specialists would be interested in a blow-by-blow account of various Democratic efforts to bring about changes in rules governing the selection of convention delegates. In 1973 the Commission on Delegate Selection drafted new rules, which were to be enforced at the 1976 convention by a seventeen-member Compliance Review Commission. The chief question, of course, was which fraction or clique of the party would have control of the commission.

United States, it is now understood that initiation and formulation may come from a wide variety of sources: the White House, the great interest groups, the mass media, powerful agencies such as the Pentagon, as well as from congressional committees, and occasionally public opinion. Because of a feedback system, the policy output itself may and often does affect the input process. It is partly because of this reason that public policies which look impeccable on paper very often have totally unintended consequences.

When a national political environment is viewed as a system, it is clear that all national systems are extraordinarily complex. This is certainly true in those democratic regimes which have proceeded furthest down the long path of political modernization.

In an effort to explore some of these interrelationships somewhat more precisely, the next part of this chapter examines the relationship of these conclusions in terms of urban politics and public policy.

New Directions

In the preceding section we examined factors and trends in the American national party system. In this section, the main objective is to examine the operations and trends in American urban politics. As a consequence of both examinations, certain key questions suggest themselves with regard to future research in the area of parties, interest groups, and public policy.

Urban Politics: Old-Style and New-Style[b]

Urban America has been changing rapidly, and so has its politics. The old style of urban politics, which emphasized the brokerage function, is on the way out. It is being replaced by a new style which has distinctive features of its own.

Close observers had known for some time that a great transformation in urban politics was in progress. But the general public was not let in on the development until the publication of the 1970 Census. That compilation revealed that for the first time more Americans were living in the suburbs than in the central cities of the metropolitan areas. The implications of this demographic development delighted ambitious suburban politicians and threw big-city leaders, reformers, and ethnic spokesmen into varying degrees of gloom.

In fact, of course, the great changes in urban politics have occurred not precipitously and in one Census decade but over an extended period of time. What is now becoming clear is the momentum, extent, and character of these

---

[b]This section of the chapter is adopted from a paper delivered to the annual meeting of the Political Studies Association, April 1973, at Reading, England.

changes. It is the purpose of this section to trace this evolution and to identify the nature and characteristics both of the old-style and of the emerging new-style politics. It is in this altered political environment that future urban decision-making will of necessity take place.

The Nature of Old-Style Politics[16]

From the end of the Civil War to the end of World War II, the old-style of urban politics served the cities reasonably well. Since that time, this style of politics has increasingly become less and less effective. The old-style politics which dominated the urban political system was—and where it still survives is—characterized by a brokerage function. In a manner somewhat akin to a commodities exchange, sales and purchases are handled by specialists operating under carefully drawn procedures. No one is required to engage in the acquisition, trading, or selling of the commodities. But if he chooses to participate, he places himself under the accepted rules and regulations of the exchange.

In its political manifestation, the brokerage system is built around a leader and his largely personal organization. Persons or interests desiring to arrange a political accommodation must do so through the cooperation, intervention, and assistance of the dominant political group. In working out a solution to a problem—for instance, does a community group, a factory, or a school get the use of a particular piece of land?—the political organization provides the means and the arena for the bargaining of the different interests to take place. There is a *quid pro quo*, a trade-off, as in a commodities exchange system. All interested parties get some "piece of the action," that is, everybody wins something, though not, of course, all that he may have desired.

Brokerage politics places a high premium on organization, and the political history of urban America is in large part a recital of the names of colorful organization leaders. One thinks immediately of William M. ("Boss") Tweed, of Thomas Pendergast, of Mayor Frank Hauge, and—among others—of the immortal George Washington Plunkitt. As Charles F. Murphy, onetime Tammany Hall leader remarked in 1905: "Senator Plunkitt is a straight organization man. He believes in party government." So, naturally, did Charles Murphy.

Yet for all of its historical glamour, the urban political system has not been working very well in the last two decades. The municipal elections of the 50s and 60s failed, in general, to produce governments which could handle substantive problems. It is now crystal clear to any one who seriously surveys the urban political landscape that the old-style politics, with its brokerage approach, is in difficulty. It is becoming less and less relevant to the social needs of our time. What is more, it has been repudiated, or is in the process of being repudiated, by significant groups in the community. This tendency is particularly apparent in the actions of the young, whose disenchantment with brokerage politics is obvious to all. But the repudiation extends to more or less alienated groups, including lower-class blacks and certain upper-class blacks and certain upper-class whites.

The Charges Against Old-Style Politics[17]

What are the principal charges against brokerage politics? In summary form, four items may be placed on the bill of indictment. First, it is widely believed that the traditional system of rewards and punishments has become ineffective. There is less and less interest in playing the historic game. Secondly, brokerage politics has failed to deal successfully with the great urban social issues of today— schools, race relations, crime, welfare, and housing. Thirdly, the brokerage system has been unable to satisfy the demands of lower-class blacks and other excluded groups in the urban community. And fourthly, brokerage politics has failed to bring about the great goal of social integration. In short, everywhere in urban America the sense of *civitas* continues to wane. Inside the cities, anomie increasingly displaces the traditional concept of community.

In addition to its inability to deal with the big problems of the present, old-style politics suffers from two additional serious disabilities. It has proved unable to establish priorities in any rational or meaningful way. In city after city, there have been increasingly serious problems in the areas of education, housing, health, crime, mass transportation, pollution, and taxation. The municipal response to this generally dismal situation has been, by and large, that of paralysis. The officials have been overwhelmed. In the absence of any agreed-on system to decide priorities, what will happen in all probability is a continued general deterioration on all sectors of the American municipal front.

But the situation should be seen in a wider perspective. Even when priorities have been decided rationally—and this has happened in a few cities—there has been an increasing inability to implement the decisions which have been made. For this, there are many reasons—inflation is a leading character in the cast of villains. But the fact remains that even those cities which have been able to determine priorities have not been distinguished by their ability to implement them.

Why is it that urban political organizations can no longer govern, although they once could? It may be useful here to retrace some historical developments. Citywide political organizations existed in most municipalities long before the Civil War. Yet with the exception of the largest cities, such as New York and Philadelphia, the organizations were under the control of a relatively small civic-minded elite. In the largest cities, the type of political organization was already present which was later to dominate the post-Civil War period. The Democratic organization in New York City—Tammany Hall—foreshadowed what was eventually to become the norm in the medium-sized and smaller cities.

During the years following Appomatox, the Tammany-style political organization—the machine based on an immigrant population—replaced the civic-minded, elitist organizations throughout the East and the North. Long before the end of the nineteenth century, the machine-style of organization was ascendant in America's principal cities.

Because of various and well-publicized abuses, a reaction against machine politics set in. This reform movement was dominated by the old-time elitists, or their children, who had been pushed out of active politics into the civic organizations. Outnumbered at the polls, they could still launch sharp, well-financed campaigns from their civic clubs and associations. The National Municipal League, founded in 1894, served both as a source of intellectual strength and as a positive symbol for the Reformers nationally.

The story of the great machines and of the reactions to them is too familiar to warrant repetition. But in retrospect it is clear that the Reformers achieved many of their objectives—a short ballot, a greater concentration of executive power, a merit civil service, the elimination of the most blatant forms of municipal corruption. *Yet the movement did not succeed in its dream of taking politics out of government.* The Reformers did not understand the nature of political power and, because of this, they let the control of events slip out of their hands. On balance, it is fair to say that while the Reform movement realized a good many of its specific objectives, it failed to win its overall goal of separating politics and government once and for all time.

The Reformers themselves rarely attributed this setback to their own inadequate analysis of power. Rather, they were inclined to be critical of the structure of government, or of the corruptibility of those who managed government, or of the supposed low levels of education of the electorate. But all of these contentions, with their highly personal and class overtones, miss the main point. The breakdown of old-style politics is not caused by structural deficiency, or ill-will, or corruption, or conspiracy. It is caused by the fact that the conditions which formerly underlay the system have been changing rapidly.

In this respect, the urban political system is not much different from other systems. When the philosophical base of any great system erodes, the system itself and its operations are in jeopardy. As an illustration, one need only recall how Newtonian physics changed man's whole outlook toward religion and philosophy. So far as brokerage politics is concerned, the philosophical assumptions which underlie it are increasingly less valid. No political leader or organization can seriously alter this situation. No great speech or inspired proclamation is likely to make much difference. No smashing electoral success will have much bearing on the matter.

The Failure of Pluralism[18]

To come quickly to the point, the foundation of old-style politics is pluralism. This is not the place to trace the fascinating intellectual history of pluralism as a political concept. But the account would certainly have to include such names and documents as the following: James Madison, in *The Federalist* No. 10; J.N. Figgis, F.W. Maitland, and Otto von Gierke; G.D.H. Cole; Sidney and Beatrice Webb; Harold J. Laski in his early work, *Authority in the Modern State*; R.M. MacIver in his study, *The Web of Government*; and contemporary investigators of community power, especially Floyd Hunter in *Community Power Structure* and Robert Dahl in *Who Governs?*. Pluralism, in short, has an ancient, honorable, and useful pedigree.

As applied to the urban political system in America, pluralism has had two outstanding characteristics. The first component, coming from group theory, is the competitive principle. In Madison's thinking, conflict among groups—or "factions," as he termed them—was inevitable in a free society. And, he continued, the chief task of government was to mediate and regulate the consequent struggles. The second component of pluralism is the idea that government should be limited. This concept can be traced directly to John Locke and, indirectly, to certain medieval and even some Roman political philosophers. But in its modern version, political pluralism was probably best stated by R.M. MacIver.

The evidence of current urban research indicates that both ingredients of pluralism are less effective, less influential, and less valid today than they were, say a quarter of a century ago. They are infinitely less valid, as working principles to support a system—pluralism—than they were at the beginning of the present century.

It is becoming increasingly apparent that the problems associated with pluralism are mounting. As Theodore Lowi pointed out in *The End of Liberalism*, pluralism is the philosophy on which modern interest group liberalism is based. And this kind of liberalism has come under heavy attack—by Lowi, among others.

Probably more significant is the criticism of pluralism in terms of justice. Traditionally, pluralists have believed that the conflict of groups has resulted in an acceptable—even a just—equilibrium. In this sense, whatever happens at the moment to be the status quo can, roughly, be equated with a kind of natural justice.

The argument against this pluralist assumption takes this form. Pluralism—the conflict of groups—results, to be sure, in the achievement of an equilibrium. But it is an equilibrium in which the strongest groups have succeeded in getting most of what is worth getting. The equilibrium, once achieved, is held to be impervious to the demands of social justice. Groups which are effectively excluded from the conflict—such as blacks and Puerto Ricans living in slums and the elderly everywhere—find themselves observers instead of participants in the political process. In this way, the traditional pluralist assumption that pluralism equals equilibrium which in turn equals justice has been more and more challenged. In my view this challenge is eminently justified. But in any event, disillusionment with urban politics on the grounds of injustice is widespread and probably increasing.

The old-style of brokerage politics is obsolescent, then, because the philosophy upon which it is based—pluralism—has become untenable. Yet there is another objection to this type of politics—an operational objection—which merits emphasis: old-style politics cannot set priorities. To pursue this for a moment, the question may be asked as to why this is so. Why, that is to say, does the old-style system of urban politics not allow the government to establish priorities and then to implement them?

To start with, under the brokerage system there are a number of competing interests. In the nature of the contest every interest of any significance must be appeased. Its acquiescence if not approbation must be purchased through the allocation of some kind of resource available to the municipal government. But because resources are limited, no interest can get everything it thinks it is entitled to. As a result, no problem is really ever solved. To temporize is better than to come to grips with the basic issues. In an age where the demands keep increasing and the resources do not, only partial or incomplete compromises—not real solutions—are to be expected.

There is a second reason why the old-style politics cannot set priorities. To put the matter bluntly, liberals—that is, those who play the game of pluralistic politics—are much too soft to make and enforce hard decisions. To set priorities and carry them out would obviously hurt some people and alienate others. But liberals want to be loved. Therefore, they must distribute a little here, a little there, in an effort to please everyone. This is exactly the opposite of the rational establishing of social priorities. For all of these reasons brokerage politics—politics premised on pluralism—has become passe.

Elements of the New-Style Politics[19]

With the old-style politics discredited, what can be said regarding the new-style which is in the process of replacing it? In response to this inquiry, we are now in a position to identify the principal elements which we may expect to be included within the new and developing system.

In the first place, the new system will have to be able to set up and to enforce priorities. It is not clear yet how this may be achieved, but it is certain that some kinds of persuasion or coercion not currently employed under the present system will have to be utilized. There will have to be a recognition of the idea that not every group and interest can advance at a rate decided on by itself (see Spadaro's concept of Influence and Value). Public authority will have to be just that—authority.

Some new forms will evolve under the new-style politics. We can reject participatory democracy, the "New Left," the students' movement, politics of "confrontation," and John W. Gardner's Common Cause on the grounds that they are all transitory or ineffective or both. Much more likely to have an impact on the evolving new-style politics is the mass movement which is now being created in the ranks of America's black citizenry. At the same time, parallel movements are slowly emerging from the Puerto Rican and Chicano populations. Two more movements which possess a political potential are the consumers' movement and the women's movement. Given sufficient organization and financing, they might develop into permanent and important factors in the urban political process.

Finally—but most important of all—is the almost spontaneous drive in the great cities for community control over certain community activities. Some—but by no means all—of the elements of this drive have their origin in local groups sponsored by the antipoverty program. Other sources include the desire for self-determination always nascent and now evident in many neighborhoods, and the generally current favorable attitude toward governmental decentralization at all levels.

An examination of the literature on community control shows that sentiment for such control is most marked in three areas: education, housing and urban renewal, and law-and-order.[20] To be sure, most thinking people will have some reservations as to the desirable extent of community control—one thinks of the conflict between individual constitutional rights and a majority determined to have its way over such rights. Yet, despite this, the concept of community control over certain activities which take place within the community possesses a very strong psychological attraction. This is especially observable in the rapidly growing black and Puerto Rican areas of the largest cities.

The movement for community control will continue to gain momentum. It will be an important factor in the new-style politics.

In addition, we may expect to witness the rise of a new type of ethnic voting based on race. Class and racial voting will be highly correlated. There will be an increasing demand for welfare-state-type programs inside the cities. This is because the disaffected do not have much use for the niceties and benefits of the free enterprise system. Finally, the cities will attempt to forge a city-federal government axis, by-passing the states as much as possible.

Whatever develops specifically, it is quite certain as a general proposition that the new-style politics will be played under a different set of rules of the game. Not only will the rules change, but there will also be new actors and new goals. In this process there will be important attitudinal changes on the part of the citizens. For example, some segments of the electorate may simply refuse to accept the losing of an election. Politics will become too serious to be considered merely a form of sport.

As the new politics replaces the old, it will become increasingly apparent that the concept of pluralism which undergirded the old system has, in effect, been repudiated on the ground of obsolescence.

*The New Urban Politics and
Decision-Making*[21]

All of these interrelated developments will, of course, affect urban decision-making in very profound ways. To begin with, the arena of decision-making will very often be shifted from one place or level to another. The problem of coordinated transport, for example, will probably have to be tackled at the state rather than at the metropolitan or citywide level. In cases involving territory in more than one state, it is likely that only federal action will be decisive.

Again, it is clear that many of the traditional actors in the political arena will be pushed aside and their places taken by new players. For instance, teachers' organizations are now dealing directly with boards of education regarding salary, tenure, and other matters. A newfound militancy has also put police associations and unions of municipal workers in the center of the political process. The day is long since past when policemen, teachers, and municipal employees would rely solely on the good will and general beneficence of the political party in control of city or borough hall.

Finally, as the area of political combat is extended and as the number of actors increases, questions as to the legitimacy of particular decisions will become more and more pointed. In what sense, for example, does a decision taken by city council become "legitimate" in the view of a hostile and antagonistic section of the community? Will it become necessary to hold referenda in such cases in order to establish legitimacy? This type of problem is bound to become more frequent as the momentum of the new-style politics accelerates. The continual posing of the question of the moral authority of law will also provide some ammunition for the most welcome revival of political philosophy.

Parties, the Political Scientist, and Public Policy

In the preceding two sections, we examined the evolution of American national and urban politics, and pointed out some areas where further inquiry is needed. In this section, the emphasis is on the study of political parties, with particular reference to the role or roles of the political scientist with a special interest in parties, policy, and policy analysis. The approach employed is to raise a series of questions or problems, and to try to arrive at what Reinhold Niebuhr once called "proximate solutions to insoluble problems." Even this formulation, it is only fair to warn, may in many cases seem overly optimistic.

In his 1964 study, Sorauf listed some of the "unfinished business and scholarly needs of the study of American parties."[22] Much of what he said at that time is also applicable to the study of British, French, and German parties. A summarization therefore is appropriate.

First, there are gaps in the descriptions of parties. Such voids include information about rural and small-town parties, about party functions over and beyond the electoral function, and about party leaders and party workers.

There is also a need, he said, to clarify certain concepts which are central to the study of parties. For example, little still is known about the party as a political organization. The concept of "competitiveness," to take another example, suffers because there is little agreement on its definition. In a related area, we use the term "faction" with great imprecision. For many other matters we are in need of concept and of definition.

Thirdly—and this is a point repeatedly made by E.E. Schattschneider—it is necessary to develop new data on which to work. Though it is easy to obtain electoral data, it is extremely difficult and expensive to obtain data on party recruitment of candidates, endorsements in primaries, authority relationships within the party, and modes of organization. The basic reason for the difficulty is that in these areas one must rely on local informants and observers.

Lastly, Sorauf contends, scholarship on the parties "must press its search for more middle-range theory of the political party."[23] For example, it might be advantageous to apply to the study of parties the entire body of knowledge about large-scale organizations which has been developed in recent years.

The lacunae about which Sorauf complained still remain largely unfilled, despite the appearance during the decade of a torrent of empirical studies of American, British, and French political parties. Particularly disappointing has been the failure to produce some sort of a "break-through" in the development of middle-range theory concerning parties, including the function of public policy analysis.

Though this assessment may seem unduly harsh, it has been recently concurred with by Evron M. Kirkpatrick in a comprehensive examination of the study of American parties.[24] Using as his starting point a re-examination of the 1950 *Report* of the Committee on Political Parties, Kirkpatrick (who was a member of the committee) goes on to criticize political scientists for their failure to develop a policy science approach, especially in the field of parties.

In his analysis, Kirkpatrick singled out four general deficiencies of the political science profession in the field of public policy. The charges are important—at least to political scientists—and they are summarized in the next few paragraphs.

1. Inadequacies in goal and derivational thinking. The problem here is to identify and clarify the aims of action. This is the essence of goal thinking. In addition, aims and goals must be narrowed so that they are relevant to specific problems and situations. Derivational thinking is concerned with the justification of values. To be effective, such thinkig must deal with clearly stated, understood, and explicit norms. Anything short of this tends to end up as shoddy thinking.

2. Inadequate value institutional analysis. The charge here is that political scientists have failed to explore systematically the relations between political institutions and policy outcomes. This is true generally, but it is especially observable in the study of political parties.

3. The emphasis on scientific thinking. The point here is that the emphasis on science and scientific method has led to a deemphasis on other kinds of thinking. As a result, goal and derivational thinking have suffered. So has concern for trends as instruments for evaluation, along with the invention of alternatives. Kirkpatrick's principal complaint is that political scientists are oriented to what exists. What is required is that they become future-oriented.

4. Insufficient data and inadequate empirical theory. This allegation is parallel to that already noted by Sorauf. Kirkpatrick finds that the existing levels of knowledge are inadequate. In general, political science remains a "data-poor discipline."[25]

In conclusion, Kirkpatrick laments: "Perhaps the most important lesson is simply that the job of the policy scientist is not easy."[26] Beyond any doubt, political scientists who study parties, interest groups, and policy politics would agree with this judgment. Yet it is equally certain that they will continue to attempt to develop a more adequate understanding of policy science than we have at present. Though there is no very solid ground for joy, there is also no compelling reason for despair.

The Party Specialist—Scholar?
Politician? Or Both?

Specialists in parties, interest groups, and public opinion have generally found it comfortable to approach their subjects with a certain degree of personal detachment. Though recently a minority of social scientists has been calling for a determined—and even ideological—activism and relevancy on the part of their colleagues, the dominant tone is still that set half a century ago by Max Weber. The ideal was held to be a separation of scientific verities from personal values. It has become clear, however, that in the real world of politics this detachment is often difficult to achieve, let alone maintain. But the ideal continues to command at least widespread lip-service.

A difficulty arises when a political scientist holds the conviction that he or she possesses superior skills for insights into the solution of certain questions than do persons with no formal training in the discipline of political science. So far as psychologists and economists are concerned, this is a ballgame they have won. So far as political scientists are concerned, the general impression is that all citizens who can read the newspapers are specialists in political matters, with or without the benefit of any formal academic training.

For any one who has ever "taken" a course in party politics, or has taught one, nothing is more familiar than the visiting councilman, representative, or senator, whose job is conceived to be to bring "the real world" into the classroom. The fact that such appearances are usually disasters does not make their occurrences less frequent. For even if the students and the instructor merely pick up a few easily given and easily forgotten anecdotes, the word quickly reaches higher university and "outside" circles that the particular class is "relevant." Relevant to what is never very clearly spelled out, but the impression is one of progress—an impression many students and all university bureaucrats wish to foster. There are, of course, some relatively splendid examples of a scholar turning politician with conspicuous success, for example, Governor and later President Woodrow Wilson, Mayor Samuel Eldersveld, Senator John Tower, to cite a few. But they are the exceptions. The more usual sequence of events is for the scholar to serve as an advisor to a candidate. And in the event of victory the advisor may continue in an appointed position.

In short, there seems to be no magical formula whereby a student can take X, Y, or Z courses in the area of parties, interest groups, and public opinion and breeze into the political arena. What then is the best background? Obviously, opinions will differ widely. At a convention of political scientists held in Washington several years ago, this question was put to a distinguished panel of political scientists. All of them had had considerable experience in government, usually as advisors or staff personnel. John P. Roche, a former top advisor to President Lyndon B. Johnson, gave it as his considered view that the most useful people to have in high policy positions were "policy-oriented lawyers." He named one-time Secretary of State Dean Acheson as a prime example. Queried on this point, Roche said that the superiority of the policy-oriented lawyer, over, for example, businessmen, lay in the ability of this special breed of lawyer to absorb vast amounts of data, arrange the data into patterns, and come forth with well-founded policy recommendations.

Again, there is the old question of whether the roles of the party-specialist-scholar and of the party-specialist-politician are in conflict. Certainly this conflict of interests is a possibility, as it has been in recent years when legal scholars accepted positions as White House counsel.

But if Clara Penniman is right—and she probably is—political scientists in recent years have tended to stay clear of major policy debates, at least in comparison with economists and lawyers.[27] This means that the conflict of interest temptation only infrequently arises. In brief, it is not at present a major problem.

Policy Analysis in Relation to Parties

As has been previously noted, the historic view of parties stressed the role of parties in the formulation of public policy. This view has, as we have seen, come under consistent attack for many years, and the prevailing approach today is to treat the party more as a dependent than as an independent political variable.

But it is possible to go even further, as David Broder, a political journalist, and Walter Dean Burnham, a political scientist, have recently done. It is the gist of their argument that American party politics has been falling apart for at least the last decade. Broder's presentation is familiar and traditional, but Burnham, in a 1969 analysis, adds some new elements to the debate.[28] His first important point deals with the theory of "critical elections," first clearly enunciated by V.O. Key, Jr., in 1955. The idea is that some elections have a permanent realigning effect on American politics, for example, those of 1800, 1828, 1860, and 1932. On the whole, the results have been beneficial. But, Burnham wonders, what are the socioeconomic currents which bring about such realignments, and what are the chances of a meaningful realignment in the future. (Undoubtedly, he would not consider 1972 to be a "critical election," even if Kevin Phillips and other Republican theoreticians did—for about a year.)

Turning to what he calls "the second major dynamic of American electoral politics during this century," Burnham addresses himself to the withering away of the parties—the phenomenon of "electoral disaggregation." The evidence for this allegation is familiar, and it depends heavily upon the shifts in party loyalties and the increasing numbers of voters who consider themselves to be Independents.

From all of this, it follows that if the long-term trend of "politics without parties" continues, there will be profound policy consequences. One possibility is the continuation of traditional Lockean individualism into the era of Big Organizations. If that happens, Burnham concludes: "One may well doubt whether political parties or critical realignments have much place in such a political universe."[29] In short, there will be nothing left for the specialist in parties to study, particularly in relation to policy.

Yet there are other prominent political scientists who do not necessarily share Burnham's brooding pessimism. In a significant work, also published in 1969, Robert Golembiewski, William Welsh, and William Crotty arrived at a more optimistic conclusion.[30] Their method was to examine the methodologies in the leading books of M. Ostrogorski, Robert Michels, Maurice Duverger, and Samuel Eldersveld. The discussion is informative and illuminating, but not all of it is directly related to the present analysis. The general finding was that "... research on parties generates a substantial optimism."[31] On the other hand, the authors concluded that there is a "methodological barrenness of research" on parties, which is most notably apparent in its failure to produce "theoretical constructs able to support cumulative research."[32] The cheerful disposition stemmed from the increasing probability that conceptual schemes and a common focus to guide research efforts, may emerge in the next decade or so.[33]

Golembiewski, Welsh, and Crotty, in the same book, also raised serious questions about the value of the traditional voting studies. Again, their critical review of the major studies deserves to be read in its entirety. But their overall finding is encouraging: ". . . research on electoral behavior has progressed far in a relatively short period of time."[34] The degree of methodological sophistication shown in the leading voting studies is, unhappily, somewhat rare in political science. If and when a true science of electoral behavior is developed, it is reasonable to assume that it will have some bearing on various aspects of policy analysis of interest to specialists on parties.

What Should Be Included in
the Study of Parties?

Though the academic study of parties goes back many decades, one associates its modern development in American colleges with such names as Charles Merriam and Robert Brooks. Further refinement came, of course, with the succeeding publications of V.O. Key, Jr.'s synthesizing textbooks in the post-World War II period. Indeed, the influence of Key is perhaps the greatest single factor in systematizing the subject of political parties, interest groups, and public opinion in American academic circles.

Since the death of Key a decade ago, the subject-matter which he saw as highly interconnected has tended to become relatively fragmented. A perusal of recent textbooks in the area once covered by Key and his disciples reveals that a profusion of specialized undergraduate courses has replaced the synthesis that was earlier envisaged. Sorauf, in his writings, deals only with parties, while Zeigler gives most of his attention to interest groups, and Childs and other specialists focus on public opinion and related problems. There are, of course, many further specializations, as illustrated by Fred Greenstein's studies of the political socialization of children, or the various specialized studies of urban and suburban politics.

At the undergraduate level, the problem is how to cover a meaningful fraction of these materials with any degree of depth and of sophistication. Happily, there seems to be some general agreement, at least in the area of research and methods. Most undergraduate studies in political parties now require at least some field research work. At the very least, students are encouraged to participate actively in political party campaigns or, alternatively, in the activities of leading interest groups. At a minimum, this effort has added a behavioral dimension to studies of parties and interest groups. When coupled with survey and questionnaire techniques, the results of such field studies are often of a very high level.

Another spin-off in recent undergraduate studies has been evidenced in the apparently increasing number of students who have become not only partici-pant-observers but party officials and candidates. Of course, no one has any exact figures on this, but one illustration is suggestive. Of about 360 upper class political science majors at Temple University during the 1973-74 academic year, at least a dozen held positions as committeemen or committeewomen with one of the major parties. In addition, several had been candidates—successful or otherwise—for various municipal and educational offices. Undoubtedly, the lowering of the voting age to 18 has spurred this trend. But it was in evidence long before the change in the voting age was made.

There are other developments which deserve highlighting. For decades, students of parties have made extensive use of Census data, and the breaking down of electoral districts by Census tracts is old hat. Another tried and true device is to employ public opinion data, whether that supplied by commercial organizations like Gallup and Harris, or the more detailed data made available by the Survey Research Center.

But since 1960, a further development has taken place, and it has shown and continues to show great promise, even for undergraduate work. The device is known as political simulation, or, more technically, simulation-gaming. The principle involved is that one learns by doing. The idea is to simulate a realistic, though admittedly artificial, representation of the world.[35]

Originally used in political science mostly in international relations and war studies, political simulations have been developed in other fields, including campaigns, elections, and parties. The advantages of learning by the use of simulation methods are numerous, and they include the following: (1) The learning experience is often better than in real life. (2) Simulations are usually faster than the real-life equivalent, and they can be repeated many times. (3) Simulations may result in giving the players a very high degree of motivation, as well as learning how to play the game expertly. (4) Though in real life errors in judgment may be prohibitively costly—thus discouraging the effort in the first place—in simulations the risks are not actual ones. And (5) Simulations are of value in making an ex post facto analysis of what may actually have happened in, say, an election or may happen in relation to values.

Of the many games developed by simulation specialists, one of the most useful for the study of municipal politics is the Woodbury Political Simulation. Developed by H. Robert Coward, Bradbury Seasholes, Marshall Whithed, and Robert Wood, the Woodbury game involves a mock election in a hypothetical community—Woodbury. At the start of play, student participants are given background data on the basic socioeconomic characteristics of each ward: ethnicity, income, religion, and so on. Information about past voting trends, potential campaign issues, and the condition of the mass media are also made available.

In ordinary mock elections, there are usually no statistical controls. In this respect, the Woodbury Political Simulation is different. For each ward, there is an umpire, who calculates, on the basis of the vote distribution worked out beforehand, the effect of various moves on the votes for the candidates. Therefore, there is a statistical outcome to the election: one candidate wins, another loses. In its computerized version, the computer replaces the human umpires. To play the game through the stipulated twenty-one campaign days requires about 200 separate moves and takes approximately nine hours. But the result is—by general agreement—the best substitute yet invented for actual high-level participation in a real electoral situation.

It is possible to apply the technique of simulation to actual elections, and potential public policy outcomes. In an experiment in De Kalb, Illinois, Marshall Whithed and Clifford Smith were able to compare simulation results with the actual results of an election held four days after the simulation run. The uses of this technique—and possible misuses—are evident.

In short, for undergraduate teaching, simulation games may be superior to the use of case studies, which tend to be dated or in other ways seem to lack reality. In addition, they have the advantage over real elections in that they may be played at any time, for example, in the middle of an election-less summer session.

In summary, then, the undergraduate curriculum in political behavior (parties, interest groups, voting, public opinion, and sub-topics of these areas) seems to have found some measure of agreement as to what should be studied and as to methods of presentation and experimentation. The overall trend is clearly in the direction of more field studies, using as sophisticated research methods and tools as are available to a particular department of political science, and eventually the exciting possibilities of Spadaro's discussion of psychorational and biophysical tools.

At the graduate school level, the picture is less clear. Just as political scientists are having difficulties redefining—in the post-behavioral age—the core areas of their discipline, so are the specialists in political behavior (including parties) running into the same obstacles. At the heart of the problem is the need to master a vast amount of materials and techniques in a relatively short period of time.

Under the circumstances, the temptation is to concentrate one's attention upon a highly specialized area and master the techniques most relevant to that area. For example, a student of French politics must obviously be able to read technical French and to conduct interviews in France in non-technical French. If French happens not to be the native tongue of the student, this mastery of the language may take some time. But in addition, the student will have to become familiar with French electoral history, French campaign methods, and French public opinion polls. All of this is over and beyond the necessary minimum standards of familiarity with the newer methods of research, including perhaps model-building, simulation, and computerization. This task, seen in this perspective, is formidable, and more likely to take one's lifetime than it is to be achieved in the compass of several years of graduate study.

To put the matter differently, it is desirable to learn everything related to one's special interest, and it becomes increasingly less possible to do so. Is there any hope at all? There is some reason to believe that there is.

Some Hopeful Signs for the
Study of Parties

During the last fifteen or twenty years, two developments have taken place which lead to an optimistic prediction for the future and further study of political parties. The first has already been hinted at, but some elaboration is in order.

The reference is to the computer revolution, which is being increasingly applied to all phases of the scientific study of politics, including political behavior and parties. Political science is not, of course, the sole beneficiary of this revolution. In social science generally calculations may be completed in a few moments which were previously beyond the capability of calculating machine computations. But it is not only the speed of calculations which has benefited from computer science; it is also the absolute extension of the frontiers of what can be learned and explored.

It is now possible, for example, to isolate a large number of political or other variables, and to assess their relative importance to other factors, in a way which was totally inconceivable prior to the computer revolution. Dye and his associates have shown how effectively this can be done. While they are probably not infinite, the uses of the computer stagger the imagination. An illustration cited earlier in this chapter related to the simulation of elections, in which the calculations needed in the Woodbury Political Simulation may be immensely improved and also accelerated by tying in terminals to data banks. This is, literally, only one of hundreds of possible examples, and the field is wide open for experimentation and advancement.

Nor is it any longer necessary for the advanced political science student who wishes to make use of computerization to be an expert on the internal operations of computers themselves. The analogy is with a television set. To operate a television receiver successfully it is not necessary to understand the internal workings of the machinery. So it is with computers. As Whithed has remarked, his generation is the last which will need to know both how computers work and what their uses are.

Various computer centers can program and help analyze any problem which students (or instructors) can define with sufficient precision (and obtain data on) so that computer analysis will pay off. A person who studies independent voting, for example, can collect basic data prepared and made available through the Inter-University Consortium on Political Research (a membership organization), define the problems he wishes to analyze, and turn to his computer center for the technical job of handling the necessary programming and print-outs. The Survey Research Center at Ann Arbor has shown what can be done in this area, but almost any first-rate university nowadays can play the same game and this increases the potential analysis of party "policy" as an independent variable.

For the advanced student of parties and related subjects, there is a second reason for cautious optimism. This comes from the continuing advance of systems analysis, and the increasing application of its suggestions and findings to the study of parties.

In political science, systems analysis grew out of a concern to advance the study of comparative politics from a kind of county-by-country Cook's tour to a genuine comparative undertaking. The first step beyond a country-by-country approach was to develop a method whereby institutions in differing political systems were compared, for example, the legislatures. Yet this institutional approach, while interesting, possessed inherent limitations when it came to developing cumulative studies, that is, those which could be built on each other.

The next step, therefore, was to work out a scheme in which it was possible to isolate functions which were performed in all political systems, and to compare them from the points of view of relative development, impact, and trends. An example is the articulation of interests as evidenced in differing political environments (or possibly the use of set theory).

In its modern phase, systems analysis has multiple origins, including the pioneering work of Gabriel Almond, Sidney Verba, and G. Bingham Powell, and the various conferences sponsored by the International Political Science Association and related organizations. Of particular importance was the Florence Conference of 1954, which was financed by UNESCO and attended by the leading scholars in the field of comparative government (now usually called comparative politics).

It may well be, as is often charged, that the systems approach is more a framework, at present, than a genuine theory.[36] But the framework itself has suggested a wide variety of useful applications. As an illustration, the techniques used in comparative politics (among nation-states) have increasingly been applied to the study of state politics (among the states of the American Union). Department-by-department behavior may be studied in France, as may county-by-county behavior in Texas. The possibilities are both numerous and challenging, though Spadaro raises serious limitations on its operational caveats.

In short, with the problem of data analysis brought under control by the use of automatic equipment, the task of comparative analysis has been advanced by the utilization of the systems approach. Even though we are still in the infancy of this development, we may well be on the threshold of major advances in this aspect of the study of parties. When this approach is coupled with rigorous data requirements, imagination, and hard work, there is therefore a reasonable basis for optimism.

The New Interest in Policy Politics

The decreasing importance of parties has been matched by the increasing importance of policy politics.[37] The evidence for this generalization is multifold, but a few examples will illustrate the point.

In the politics of urban areas, it no longer makes much difference whether the electoral system is partisan or nonpartisan. Even where the system is partisan, that fact is usually of little importance. This is because of the general tendency for the organization which holds power to remain in power, possibly for decades. What is therefore important is the factionalism inside the major party or organization.

But factionalism is a poor and inadequate substitute for policy formulation. Factionalism tends to be built around personality and personnel politics. Yet somewhere along the line substantive issues do come before city councils, and laws are passed. Hence, the emphasis of scholarly attention has shifted to the issues which are the subject of the more important laws.

Such issues would include education as Zeigler argues in Chapter 5, law and order, housing and urban renewal, and transportation. For many political scientists, the politics of education, for instance, is more worthy of study than the political campaigns of a particular party or organization. Indeed, we may be in the process of following upon the steps of the sociologists. Their technique is simple, but it pays off. One simply takes the word "sociology" and follows it with "of" and adds any important noun. Thus, there is the sociology of knowledge, the sociology of law, the sociology of religion, and so on indefinitely. Judging from recent publishers' lists, political scientists are also finding this approach attractive. What this amounts to is a recognition that the decline of the parties has been followed by a decline in the scholarly interest in parties. At the same time, the increasing interest in substantive issues has been paralleled by an increase in the scholarly concern with policy politics.

It may, of course, be argued that what is being developed is merely a new and up-dated description of what used to be called in political science circles "public law." But what seems to be different now from, say, thirty years ago, is the fact that during the last decade persons trained in the behavioral approach to the study of parties and interest groups have increasingly turned their attention to policy politics. To put the matter differently, these scholars have become and are becoming both as a matter of principle as well as of practice more and more policy-oriented. On balance, this may be considered a very welcome and positive development.

Policy Politics and Policy Sciences

In other chapters of this book, the question is raised in a number of ways as to the actual as well as the appropriate relationship between political science and policy science(s). Here, the focus is on the relationship between policy politics—the newer emphasis of specialists in political parties and political behavior—and the policy sciences.

To begin with, the whole area is something of a terra incognita. While we can fairly well define "policy politics," there is little agreement on what constitutes "policy sciences." To be sure, there is no dearth of definitions, but on balance they are more confusing than helpful. The pioneering work of Harold Lasswell of four decades ago has simply not produced the kind of follow-up that many social scientists had anticipated. This is, of course, regrettable, if for no other reason than that some of the ablest academic brains of our time have spent innumerable and largely unprofitable hours trying to develop the Lasswellian insights into some sort of an applied social science.

A related problem arises when one asks who the policy scientists envisaged by Lasswell are going to be, and where they are expected to be found. In a friendly but sharp review of Lasswell's *A Pre-View of Policy Sciences*, Charles O. Jones has expressed several reservations about the policy science approach.[38] He doubts that it will be possible to develop policy scientists with the ability to comprehend and to integrate the kind of knowledge Lasswell calls for. He wonders whether such a class of policy scientists, if put in decision-making posts, might not be incompatible with the maintenance of a democratic order. In any event, Jones continues, with policy scientists in mind, "At the risk of insulting Dr. Kissinger, I am compelled to say that I don't know any such persons presently in decision-making capacities."[39]

Finally, in his *coup de grace*, Jones adds: "I can understand the policy science role of academic advisers who are broadly trained, as well as of decision makers who are told 'be comprehensive.' What is never made concrete to me in this book is where I should expect to find these super-integrators in our system of political decision making."[40]

At an operational level, other difficult problems arise. Across the country, for example, there are springing up a large number of institutes, centers, and even departments of policy sciences. What it is that they are expected to do is not particularly clear. So far as a casual utilizer of their wares can see, the new studies are not very much different from the older studies. They simply bear new imprimaturs.

To focus directly on political science, one might begin by asking whether policy sciences should be taught as part of a political science curriculum, and why. At first glance, the idea is an attractive one, for in many respects it seems a logical extension of the current interest in policy politics. But this is not really what Lasswell is driving at: he is driving at the development of a science of decision-making.

Now few political science departments have any special claim to expertise in that area. Unfortunately, it is all too often true, as Schattschneider was ruefully fond of remarking: "Political scientists are never happier than when studying the past." But the problem with Lasswell is that he is almost entirely future-oriented. There seems to be little in the academic study of policy politics that inevitably propels political scientists to join in the Lasswellian avant garde. Rather, the temptation is to concentrate on the study of problems which are at hand, and which may be affected by the devices of applied social science. And it may be added that there are considerable internal and external pressures impelling political scientists in this direction.

As has been implied above, another problem is the location of policy sciences within the academic community. Most social science departments, including those in political science, are poorly equipped to carry on continuing and collective research.[c] Yet policy scientists themselves admit that the policy sciences require for their development and enrichment an interdisciplinary approach on a research team basis. Thus, the most a political science department could do would be to contribute the services of some of its political behavior personnel, including party specialists, to a research center devoted exclusively to the policy sciences. But again, in actual life, it is hard to serve two masters. In the long run, it seems likely that the political scientists in question would have to choose between mainly working in the research center or mainly living within the department. In the latter case, the problem of isolation from the scholarly interests of the majority of one's colleagues in the department might become a very serious one.

For these reasons, it seems likely that the type of model which will ultimately prevail will be along the lines of the various and highly successful research institutes developed at the University of Michigan and the University of Illinois. There are, of course, many other possibilities, but the temptation is usually rather overwhelming to imitate, at least in the first go-around, those models which have proved their worth.

Policy as Independent Variable

Nevertheless, Theodore Lowi has posed this question: What differences, if any, do the policies of political parties account for? As usual, Lowi's approach is somewhat at variance with that of other scholars, but his argument is worth summarizing.[41] In the United States, he says, a party institutionalizes, channels, and socializes conflict over control of the regime. Or, to use his more specific language, an American party performs "a *constituent* or *constitutional* function" in the polity.

Lowi has underscored the importance of this function as follows:

That is to say, the significance of democratic party systems is to be found first in the *regime* and in the *type* of regime rather than directly and specifically in the

[c]It would be interesting to know how many political science departments as departments carry on continuing and collective research. The usual pattern, of course, is to establish a separate institute for research and/or activist functions. An example is the coexistence at Rutgers University of the Department of Political Science and the Eagleton Institute of Politics. Some of the personnel overlap, as would be expected, in that they hold appointments in both organizations.

substantive outputs of the regime. The consequences of party and party development ought to be sought in *government* rather than in *governing.*[42]

From this it follows that a meaningful distinction may be drawn between political parties that emphasize constituent processes and functions and those that rely on policy processes and outputs. Obviously, party systems, as in the European democracies, *may* perform both sets of functions, in which case they are called "responsible" parties. In the United States, the main stress is placed on the constituent functions. Lowi continues: "The key to understanding American political development and modern American party politics lies in this distinction: it is decisive to distinguishing between European and American party experience."[43]

Lowi then examines American party history from this point of view, and his argument that American parties have had a negligible effect on policy is persuasive. The argument is based mostly on empirical studies.

His concluding remarks on the constituent thesis are in accord with observations found in this chapter. Some of Lowi's conclusions are worth restating here. The constituent thesis

leaves us with a party system that splits regime off from policy. It leaves us with parties that virtually exist to keep leadership, succession, and the constitutional structure separate from the actual settlement of issues. Just as responsible, programmatic parties, like Europe's, tend to centralize authority, so programmatic parties tend to democratize regimes by keeping legitimacy and policy in close association.[44]

As a result,

One of the secrets of political stability in democratic development is the indirectness of the relation between the mass and the authoritative policies by which they are governed. Plebiscitary democracies are either unstable or totalitarian; and in this sense Great Britain, not the United States, is the exception.[45]

That is not to say that the United States does not possess conditions of instability, but that our "irresponsible" parties have managed to separate legitimacy and policy. Even allowing for the skepticism toward American government that followed Watergate, and for the instability of the British parliamentary system during the mid-1970s, Lowi's words still carry an aura of conviction.

In short, as John Kessel, one of the most significant writers on political parties in recent years, suggests, parties *generally* do not develop policies (at least in the American context), except by very *particularized* parts in narrow areas towards specific targets—usually as response actions that lead to feedback, and to recruitment by "philosophy."[46] In effect, party "policy" or philosophy also then can be viewed as an independent variable. But we need to know much more about how to measure these effects, particularly when they are symbolic. Thus perhaps Spadaro's PL = Political Leaders, emphasis on leadership and decision-making rather than parties as such, is appropriate, PL viewed either dependently or independently.

Summary

In summary, then, there is unlikely to be—to any great extent—the development of a network of organic relationships between departments of political science on the one hand and policy sciences institutes, centers, or laboratories on the other hand. At the same time, it would be almost a criminal offense to our profession if individual political scientists were barred for purely institutional reasons from taking positions in policy sciences centers. There is no iron law which decrees that all political scientists must be in the employ of political science departments.

If any real progress is to be made in the development of the policy sciences, surely political scientists will have a positive role to perform, even if it is only to see to it that "the right questions" are asked. And as readers of this book are acutely aware, asking the right questions is usually the toughest intellectual aspect of any worthwhile research project.

Notes

1. Woodrow Wilson, *Congressional Government* (New York: Meridian Books edition, 1956), p. 24.

2. E.E. Schattschneider, *Party Government* (New York: Holt, Rinehart and Winston, 1942), p. 207.

3. Committee on Political Parties of the American Political Science Association, *Toward a More Responsible Two-Party System*, supplement to *American Political Science Review* 44 (September 1950).

4. Woodrow Wilson, *Constitutional Government in the United States* (New York: Columbia University Press, 1908).

5. See Maurice Duverger, *Political Parties* (New York: John Wiley & Sons, 1954). The original French edition appeared in 1951.

6. Frank J. Sorauf, *Political Parties in the American System* (Boston: Little, Brown and Co., 1964).

7. Ibid., p. 2.

8. Ibid.

9. Ibid., p. 3.

10. Ibid.

11. Ibid., p. 4.

12. Ibid., p. 5.

13. Ibid., p. 169.

14. Ibid., p. 168.

15. For an assessment of Independency in recent American national elections, see Robert D. Cantor, "Critique of Theories of the Independent Voter," Ph.D. dissertation, Temple University, 1972.

16. The old-style politics was brokerage politics. The brokerage operation is perhaps best explained in Anthony Downs, *An Economic Theory of Democracy* (New York: Harper & Row, 1957). The flavor of this politics is wonderfully captured in William L. Riordon, *Plunkitt of Tammany Hall* (New York: E.P. Dutton, paperback edition, 1963). (First published in 1905.) The best analysis of a political machine continues to be Dayton D. McKean, *The Boss, The Hague Machine in Action* (Boston: Houghton Mifflin, 1940). There are two main elements to the "official" model of brokerage politics—the state/community dichotomy, from Robert M. MacIver, *The Web of Government* (New York: Macmillan, 1947), and the group component, from David Truman, *The Government Process* (New York: Knopf, 1951).

17. In general, see M.S. Stedman, Jr., *Urban Politics* (Cambridge, Mass.: Winthrop, 1972), pp. 86-93. The National Municipal League and its excellent journal, *The National Civic Review*, have kept city politics under a reformer's microscope for many decades. The erosion of the base of political machines is treated in Elmer C. Cornwell, Jr., "Bosses, Machines and Ethnic Groups," *The Annals* 353 (May 1964): 27-39. Various writers have charged that the old-style politics fails to regulate private economic empires. On this theme, see Robert Engler, *The Politics of Oil* (Chicago: University of Chicago Press, 1961; paperback edition, 1967); Grant McConnell, *Private Power and American Democracy* (New York: Knopf, 1966); and C. Wright Mills, *The Power Elite* (New York: Oxford University Press, 1956; paperback edition, 1959).

18. The earliest authoritative statement of American pluralism is, of course, James Madison's No. 10 of *The Federalist Papers*. Jumping ahead 160 years, the re-formulation by R.M. MacIver in *The Web of Government* (New York: Macmillan, 1947) is as appropriate today as when it was first published. For a recent and very forceful attack on pluralism, see Theodore J. Lowi, *The End of Liberalism* (New York: W.W. Norton, 1969). This work attracted considerable attention in American academic circles.

The community studies came to grips with pluralism in trying to locate power inside particular communities. The classic study using the "sociological" approach—which finds power monolithic—is Floyd Hunter, *Community Power Structure* (Garden City, N.Y.: Anchor Books edition, 1963). (First published in 1953.) The classic study using a "political science" approach—which finds power pluralistic—is Robert Dahl, *Who Governs?* (New Haven: Yale University Press, 1961). An attempt to reconcile the differences between the two approaches, only partly successful, is Arnold M. Rose, *The Power Structure* (New York: Oxford University Press, 1967).

19. There is an identification of these elements in Stedman, *Urban Politics*, Chapter 12. John W. Gardner, formerly Secretary of Health, Education and Welfare, is the founder and leader of Common Cause, which likes to call itself a "citizens' lobby." While it has had some success in what it exposes, it has had little acceptance of what it proposes.

A carefully selected book of readings dealing with recent protest politics is Samuel Hendel, *The Politics of Confrontation* (New York: Appleton-Century-Crofts, 1971). Otherwise, the serious literature is mostly periodical.

20. For an analysis of these questions in depth, see Murray S. Stedman, Jr., *Urban Politics* (Cambridge, Mass.: Winthrop, 1972).

21. One of the basic emerging problems is the moral basis, or legitimacy, of decision-making in an urban environment. On this, see Lowi, *The End of Liberalism*, and also Peter Bachrach, *The Theory of Democratic Elitism* (Boston: Little Brown, 1967). A different but interesting approach to the same question is found in Samuel Lubell, *The Hidden Crisis in American Politics* (New York: W.W. Norton, 1970), especially Chapter 2, "Revolt of the Voters." An overall survey which gives attention to the legitimacy issue is Kenneth M. Dolbeare and Patricia Dolbeare, *American Ideologies: The Competing Political Beliefs of the 1970's* (Chicago: Markham, 1971).

22. Frank J. Sorauf, *Political Parties in the American System* (Boston: Little, Brown and Company, 1964), p. 176.

23. Ibid., p. 177.

24. Evron M. Kirkpatrick, " 'Toward A More Responsible Two-Party System': Political Science, or Pseudo-Science?" *The American Political Science Review* 65, 4 (Dec. 1971):965-990.

25. Ibid., p. 990.

26. Ibid.

27. Clara Penniman, "Political Science and State and Local Government in the Seventies," in *Political Science and State and Local Government* (Washington, D.C.: The American Political Science Association, 1973), pp. 118-129. It would be useful to have a parallel book on political behavior and parties.

28. Walter Dean Burnham, "The End of American Party Politics," reprinted in *Institutions, Policies, and Goals: A Reader in American Politics*, edited by Kenneth M. Dolbeare and Murray J. Edelman with Patricia Dolbeare (Lexington, Mass.: D.C. Heath, 1973), pp. 145-159.

29. Ibid., p. 159.

30. See Robert T. Golembiewski, William A. Welsh, and William J. Crotty, *A Methodological Primer for Political Scientists* (Chicago: Rand McNally, 1969).

31. Ibid., p. 356.

32. Ibid.

33. Ibid., p. 384.

34. Ibid., p. 419.

35. See Murray S. Stedman, Jr., *Urban Politics* (Cambridge, Mass.: Winthrop,

1972), pp. 99-100, for a brief summary of political simulation in the study of elections.

36. For an excellent analysis of the uses as well as the abuses of models in social sciences, see Eugene J. Meehan, *The Theory and Method of Political Analysis* (Homewood, Ill.: Dorsey Press, 1968).

37. On this point, see Stedman, *Urban Politics*, especially Part Five, "Policy Politics," pp. 203-295.

38. See Harold D. Lasswell, *A Pre-View of Policy Sciences* (New York: American Elsevier Publishing Co., 1971). The review of this work by Charles O. Jones appears in *The American Political Science Review* 67, 4 (Dec. 1973):1363-1364.

39. Jones, "Review," p. 1364.

40. Ibid., p. 1365.

41. Theodore J. Lowi, "Party, Policy, and Constitution in America," in William Nisbet Chambers and Walter Dean Burnham (eds.), *The American Party Systems* (New York: Oxford University Press, 1967), pp. 238-276.

42. Ibid., p. 239.

43. Ibid., p. 240.

44. Ibid., p. 276.

45. Ibid.

46. John H. Kessel, forthcoming book to be published by Duxbury in late 1975.

5

Pressure Groups and Public Policy: The Case in Education

L. Harmon Zeigler and Michael O. Boss

Pressure Groups and Public Policy

Emerging from the behavioral revolution of the years following World War II, after years of neglect, pressure or interest groups once threatened to assume the role of a "first cause" of public policy. A veritable flood of case studies, dealing with either a single group or a single issue, has appeared, all paying either tacit or overt homage to the patron saints of the "group approach," Bentley (1949) and Truman (1951). The difficulty with such studies is that most of them *began* with the assumption that interest groups were powerful (otherwise why would we study them), as compared to Spadaro's discussion of their *latent* potential. Further, no matter how laudable the case study method may be, it is extraordinarily difficult to reach valid generalizations from studies of single issues or single groups.

Whatever the validity of case studies, they were soon challenged by a new group of research efforts, relying more on comparative and (within the limits of measurement) systematic observations (Milbrath 1963; Bauer, Pool, and Dexter 1963; Zeigler and Baer 1969). While no useful purpose would be served by an enumeration of the specific findings of this research, there was a theme common to it: interest groups are far less influential than the case studies would lead us to suspect. Thus, we have come full circle. Where interest groups were once thought to be the basic catalyst for the formation of public policy, they are now described as only one of a number of competitors for power, and frequently the least effective combatants.

Some Problems in the Study of Interest Groups

In spite of the vast amount written on the subject of interest groups, we have not really made very much progress. The fault lies not so much with theory as with data. It is very difficult to measure the contribution that interest groups make in the formation of public policy and the resolution of policy disputes. Other political variables lend themselves much more readily to quantification; e.g., financial resources, malapportionment, party competition, and so forth. It

173

is quite significant that the major efforts in developing systematic, empirical descriptions of the formation of public policy at the state level make absolutely no mention of interest groups (Dye 1966). Their exclusion is clearly the result of the fact that nobody has developed an inexpensive and reliable method of measuring interest group strength (see Chapter 4). For instance, both Zeigler (1965) and Froman (1966) used the assessment of political scientists as an indication of interest group strength, hardly the sort of measure in which much confidence would be placed. In fact, the only effort—that of Francis (1967)—to develop a measure of the activity of interest groups in state politics (group competition rather than group effectiveness) is at odds with the conclusions reached by Zeigler.

School Districts as Foci of Inquiry

This concluding chapter is more pragmatically oriented to describe policy and "value" formulation, and while not pretending to solve the problems of measurement to the satisfaction of all, does offer the opportunity for systematic analysis using a relatively large number of units of analysis: local school districts. The use of school districts as units of analysis can be justified on grounds quite independent of their methodological advantages. Both in terms of formal governmental organizations and in terms of governmental office holders, the school districts supply an inordinate proportion of all such organizations and officials in the United States. Further, as the recent brouhaha over sex education, dress codes, decentralization, tax support, and student revolutions demonstrates, people are apt to become quite concerned about educational policy. If the interest group theorists can make an argument in support of their assertions, school districts provide an ideal setting, and an ideal example for this book. There are, indeed, plentiful examples of interest groups having profound effects on local school politics (Gross 1958).[1] On the other hand it is not very difficult to find examples of interest groups accomplishing very little in educational politics. The major point is that the evidence is sporadic and incomplete.

Obviously, the time has come to make a stab at something more systematic. The questions which such an inquiry ought to address are really quite simple. We need to specify both the antecedents and the consequences of interest group activity.

The antecedents of interest groups, or more specifically the conditions leading to their formation, have recently been subjected to some critical assessment. The traditional position, as enunciated by Truman, is described by Salisbury (1969) as the "proliferation" hypothesis. Briefly stated, the argument is that social differentiation leads to specialization. Specialization, especially economic specialization, leads to a diversity of values and—under some not clearly specified conditions—formal organizations. To specify the conditions under which specialization results in the formation of an established equilibrium by disruptive factors (e.g., changes in the business cycle, energy crisis, technological innovation) leads disadvantaged groups to seek a restoration of balance by political activity.

Recently, both Olson (1965) and Salisbury (1969) have challenged Truman's assertions by use of an exchange theory of the origin of groups. They argue that entrepreneurs offer benefits (only some of which are political) to potential members in exchange for membership. Entrepreneurial activity is the first visible evidence of group formation. In essence, Olson and Salisbury look at formal organizations as business enterprises, and focus upon the key role of the organizer. In so doing they have added an important dimension to Truman's offerings, for it is apparent from the case material they present that individual entrepreneurs play a significant role in group formation.

Yet they have not rejected either the proliferation or the disturbed equilibrium hypothesis. It is clear, even in the Olson-Salisbury argument, that groups originate in response to unsatisfied demands on the part of potential group members. Although unsatisfied demands may be insufficient to stimulate group activity, they are functions of environmental change (proliferation) and unresponsive political systems (inability to restore equilibrium). Demands lie at the heart of interest group formation even though groups ordinarily need an individual leader (entrepreneur) to channel unsatisfied demands.

We assert, then, that there is still merit in "traditional" group theory. One purpose of this chapter is to see what use can be made of such theories, if we do not rely (as Truman, Olson, and Salisbury have done) on case histories of particular kinds of organizations.

With regard to the consequences of group activity, less serious theorizing has been done. As noted previously, most of the debate has centered around the empirical question of how much influence a particular group is able to achieve. We wish to address ourselves both to this kind of question and also to the more fundamental problem of the effect of formal organization upon other components of the political system. The question is one of uncovering both the influential groups in educational decision-making and assessing the *overall* impact of group activity upon the decision-making process.

In the process, we will have a better understanding of both influencing public policy and to some extent what differences policy (as independent variable) can make, and at least some idea for the reader of "how to do it" since the preceding chapters are more theoretically oriented. Thus too we can gain increased understanding and bases for operationalization of the role of pressure groups in models such as Spadaro's Quantum Dynamics policy approach.

Public Policy and Education

A variety of recurring or crucial problems arise within any institution or system.[2] We find within the schools system, for example, that classrooms are overcrowded, that playground discipline breaks down, that administrative log-jams develop, that finance measures are defeated at the polls, that children are not learning to read, that community groups object to racism or sexism in the schools, that teacher behavior causes controversy in the community, that textbooks are dated, that expanded vocational or science programs are very expensive, and so on. Policy-making concerns the development of a guide to action for dealing with such problems.[3] Policy is formulated within the schools system in response to community relations problems, to instructional problems, to personnel problems, to student behavior problems, to facilities problems, to administrative problems—in response to any particular problem that may be recognized as demanding action or attention.

Policy-making includes, but should not be equated with, problem-solving, for policy-making does not deal with single, identified problems.[4] Rather policy-making concerns all of the problems that arise within an institution. Needless to say, since there are far too many problems, large and small, simple and complex, it is not possible to deal with them all. Depending upon how goals and values are organized within an institution, different problems are given different priorities and are allocated different resources (a point Spadaro also makes). The primary task of policy-making is to identify just what the most important and crucial problems within an institution are. We find within the schools system, for example, that the problem of providing equal educational opportunity may be given priority over the problem of maintaining neighborhood contiguity, that the problem of providing college preparatory training may be given priority over the problem of providing vocational training, or that the problem of maintaining administrative economy may be given priority over the problem of administrative backlogs.

Policy-making is ultimately a political matter, for the ordering of problem priorities involves a variety of political activities.[5] Policy-making does not concern so much how a problem should be solved—a technical question—as just what problem is worth solving—a value question. Policy formation depends upon value positions which can be articulated only through the political process. Occasionally, this aspect of policy-making evokes the great controversy and emotion we usually associate with politics. Perhaps for this reason alone, policy-making is a task most view as belonging to the politicians rather than to administrators. In the schools system, a guiding axiom is that the school board sets the policy and the superintendent administers that policy. But if policy-making is ultimately a political activity, it is hardly separate from administration (similar to Golembiewski's Phase IV in Chapter 3).

Policy-making in most large, modern institutions or systems increasingly depends upon the "expert" administrators or managers who have a virtual monopoly on the technical information essential to effective policy-making. Politicians may set problem priorities—but only the administrators are able to identify and specify what those problems are. A school board may suspect that something is wrong with the reading program, or the vocational instruction program, or facilities construction program within the schools system, but it relies upon the school superintendent to identify exactly what the nature of the problems might be and what can be done about them. The crucial point here is that the identification of problems is not a neutral activity. By controlling the kinds of problems that are raised and the manner in which they are raised—by maintaining the dependence for information—administrators are able to influence significantly the priorities given to certain problems and the resources allocated to deal with these problems. Administrators, like everyone, have their own preferences, and whether consciously or unconsciously, they utilize their monopoly on technical information to influence (and, if possible, control) policy-making.

The administrator's contribution of technical skill and information is essential to effective policy-making. Most certainly we could not and would not want to remove the administrator from policy-making. We must ask to what extent the growing technical complexity of institutions or systems has transferred the job of policy-making from the political realm to the technical realm and what this means for policy-making in a democracy.[6] Many policy-making analysts have noted the shrewd encroachment of the expert administrator upon the entire policy-making process—of the use of technical skills and information to control the political aspects of policy-making. Very little is kown, however, about the extent of this encroachment, or more important, what effect it has on overall policy-making outcomes or performance.

The examination of educational policy-making provides an important and fascinating example of the expert administrator as a policymaker. Schools in America have traditionally been founded on the democratic principle of local community control. In the most common form, the local community elects a school board. The school board, in turn, appoints a superintendent. The superintendent acts as the chief executive for the schools, The fundamental axiom guiding school board-superintendent relations, at least in myth, is that the school board, acting for the community, establishes policy and the superintendent administers the policy. The idea of community control of schools and democratic policy-making within the schools is so well established that it is apparently taken as an article of faith by nearly all Americans, laymen and professional educators alike.[7]

Most superintendents, whether they genuinely believe it or not, strongly support the traditional separation of education and politics. They appear very willing to let the school board take responsibility for policy-making—for setting and legitimizing problem priorities. Meanwhile, superintendents have increasingly redefined problems within the schools systems as "technical" problems that fall within the strict domain of the educational expert. Let us caution at this point that the governance of education has not been examined in much depth. Some of the most significant research into educational policy-making to date, however, serves to demonstrate the degree to which the superintendent dominates policy-making within the schools system.[8]

How the school system makes decisions in the hands of the professional superintendent is a matter of great debate and speculation.[a] The performance of superintendents can vary considerably. But more important, the integration of various political inputs—community opinion, interest group activity, school board representation, elite influence—together with superintendent expertise in educational policy-making can also vary considerably. Obviously this integration affects the shape of educational policy. The fact of the matter is that despite the great debate, we still know very little about this aspect of educational policy-making.

This chapter undertakes a brief examination of educational policy-making, focusing on the superintendent as an expert on the one hand and the school board and community groups as political actors on the other. Our concern is both objective and evaluative. We first examine the basic problem orientations of the superintendent, the school board, and the community, identifying the significant patterns of symmetry and asymmetry. We then examine both the structural or environmental factors and the political factors that appear to underlie basic problem orientations. This exercise provides an initial objective understanding of the political and administrative inputs to educational policy-making. We finally attempt to assess educational policy-making in terms of the degree to which policy appears to respond to superintendent, school board, and community identified problems. We caution here that our view is that the school system performs social and political as well as educational functions. We thus evaluate educational policy-making in terms of its responsiveness to broadly defined community demands more than its responsiveness to narrowly defined educational demands. We attempt as far as possible, however, to put our assessment into positivistic terms. Hopefully this provides an evaluative understanding of the political and administrative inputs to educational policy-making which can and should properly be expanded upon and reinterpreted.

The Study

Study Sample

As we noted above, examination of the area of concern to us is just beginning. Our investigation is therefore based principally upon original data. Our data are drawn from eighty-eight school districts from throughout the continental United States weighted to form a national probability sample. A technical description of the data is given in the Appendix. The data include basic information about each

---

[a]Political scientists generally argue for greater political control over education while educators generally argue for less political control and more superintendent autonomy.

school district, and in-depth interviews with individual school board members and superintendents in each school district. In addition, the data include interviews with a sample of the mass public within the school district for about two-thirds of the total districts. Our analyses indicated no significant differences between the school districts for which data pertaining to the mass public are available and the school districts for which data pertaining to the mass public are missing. Missing data were evident in certain instances. Again, our analyses indicated no significant differences between school districts for which data are available and school districts for which data are missing. The largest available and appropriate sample space is utilized whenever possible. Analyses of the superintendent and the school board include the total sample space. Analyses of the mass public include a reduced sample space. All analyses reported in the chapter are based on weighted N's.

Democratic Model of Community Control

We take as the point of departure in our examination of educational policy-making the traditional democratic model of community control of the schools. The model, as we suggested in the introduction, is quite simple. The community elects a school board which appoints a superintendent who administers the schools. The model can be expressed as a set of completed links between the community and educational policy outputs (Figure 5-1). The school board, acting for the community, establishes problem priorities and policy—a political activity. The superintendent, acting for the school board, implements policy—an administrative activity.

The model is obviously a gross over-simplification of actual educational policy-making. In a complex world, few activities can be so neatly compart-

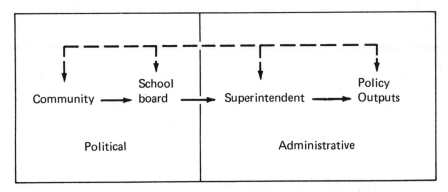

Figure 5-1. Democratic Model of Community Control

mented. The model is useful to us for several reasons however. First, the model does reflect the basic legal organization of the schools system and the legitimate chain of authority. The community does elect the board members and the community can turn the school board members out of office. The school board does hire the superintendent and the school board can dismiss the superintendent. Forced turnover of either school board members or superintendents occurs very infrequently within the schools system. The threat of this sanction, however, is sufficient to reaffirm that ultimately the schools are indeed subject to local community control.

Second, the model is a useful initial organizing device. It suggests three foci of interest—the community, the school board, and the superintendent—and the linkages between them. By utilizing the model as a base, we can more systematically determine at what points and in what manner educational policy-making varies.

Finally, the model is useful as an evaluative device. The model represents the democratic ideal. It is founded on the idea of community control of the schools system and presumes school system responsiveness to community need or demands. Educational policy-making may depart markedly from the simple form suggested in the model. Yet policy-making may nonetheless reflect the community quite well in setting problem priorities and responding to problems once priorities are established. Our choice of the model is clearly normative. By utilizing the model as a base, we can evaluate policy departure from the norm.

Examination of the principal elements in the model of community control of schools suggests several reasons why the pure model is unlikely to hold. Not the least of these is that most individuals do not take an active interest in the school system and particularly in educational policy-making.[9] This is not unique in the schools, of course. Repeated studies indicate that Americans, on the whole, are not very involved in public affairs of any kind.[10] Lack of participation does not necessarily mean that there is no community interest in the schools. Indeed, most individuals want the best possible schools in their community at the lowest possible tax cost. But for the most part, however, they prefer to leave the task of providing the best possible schools to the superintendent and the school board.

When the community does get involved in school affairs, this reaction is very likely to take the form of response to a specific issue.[11] We thus find very little community input into such matters as curriculum planning, text selection, teacher certification and hiring, site selection, or budget planning, even if given the opportunity. But quite often, we find community reactions (feedback) to the inclusion of a particular course in the curriculum, the selection and use of a particular text, the firing or granting tenure to a particular teacher, the selection of a particular new school site, or the cutting or expansion of a particular budget item. The community controversy surrounding issues like sex education, prayer, athletics, radical teachers, and book burnings illustrate the point quite well.

The general orientation of the community to the schools we have outlined briefly above is fully reflected in priorities that the community gives to problems within the schools. Members of the mass public, members of the school board, and superintendents within our sample were all asked the question: "In your opinion, what are the most important problems facing education in this school district." An abbreviated tabulation of the replies is given in Table 5-1.

The most salient feature of Table 5-1 is the high proportion of the mass public, nearly one-third, reporting that they do not know what problems might exist within their local school district. We should perhaps give credit to this sector of the mass public for being so candid—it is very likely that a substantial number of the other replies are little more than educated guesses. We suspect that only a minority of the replies are indeed knowledgeable. Opponents of community control of schools are quick to seize on this point. Obviously an unknowledgeable and disinterested mass public does not provide very wise or useful inputs into educational policy-making. We will not belabor the issue here but only raise two quick points. First, if the superintendent and the school board do an effective job, the community does not need to be very concerned about what arises within the school. Second, if a substantial proportion of a community agrees that a given problem does exist within a school, that problem must be serious indeed.

A comparison of the distribution of replies for the mass public on one hand and the school board and superintendent on the other hand in Table 5-1 is also instructive. Looking first at problems that reflect the basic functioning of the schools—curriculum, personnel, and finance—we find that the mass public recognizes and mentions such problems only about half as often as the school boards or superintendents. In contrast to this pattern, race—a problem that is more likely to emerge as a major public issue—is recognized and mentioned with equal frequency by the mass public, the school boards, and superintendents. The basic orientation of the community to problems in the schools is quite clear

Table 5-1
Major Problems Facing Education

Problem	Individual Mass Public	School Board Members	Superin- tendents
Race	18%	16%	22%
Curriculum	16%	31%	39%
Personnel	29%	45%	28%
Finance	38%	67%	68%
Other	22%	59%	58%
Don't Know	31%	0%	1%
N	1318	1138	182

Note: Total percentages exceed 100% due to multiple replies.

here. The community is not very interested in the more routine or basic school problems but can become very interested in isolated, episodic problems of a more conflict laden or controversial nature. This basic orientation is reflected in the style of educational policy-making.

Turning from the community to the school board, we find again a significant departure from our model. The school board is presumably the elected representative of the community. We will deal only briefly with the representative—or perhaps more accurately, the unrepresentative—character of the school board here. This has been reported in detail in a previous study using our same sample base.[12] Let it suffice to note that school board members do not perceive their role as that of a representative of the community and that school board members are not representative, on the whole, of the community. School board members tend to come from an upper-class, conservative, apolitical background. They tend to favor orthodoxy and tradition—they eschew controversy and conflict. Less than one-half of the school board members faced any meaningful electoral competition when they ran for the school board. A majority were the products of self-perpetuation by the school board; the recruitment of members of like mind who will minimize conflict on the school board. Not surprisingly, the school board often appears as a better representative of the educational establishment and the schools than the community.

School board members are recruited into and occupy positions within the educational establishment, and their perceptions of problems within the schools appear to take on the pattern of the educational establishment rather than the community at large. Looking again at Table 5-1, we find first that the school board appears to be knowledgeable about problems in the schools. Most school board members, like the superintendents, cited at least two and some three or four major problems within their school districts. Further, the pattern of replies given by the school board matches the pattern of the superintendent closer than the pattern of the community. The school board gives greater relative stress to problems that reflect the basic functioning of the schools—curriculum, personnel, and finance—and less relative stress to race, even though the latter has appeared to have a much higher priority in the community. We might well expect the school board and the superintendent to appear to have similar problem orientations, however, for the school board depends largely upon the superintendent for knowledge about such problems in the schools.

We have left the superintendent for last, but as we shall see, the superintendent is the most dominant element in educational policy-making despite, or perhaps more accurately because of, the formal administrative role. The superintendent is closer to the schools than either the community or the school board, monitoring on a full-time basis the conditions within the schools. Presumably the superintendent will recognize problems arising within the schools long before either the community or school board does and when neither the community nor school board does so. This position provides the superintendent with the immediate opportunity to expand his influence over educational policy-making and warrants brief discussion.

First, most of the problems that arise in any modern, bureaucratized system like the schools are routine in nature. They are the minor, ordinary, day-to-day problems that are handled with dispatch and according to standard procedures. It almost goes without saying that the administrative staff, under the direction of the superintendent, handles most of these problems. Few individuals outside of the school staff are aware of, let alone care about, such problems unless they happen to have a direct personal interest in a specific matter. Even then, concerned outsiders usually focus on the narrow problem and have little interest in the routine policy-making apparatus in its totality.

If no single routine problem is very important by itself, taken altogether routine problems must be considered as constituting a very significant share of all of the problems that enter into educational policy-making. The sheer number and predominance of routine problems alone give them significance. Yet policy-making with regard to these problems lies effectively beyond the political realm. Pity the school board that does get involved in these routine problems, for it is very likely that they will become so overloaded by routine problems that they cannot deal with either very many trivial problems, or more important, with more crucial problems. The paradox is complete. School boards are deterred from involvement in most routine policy-making. The superintendent, by defining and treating most problems within the school system as routine problems, immediately establishes the dominance of influence over a large part of educational policy-making.

A substantial number of problems that arise within the school system increasingly appear to be highly technical in nature. Certainly this is the case in all modern systems where one goal is greater precision. Problems with reading programs within the schools thus take the form of complex analyses of achievement scores, often involving multiple covariates, reliability and validity measures, and similar statistics. Problems of budgeting and finance take the form of complex analyses utilizing PPBS or similar comprehensive planning and budgeting methods. Problems of drawing school boundaries or mapping bus routes take the form of complex "mini-max" criteria utilized in linear and other mathematical programming of such problems. Members of the community and members of the school board, whatever the depth of interest and involvement in education, seldom have the skills necessary to understand problems cast in these very technical terms. They must rely upon the superintendent, who has special training and expertise in such matters. As an added irony, the more that a community and school board value technology—a hallmark of the more sophisticated communities—the greater is the dependence upon the superintendent.[13]

The superintendent is able to buttress this technical dependence in several ways in order to increase his influence over educational policy-making. First, strictly educational issues are designated as problems on which only the educational expert, primarily the superintendent, has sufficient knowledge and understanding to act. Laymen, lacking special training and competence in education, are simply deemed unqualified to deal with most educational matters. It thus becomes the professional educator's exclusive function to make expert judgments or decisions regarding "pure" educational problems like curriculum design, text selection, or teacher performance.

The effort to create an exclusive preserve dominated by the educational expert is reinforced by the traditional myth that politics and education are separate. Educators have capitalized on the reforms at the turn of the century designed to remove the schools from partisan and machine politics and to remove the schools from community politics as well. Certainly few superintendents genuinely believe that education and politics are not intertwined. But the more that educational decisions are kept out of community political processes, the more that the superintendent is able to dominate educational policy-making.

The development and application of educational technology to the schools is highly value laden and politically potent. Educators have seized upon those technical measures or production functions which best serve their own communities' interests. It is not entirely accidental, for example, that the increased application of educational technology has resulted in a larger rather than smaller educational establishment.[14] The shrewd superintendent is always ready with the technical information to support the addition of his pet programs.

Finally, problems arising *within* the schools are defined and specified as strict educational or technical problems whenever possible. Once so defined, such problems are then left to the province of the educational experts. During this process, problem priority is implicitly set, not through the political process but through the administrative process. We thus find it is the superintendent rather than the school board or the community who allocates resources to most educational problems.

To appreciate fully the consummate skill with which the superintendent dominates strict educational problems, we need only consider who initiates changes in the educational program within the schools. Both the superintendent and the school board members were asked what the sources of change in the educational program in their school districts were. Multiple replies were coded. A summary of replies is given in Table 5-2. The distribution of replies in Table 5-2 leaves little question that professional educational experts, the superintendent and staff, control nearly all changes in the educational program. Both the school board and the superintendent indicate that the community plays a minor role, at best, in initiating any change. Although the school board claims somewhat of a role for itself in initiating change, the superintendent replies suggest this claim is overblown. Even taken together, the community and the school board can hardly be considered more than a very marginal input. The fact is that the superintendent has a basic problem orientation to technical,

Table 5-2
Sources of Change in Educational Program

Source of Change	School Board Members	Superintendents
Superintendent	75%	62%
School Staff	35%	58%
School Board	13%	4%
Community	3%	2%
Other	2%	11%
N	1069	173

Note: Total percentages exceed 100% due to multiple replies.

educational problems for this orientation allows him to dominate educational policy-making.

Looking once again at Table 5-1, we find that superintendents are far more likely to see curriculum problems as major problems within their school districts than either the community or the school board. If we look at specific curriculum problems, the differences are even more pronounced. Nearly all of the superintendents who cite curriculum problems cite specific curriculum problems. In contrast, about one-half of the individual mass public and school board members who cite curriculum problems do so from a very general perspective. A typical community or school board view is "the need to improve basic education." In other problem areas, the superintendent and the school board appear fairly similar in relative distributions. Again, however, superintendents tend to be more specific and technical in their replies.

Our aim in this section has been to examine the basic problem orientations of the community, the school board, and the superintendent. We have suggested fundamental differences in perspective among the three groups and our initial exploration of major problems that are recognized within the schools confirms this. We now turn to the question of how community, school board, and superintendent problem orientations are linked to the basic structure of the school district.

Affect of Structural Variables on
Orientations of Community, School
Board, and Superintendent

Problems are not the same in all school districts. Substantial differences in the social, political, economic, and geographic structure among school districts have a major bearing on the kinds of problems that are most likely to arise within the schools. We would hardly expect problem priorities in school systems located in suburban California, metropolitan New York, and rural Mississippi to be identical, although some problems are surely common to all. Our aim in this section is to examine the differences, if any, in which selected structural variables appear to affect the basic problem orientations of the community, school board, and superintendent.

In order to explore the linkages between problem recognition and structure, it is necessary that we move our level of analysis from the individual to the school district level. We therefore define a school district in which the public recognizes a particular problem if at least one-fifth of the individual mass public sampled in that district report that problem. Similarly, we define a school district as a district in which the school board recognizes a particular problem if at least one-third of the individual school board members in that district report that problem. Our criteria here are somewhat arbitrary; we might well have used higher or lower proportions for either the public or the school board. We feel, however, that in any school district in which there is concurrence among one-fifth of the public or one-third of the school board, we have evidence of an indication that a given problem is widely evident. Note also that the level of the criteria affect only the absolute distributions while our analyses are based primarily upon relative distributions.

We restrict our analyses of problems within the schools to just two problem areas—curriculum and race—from this point on for purposes of economy. Curriculum serves as an excellent example of the basic educational and technical issue while race serves as an equally excellent example of the episodic, public issue. The distributions of school districts in which race and curriculum problems are evident to the community, the school board, and the superintendent are given in Table 5-3. The findings in Table 5-3 are largely informational but serve to reaffirm our earlier findings. Superintendents and school boards appear to give greater relative attention to curriculum problems reflecting the basic orientation to the educational establishment. The public appears to give much

Table 5-3

School Districts with Problems Evident to Public, School Board and Superintendent

	Public	School Board	Superintendent
Curriculum Problems	31%*	40%	39%
Race Problems	28%	22%	22%
	N =127	N =185	N =182

Note: Percentage of the school districts in which at least 20% of the public, 33% of the school board, or the superintendent report given problem evident.

greater relative attention to race problems reflecting the basic orientation to episodic issues.

Race Problems. Looking first at race problems, we would expect that evidence of race problems in a school district would be closely linked to the racial structure or makeup of the district. The percentage of nonwhite students within a school district was utilized as a measure of district racial structure. The relationships between public, school board, and superintendent recognition of race problems and district racial structure are given in Table 5-4. The correlations given in Table 5-4 are all positive and moderate to strong. This indicates first that the occurrence of race problems in the schools is in fact higher or more likely where the proportion of nonwhite students is higher. But more important, this indicates that the measure of district racial structure is quite a good indicator of probable racial problem conditions in a school district.

A major difference in problem-structure relationships between the superintendent on one hand and the school board and the community on the other hand is evident in Table 5-4. We find that superintendent recognition of race problems appears to be less closely linked to district racial structure ($r = .42$) than either the school board ($r - .68$) or the public ($r = .61$). If district racial structure is the predictor of race problems in the schools that the strong school board and public correlations indicate it is, our findings suggest that the superintendent may have a fundamental insensitivity to race problems in the schools.

The explanation of why the superintendent, the policymaker closest to the schools, would be least sensitive to race problems in the schools may well be the professional education ideology. First, norms under the prevailing ideology are highly universalistic with nearly perfect equality for both white and nonwhite students.[15] Questions of race or color simply do not arise. The irony of the equality ethos, of course, is that any special needs of nonwhite or minority students in a white society are totally ignored. This set of conditions is clearly not satisfactory to the nonwhite population, and over the course of time, is not likely to be very satisfactory to the white population either. Second, the

Table 5-4
Racial Problems and District Racial Structure

Problem Evident To	Relationship with District Racial Structure	N
Public	.61*	129
School Board	.68	185
Superintendent	.42	182

*Figure given is Pearson r.

fundamental "rationality" within the school system precludes any form of conflict. All issues are presumed to be resolvable through reason and logic. There are explanations for race problems but none based upon rationality. The difficulty then is that within the context of the schools, race problems are simply undefinable and thus unrecognizable even though such problems may exist. Finally, education is narrowly and strictly defined. Educational functions are separated from social and political functions. The school system is separated and isolated from political and social problems. Race problems evident in American society as a whole are therefore not associated with the schools. Taken altogether, the above three factors in the educational ideology form a solid screen that may blind the superintendent to race problems that are very evident to others.[16]

Curriculum. Turning to curriculum problems, we would expect that evidence of curriculum problems in a school district would be closely linked to the complexity of the community served by the school district. Very generally, school districts with a sophisticated and heterogeneous population are likely to experience more serious curriculum problems in greater numbers than school districts with homogeneous and simple populations. The more complex and diverse the demands placed upon the educational program, the more difficult it is to accommodate such demands, and the more problems like curriculum problems that arise.

We have no direct measure of the complexity of school district population. However we can approach the measurement indirectly by considering the metropolitanism of the school district. Generally, populations in urban and suburban metropolitan areas are much more diverse and complex than populations in rural areas. The distributions of community, school board, and superintendent recognition of curriculum problems in the schools by urban-suburban-rural area are given in Table 5-5. The percentage figures reported in Table 5-5 are markedly higher in suburban and urban areas than in rural areas.

Table 5-5
Curriculum Problems and Metropolitan Structure

Structure	Problem Evident To		
	Public	School Board	Superintendent
Rural	12%*	30%	37%
Suburban-Urban	33%	40%	48%
Eta	.29	.17	.09
N	129	185	182

*Figure given is the percentage of school districts in which curriculum problems are evident to indicated element.

This suggests that curriculum problems in the schools are in fact more likely to arise in metropolitan areas. Metropolitanism thus appears to provide a usable, if very rough, indicator of probable curriculum problem conditions in a school district.

A major difference in problem-structure relationships between the superintendent on one hand and the school board and the community on the other hand in Table 5-5. We find that superintendent recognition of curriculum problems appears to be less closely linked to metropolitanism (eta = .14) than either the school board (eta = .41) or the public (eta = .36). Our findings suggest that the superintendent may have a fundamental insensitivity to curriculum problems insofar as such problems relate to structure.

The explanation of why the superintendent would be at least sensitive to problems posed for curriculum by the complexity of social structure may again be the professional education ideology. The development of curriculum by professional educators in the American public schools appears to engender four broad elements: tradition, individual development, community, and science.[17] There is considerable debate among educators, to be sure, over which of these elements should be given the greatest stress in curriculum. But all of the elements, with the possible exception of science, which has emerged only recently as an important element, have deep roots in the philosophy and history of education. They reflect broad educational perspectives rather than immediate social or political concerns. While the prevailing educational ideology acknowledges at an abstract level that education and society share values—for example that education (may) function to transmit and maintain the values of society— educational needs and thus curriculum are presumed to be quite universal within a society regardless of specific societal subsettings. The salience of education in the day-to-day political and social processes within a community—for example, as a potent politicizing or legitimizing force—and the implications of this for the educational program including curriculum development are largely disregarded. Put alternatively, the prevailing educational ideology that guides curriculum reflects educational values more than community values even though both values may have common roots.

Our examination of problem recognition and basic structural variables suggests that the superintendent has a very ethnocentric view of his milieu. The superinentendent, reflecting the educational ideology, tends to define problems in the schools very narrowly, considering only educational factors and ignoring significant community factors that impinge upon the schools and certainly have some bearing on the problems that arise within the schools. We would hardly argue in favor of structural determinism. However, we must suspect a policy-making deficiency when the superintendent, the dominant policymaker in the schools, has such an unbalanced problem orientation when compared to the community and the school board.

Interest Group Activity

We have focused our attention earlier on the role of the community as a whole in educational policy-making. An alternative mode of community participation in educational policy-making is through formal or informal interest group activity. We need not reiterate the significance given to interest groups in American democracy by some theorist here—the substantial body of literature positing interest group activity as the key element in maintaining a viable democratic system is well known.[18] The proximate setting of the schools provides a readily accessible target for interest group activity. Moreover, the principle of local community control of the schools should provide a ready entrance for interest group activity into educational policy-making. The separation of education from politics, however, provides a barrier to effective interest group participation in educational policy-making. The more political a particular interest group appears, the less legitimacy it has within the school system, and the less potency it has as a participant in policy-making.[19] The result is that those interest groups most effective within the school system are those that are the least political and most biased to the educational establishment.

To appreciate this point, we need only look at the kinds of interest groups that appear most salient within the school system. Our measures of interest group activity are constructed from school board member and superintendent replies to seven open-ended questions dealing with the activities of organizations and groups within the local school district. The seven questions in abbreviated form are:

	Maximum Coded Responses
Organizations most interested in the board	3
Organizations working for passage of financial referenda	3
Organizations working for defeat of financial referenda	2
Organizations critical of the board	2
Organizations attempting to influence educational program	3
Organizations which attack teachers	2
Organizations which defend teachers	2
Total	17

The replies of each school board member and superintendent were coded into fourteen possible interest group categories. The distribution of school board member and superintendent replies is given in Table 5-6.

Our measure does not indicate the objective level of interest group activity

Table 5-6
Interest Group Activity in the School District

Type of Interest Group	Superintendent	School Board Members
PTA	57%	60%
Teachers	27%	31%
Left-Wing	24%	28%
Business-Professional	35%	16%
Civil Rights	24%	17%
Taxpayers	24%	16%
Right-Wing	25%	12%
League of Women Voters	18%	14%
Citizen Advisory Committee	21%	13%
Religious	19%	11%
Service Clubs	7%	20%
Neighborhood	7%	5%
Political	4%	5%
Labor	2%	3%
N	175	1069

within the school system. Rather the measure concerns only the distribution and intensity of interest group-policymaker interaction over a broad range of issues common to most school districts. The measure should therefore be interpreted as an indicator of interest group salience or effectiveness—put alternatively, as an indicator of the impact of particular interest groups on educational policy-making.

The most salient interest group indicated in Table 5-6 is that group directly associated with education: the PTA. By comparison, all other groups clearly take a secondary position. The PTA, most often an alliance of parents, teachers, and administrators, is the very embodiment of the educational establishment. The PTA does not perform the normal interest group function of translating general community dissatisfaction or discontent with a public agency into specific demands upon that agency. Rather it coopts potentially disruptive or disgruntled parents, defuses public conflict before it gets started, communicates school policy to the community, and acts as a defense mechanism or buffer for the schools. The PTA may have an important role in educational policy-making but it is clearly not a representative role that would contribute to a viable democratic model.

Turning to the secondary interest groups, we find that teachers groups rank a distant second in Table 5-6. It is perhaps somewhat surprising that teachers appear to have so little impact. Of all the groups attempting to influence educational policy, teachers would seem to be one of the most important.

Teachers are directly associated with education, they are not outsiders like other groups. Moreover, teachers generally have a sound understanding of the issues and can direct their activity to well-defined issue areas. Yet the impact of teachers groups appears minimal. We will not attempt to explain the failure of teachers groups here.[20] Our point is that if teachers groups, working from a position of advantage within the school system and representing specific educational interests are ineffective, how can non-educationally related interest groups fare any better?

Looking at the non-educationally related groups in Table 5-6, we find that they receive infrequent notice at best from school policymakers. Moreover, groups with an "establishment" tinge like service clubs and business and professional groups are equally salient with ideologically-oriented groups of either the Left or the Right, even though the latter tend to be much more active in the general community and in lobbying with both the school board and the superintendent. We need not argue here whether establishment groups or ideological groups are best representative of the community for neither appears to have much more than a marginal overall impact on educational policy-making. This in itself has important implications for democratic group theory. We will delay our judgments about the implications for our democratic model, however, until we examine both the curriculum and race issues closer with particular attention to interest group impact.

Curriculum. Very little interest group activity organized exclusively around curriculum issues is evident within most schools or communities. Rather the interest groups who do get involved in curriculum issues in the schools—when indeed, there is any significant interest group involvement at all—take in a wide spectrum of interest groups, most with only a peripheral interest in either curriculum or in the schools as a whole. This condition is not surprising given our earlier discussion of community interest in curriculum or other narrow educational problems. Most curriculum problems that come to the attention of the community are episodic in nature. Few of the problems persist as issues long enough to allow specific interest group organization. Consequently, interest groups simply articulate their own or public reaction to a particular problem when it flares as a public issue.

Different interest groups obviously take different positions on curriculum issues, and depending upon the group and its position, have different impacts upon educational policy-making. We do not attempt to unwind these specific group differences here, however, but consider only in very broad terms the general nature of interest group impact upon curriculum policy-making. Our measure of interest group activity in the area of curriculum policy is based upon school board member and superintendent reports of interest group attempts to influence curriculum policy in their school district. Such interest group activity was evident to 61 percent of the superintendents but to only 38 percent of the school board members. Measures for the school board and the superintendent were computed separately so that differences between the two policymakers can be explored more fully. The proportion of individual board members reporting interest group activity was utilized as the aggregate measure for the entire school board. The measure for the school board has a range from 0 to 100, a mean of 36, and a standard deviation of 29.

Recall from our examination earlier that the superintendent and the school board show generally similar patterns of awareness of interest group activity. It is significant here, however, that the superintendent clearly shows much greater awareness of interest group attempts to influence curriculum policy than does the school board. The difference in part reflects the extra-sensitivity of the superintendent to political infringement into strict educational matters. What the school board perceives and interprets as a part of the general interest group activity that is evident in the school district and community, the superintendent interprets as a specific threat. But more important to us here, interest groups may well direct the greatest part of their activity concerning curriculum matters toward the superintendent rather than the school board because interest groups astutely recognize that the superintendent dominates educational policy-making to such a great extent. Interests have little reason to direct their activity toward the school board when the superintendent, even if less receptive to interest group activity and demands than the school board, plays the greatest part in responding to such activity and demands.

Interest group activity in the curriculum area, as we suggested initially, has its roots as much in the existing interest group structure as in the emergence of a particular curriculum issue in the schools. This is directly demonstrated by a simple model linking interest group activity to both public recognition of curriculum problems and metropolitanism like that illustrated in Figure 5-2.

Interest group activity in the curriculum area appears to have some linkage to public recognition of curriculum problems but the linkage is only moderate for the school board (beta = .24) and even less for the superintendent (beta = .15). This suggests that interest group impact upon the school board and the superintendent does serve to articulate community interests, but only marginally so. But equally important, interest group activity in the curriculum area also appears to have some linkage to metropolitanism (betas = .27 and .12 for the school board and superintendent respectively). The more complex social structure of the metropolitan areas supports a generally greater level of interest group support that can be readily mobilized when a curriculum or similar issue arises within the schools.

Policymakers not only perceive interest group activity but also interpret interest group activity, judging what interests are represented and how, and this interpretation affects interest group impact upon both the policy-maker and the policy-making process. The differences evident in Figure 5-2 between the school board and the superintendent in the interpretation of interest group activity are

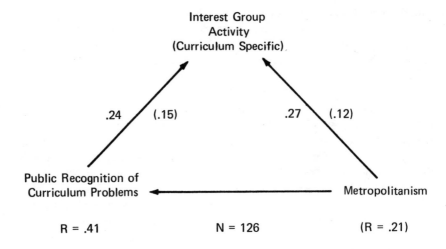

Figure 5-2. Curriculum Specific Interest Group Activity, Public Recognition of Curriculum Problems, and Metropolitanism. Note: Figures given are standardized regression coefficients for predicting to Interest Group Activity from Public Recognition and Metropolitanism. Figures given in parentheses are for superintendent.

not major but sufficient to warrant brief comment. The apparent interpretation of interest group activity in the curriculum area by the school board, indicated by the ultimate recognition of such activity, is more closely linked to community recognition of curriculum problems (beta = .24) than is the interpretation by the superintendent (beta = .15). This suggests that the school board gives somewhat greater note to interest group activity that is representative in nature than does the superintendent. To reiterate, however, in neither case does interest group activity appear to have much more than a marginal representative impact.

Interest group activity in the curriculum area appears to have very little impact upon school board and superintendent recognition of curriculum problems and thus curriculum policy, regardless of whatever efforts they might undertake. This is directly demonstrated by a simple model linking school board and superintendent recognition of curriculum problems to interest group activity in the curriculum area and controlling for metropolitanism like that illustrated in Figure 5-3. Any linkage evident between interest group activity in the curriculum area and school board or superintendent recognition of curriculum problems is slight, to say the least (betas = .20 and .08 for the school board and superintendent respectively). This suggests that even though the school board, and to an even greater extent, the superintendent may recognize interest group demands, they are unlikely to respond to such demands in narrow educational

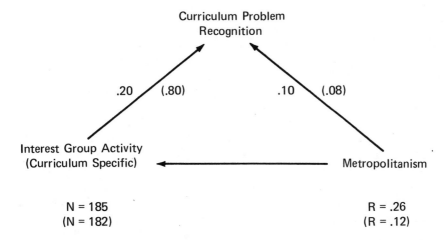

Figure 5-3. Curriculum Problem Recognition, Interest Group Activity, and Metropolitanism. Note: Figures given are standardized regression coefficients for predicting to School Board Curriculum Problem Recognition. Figures given in parentheses are the superintendent.

areas like curriculum. The difficulty here is that so long as professional experts can claim sole legitimacy in the areas of basic education, political interests are not likely to have much effect upon actual policy-making.

Race. We have seen that interest groups are not very effective in the area of curriculum. We now turn to a different type of issue, race, which is more a public issue than an educational issue. Our concern is with whether interest group activity appears to have a greater impact when issues are defined as political issues compared to when they are defined as educational issues.

Two groups in the community appear to have a particular bearing upon school governor sensitivity to racial problems in the schools: civil rights activity and white concern or tension over racial matters. We do not attempt to unwind the sources of civil rights activity here but treat the activity as an exogenous variable that impacts upon the school system. Our measure of civil rights activity is based upon the proportion of school board members plus the superintendent in each school district noting that civil rights groups had been active in school district affairs or critical of the schools. Our measure does not indicate the objective level of civil rights activity in the community or in the school district, but rather the effectiveness of civil rights activity in impacting upon the school governor. It is thus simple and direct. The measure of civil rights activity has a range from 0 to 86, a mean of 11.9, and a standard deviation of 22.5.

Our measure of white racial tension is based upon the proportion of school board members plus the superintendent in each school district noting that racial issues were matters of tension, conflict, or concern among white population within the school district. Like our measure of civil rights activity, our measure of white racial tension does not indicate the objective level of tension in the community but rather the school governors' perceptions of the state of the community. The measure does not necessarily indicate anti-integration or racist feelings but rather it represents a broad complex of concern, anxiety, and fear over racial issues in general and the impact of racial problems and conflict upon the welfare of children in the schools.[21] The measure of white racial tension has a range from 0 to 100, a mean of 18.6, and a standard deviation of 25.2.

White racial tension over racial matters is positively linked to district racial structure, its evidence increasing as the percentage of nonwhite students increase ($r = .54$), and to public recognition of racial problems, its evidence increasing in districts where the public reports racial problems in the schools ($r = .39$). Civil rights activity, however, appears to be the key factor in the mobilization of white racial tension, having much greater importance than either district racial structure or community recognition of racial problems in accounting for the evidence of white community concern. This is clearly evident in a simple model linking white racial tension to Civil Rights Activity, District Racial Structure, and Public Recognition of Race Problems while controlling each of the underlying factors for the effect of the other. Such a model is illustrated in Figure 5-4. Civil Rights Activity emerges as the most important factor ($b = .57$), far out-weighing either District Racial Structure ($b = .20$) or Public Recognition

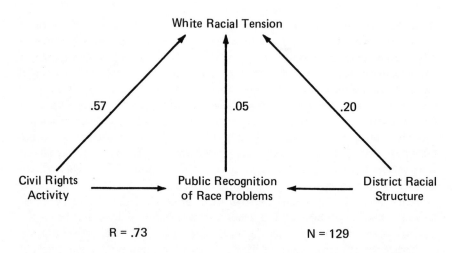

Figure 5-4. White Racial Tension and Three Structural or Political Factors. Note: Values given are standardized regression coefficients for predicting to White Racial Tension.

of Race Problems (b = .05). This suggests that civil rights activity may operate in at least two different ways in the policy-making process. It may affect the policy-making process directly and it may affect the policy-making process indirectly by mobilizing white racial tension. Careful ordering of the civil rights activity and white community concern variables is thus required in the analyses that follow.

The analysis of racial problems thus far has dealt with race as a major problem with high priority. We have additional data pertaining to racial problems in the school districts from questions probing this area in detail. Each superintendent and school board member was asked specifically what kinds of racial problems had come up within their school district and what action the school district had taken to deal with such problems. The analysis in the remainder of this section is based upon the more definitive replies. School boards, as in the earlier case, were classified as recognizing racial problems in their school district if one-third or more of the individual school board members noted that racial problems were evident. Using the more detailed variable, racial problems were evident to 49 percent of the school boards and to 36 percent of the superintendents.

A model linking school board and superintendent racial problem recognition to civil rights activity, white racial tension, and district racial structure is illustrated in Figure 5-5. The coefficients in the model suggest that school board recognition of racial problems in the schools is linked to the fundamental district racial structure as indicated earlier (beta = .42) but that school board sensitivity to such problems is apparently further stimulated by the level of white racial tension (beta = .29). Interestingly, school board sensitivity to racial problems is apparently not directly affected by the level of civil rights activity (beta = −.05). In contrast to the school board, superintendent recognition of racial problems has no link to district racial structure, the weak link indicated earlier washing out entirely (beta = .02), but superintendent sensitivity to racial problems is apparently stimulated by both the level of white racial tension (beta = .27) and the level of civil rights activity (beta = .16).

The differences in the impact of civil rights activity upon the school board and the superintendent evident here are most interesting. The school board, normally more exposed to and therefore presumably more accustomed to interest group pressure, appears to show little responsiveness to a single interest group. Rather the school board seems to take into account a broad range of political, social, and educational factors. The superintendent, normally isolated from lay criticism and pressure, however, appears to show more responsiveness to interest group pressure when it does penetrate into his domain. The racial issue cuts sharply across social, political, and educational lines and is thus somewhat unusual in the extent to which it exposes the superintendent to political pressure. Our own opinion is that it is fortunate that superintendents and other professional educators can be pressured into recognizing racial

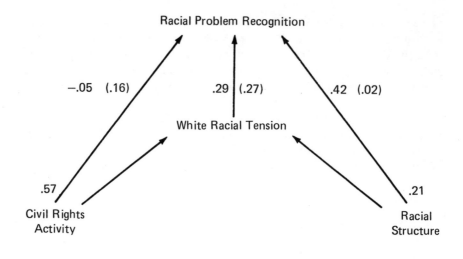

Racial Problem Recognition

−.05   (.16)   .29 (.27)   .42   (.02)

White Racial Tension

.57   .21
Civil Rights   Racial
Activity   Structure

R = .59   N = 168
(R = .41)   (N = 166)

Figure 5-5. Racial Problem Recognition and Three Structural and Political Factors. Note: Values given are standardized regression coefficients for predicting to Board Racial Problem Recognition. Values in parentheses are for predicting to Superintendent Racial Problem Recognition.

problems in the schools, if that is what is required. It is detrimental to effective school policy-making, however, if superintendents do not recognize and respond to racial problems until such problems evolve into public issues and political pressure is brought to bear. We would not argue that routine racial problems are solvable—but there may be some chance for effective action to deal with routine problems. Once racial problems balloon into public issues and take on crisis proportions, any action at all to deal with the problems is immensely more difficult and often impossible.

The indicated greater impact of white racial tension upon the school board and superintendent when compared to civil rights activity is not surprising given that nonwhite groups represent a tiny minority in most school districts (the mode for the sample is 15 percent nonwhite students). There is a strong relationship between civil rights activity and white racial tension evident ($r = .69$), however, that dictates careful ordering of the two variables. Our data suggest that white racial tension stems largely from the level of civil rights activity (beta = .58) and only to a lesser extent from district racial structure (beta = .21). Civil rights activity thus appears to have both direct and indirect effects: (1) it excites the school governor directly and (2) it excites white racial tension which in turn further excites the school governor. This is of considerable importance to civil rights group (and presumably other interest group) strategy for it underscores the importance of mobilizing a broad segment of the community in order to effectively reach or bring pressure upon school governors.[22]

Assessment of Educational Policy-Making

Our examination of the basic orientations of the community, the school board, and the superintendent to educational policy-making suggests a substantial reordering of our initial model of community control is necessary. The superintendent, serving in a full-time, expert administrative position, has a monopoly on the essential information and resources required to identify, specify, and solve most problems arising within the school system and thereby dominates educational policy-making. The community and the school board, rather than providing positive political inputs into educational policy-making by setting problem priorities and allocating resources to such problems, more often than not only reacts to policy outputs from the administrative side of the model (e.g., policy can then be viewed as an "independent variable"). The model can still be expressed as a set of completed links between the community and educational policy outputs but the order of the links is reversed (Figure 5-6). The superintendent, acting for the school board and community, establishes and implements policy—an administrative and political activity. The school board, acting for the community, monitors and reacts to policy—a political activity.

Based upon our reordered model, we should hardly expect symmetry among the superintendent, the school board, and the community in the recognition of

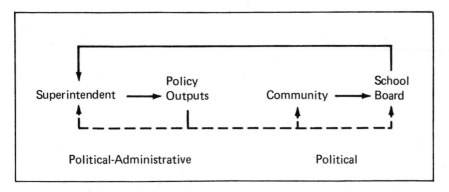

Figure 5-6. Revised Model of Community Control

problems within the schools. Indeed, we can immediately identify three significant linkage conditions, two of which are asymmetrical, if we juxtapose problem recognition on the administrative side and problem recognition on the political side of our model (Figure 5-7). Condition (1) in which neither the political side nor the administrative side of our model recognize a given problem or problem area is, of course, trivial here—even if it is the most preferred condition. The other three conditions each have special significance.

Condition (2) in which the superintendent recognizes a given problem but the school board or the community do not—a condition we call administrative autonomy for lack of a better term—probably occurs most frequently if we consider the entire range of problems including routine and strict educational problems within the schools. As we have suggested at several points, the superintendent, as the chief executive of the schools, is in the position to recognize and act on most problems long before they become issues that attract public attention from the community or the school board. This condition does carry inherent risks. The superintendent does have his own preferences and values; preferences and values that very likely reflect his educational orientation and preferences and values that may vary from those of the community and school board. These preferences and values form the bases and enter into the superintendent's policy decisions regarding problems. Unchecked administrative autonomy can thus distort and subvert even limited community control. Limited administrative autonomy may very well be a preferred condition, however. Neither the community nor the school board desire to devote any more time and attention than is absolutely necessary to the schools. It is for this reason that the

		Political	
		No Problem Recognized	Problem Recognized
Administrative	No Problem Recognized	(1) Trivial	(3) Democratic Failure
	Problem Recognized	(2) Administrative Autonomy	(4) Democratic Viability

Figure 5-7. Linkage Conditions of Political and Administrative Problem Recognition

superintendent is hired in the first place. If the superintendent recognizes and acts to deal with problems in the schools to the best interests of both the schools and the community and without political impetus from the community, so much the better.

Condition (3) in which the superintendent fails to recognize a problem evident to the school board or the community and is indicative of the possible failure of our democratic model of educational policy-making. We find in this condition that problem priorities established within the political realm are not transferred to the administration. Rather the administration appears to operate with autonomy from political demands. Two fundamental characteristics of the elements in our model of educational policy-making contribute to the frequency with which this condition arises. The first is the general intransigence of superintendents to accept lay criticism from either the school board or the community at large, especially in the basic educational areas where exclusive technical competence is claimed. Disagreement over the existence of problems is simply attributed by superintendents to public misinformation. The second is the generally unrepresentative character of the school board. Rather than providing an input of community problem priorities into educational policy-making, the school board often serves to legitimize existent conditions within the schools and to assuage the public with assurances that apparent problems are not as they seem. Of the four conditions, this is obviously the most significant and we will devote our greatest attention to it in our analyses.

Condition (4) in which the superintendent and the school board or the community are in harmony in the recognition of problems in the schools is the democratic ideal. The community, directly or through the school board, is able to communicate its views of existent problems in the schools to the superintendent. We caution that this does not insure that such problems will be eliminated to the satisfaction of the community. However when total consensus with regard to a problem exists, action to deal effectively and expeditiously with that problem is more likely. We will consider the political forces that appear to contribute to the recognition of and attention to particular problems within the educational policy-making process in two later sections. We turn first to a further examination of the above linkage conditions in two problem areas.

*Linkage Conditions in Race
and Curriculum Problems*

Our concern is with linking superintendents to their respective communities and school boards and then examining the patterns of problem recognition. To accomplish this, public and school board recognition of particular problems were crossed to form three variants of problem recognition on the political side of our model:

1. public recognizes a given problem, school board does not;
2. school board recognizes a given problem, public does not;
3. school board and public recognize a given problem.

Superintendent recognition of a particular problem under each variant was then examined. A summary of findings is given in Table 5-7 for race and curriculum problems.

Table 5-7 is designed to give the percentage of superintendents who do not recognize either race or curriculum problems even though their respective publics or school boards do. Information indicating the conditions of democratic failure (3) and democratic viability (4) are therefore given directly. Beginning in the upper-left hand cell of Table 5-7 and proceeding across or down to the lower-right hand cell, decreasing percentage figures indicate a tendency toward democratic viability. The greater the decrease, the greater the likelihood that there is democratic viability. Conversely, stable or increasing percentage figures indicate a high likelihood of democratic failure. Information indicating the condition of administrative autonomy (2) is given by the figure in the upper-left

Table 5-7

Superintendent Failure to Recognize Problems Evident to Public and School Board

Curriculum Problems			
		School Board	
		No Problems Recognized	Problem Recognized
Public	No Problems Recognized	66%* (46)**	66% (42)
	Problem Recognized	50% (15)	55% (24)

Race Problems			
		School Board	
		No Problems Recognized	Problem Recognized
Public	No Problems Recognized	87%* (79)**	100% (12)
	Problem Recognized	51% (13)	32% (24)

*Percentage of Superintendents reporting recognizing no problem under Public and School Board conditions indicated. Note that 34% of the Superintendents do recognize Curriculum Problems and 13% of the Superintendents do recognize Race Problems even though neither their School Board nor Public do.

**Cell N is given in parentheses.

hand cell where neither the public nor the school board recognize a given problem. The lower the percentage figure in the cell, the greater the likelihood of administrative autonomy.

Some administrative autonomy is evident in both the case of curriculum problems and the case of race problems. Thirty-four percent of the superintendents recognize curriculum problems and 13 percent of the superintendents recognize race problems even though neither their public nor school boards do. Based upon our earlier discussion, we would expect the superintendent to display greater autonomy on strict educational issues like curriculum than on more political issues like race and the data bear this out. Superintendents display greater fundamental interest in curriculum than in race (39 percent compared to 22 percent), however. The differences in autonomy on the two issues are thus not quite so marked as the data first indicate.

Issue type appears to make a substantial difference on the pattern of administrative-political relationships in Table 5-7. There is evidence of democratic failure in one instance and evidence of democratic viability in the other instance. Looking first at curriculum, we find only very slight decreases in the percentage figures moving down or across Table 5-7. Even more significant, we find that well over one-half of the superintendents fail to recognize curriculum problems even though such problems are evident to both the public and the school board in their respective districts. It is very clear here that the community and the school board are able to exert very little influence on the superintendent with regard to the curriculum issue and presumably to other similar educational issues. Our democratic model can hardly be considered as working well.

Turning to race, we find a substantial decrease in the percentage figures moving down and across Table 5-7. The percentage of superintendents recognizing no race problems drops from 87 percent where neither the public nor the school board recognize such problems to 32 percent where both the public and the school board recognize such problems. This suggests that the community and the school board may, in fact, influence the superintendent with regard to race and presumably similar social, as opposed to educational, issues. This supports democratic viability within our model. Note, however, that still nearly one-third of the superintendents fail to recognize race problems even though such problems are evident to both the public and the school board in their respective districts. Thus even where the democratic viability of our model appears greatest, democratic failure is still frequent.

A pattern of community-school board interaction of considerable importance is evident in the race issue in Table 5-7. School board recognition of race problems appears to have no impact on superintendent recognition of such problems as well. Reading across the top of Table 5-7, the percentage figures do not change significantly. School board recognition of race problems appears to have a substantial impact on the superintendent, however, where the community does recognize race problems. Reading across the bottom of the table, the percentage figures decrease. What this suggests is that the impact of the school board in educational policy-making is apparently much greater when it acts in a representative role for a concerned community than when it acts in a trustee role.

The Race Problem and
Policy Outputs

The implications of the above findings are considerable for they suggest that while under most conditions our democratic model is likely to fail, there are still possibilities for its viable operation. We move to a further examination of the race problem, focusing upon policy outputs. This final section of our examination provides in the form of a case study a further view of the contributions of political and administrative elements to educational policy-making.

Each school district was classified as to taking no action, public relations action, system action, or both public relations and system action in response to recognized racial problems on the basis of superintendent and school board member replies to an open-ended question asking what action the school district had taken to deal with racial problems that had come up in the district. System action pertains specifically to action or changes within the schools and includes the integration of schools through busing or reorganization of school boundaries, the integration of faculty, or the upgrading or addition of educational programs and facilities. Public relations action pertains to action focused upon the community and includes formal or informal statements of sympathy, under-standing, reassurance, or concern regarding racial issues in the schools or the formation of human relations or other citizens' groups to investigate racial issues in the schools. The distribution of policy response types is given in Table 5-8 for

Table 5-8
Distribution of School District Racial Problem Policy Response Type

Policy Response	Percentage
None	40%
Public Relations	26%
Public Relations and System Action	19%
System Action	15%
Total	100%

N* = 91

*N includes those school districts in which either the superintendent or the school board were coded as recognizing racial problems.

those school districts in which the school board or the superintendent or both recognized some racial problems.

The distribution of response types in Table 5-8 suggests that school policy action to deal with racial problems is characterized more by ambiguity than by corrective measures. Recognized racial problems have been ignored entirely in about 40 percent of the school districts. In most instances this appears to be the consequence of policy-making inaction rather than deliberate problem avoidance. Whatever the reason, however, the failure to take any action whatsoever represents an important but ambiguous policy. In about another one-quarter of the school districts, action has been limited to public relations activities. Such activities may be a necessary prelude to system action. Also, public relations action as a response to public discontent problems, if successful, may presumably eliminate any need for system action. Indeed public relations action is inherently an ambiguous policy.

System action—even minor corrective or remedial measures to deal with racial problems—is evident in only about one-third of the school districts with recognized racial problems or less than one-fifth of all the school districts. Even in these system action cases, policy is ambiguous. There is no attempt to objectively measure the effectiveness of system action. The diffuseness of responses and the contradictions in responses among school board members and the superintendent within districts with regard to specific policy, however, suggest that system action in response to racial problems is, by design or by default, woefully inadequate in a large number of cases. There is the suspicion that system action policy is often a symbolic facade to mask the lack of genuine corrective action.

Ambiguity in policy—the symbolic policy response—can be highly effective in minimizing or diffusing conflict. Unless such policy is accompanied by efforts to correct or rectify root racial problems, however, success in avoiding conflict may well be only temporary. This may well explain why racial problems appear to persist, smoldering under the surface and threatening to erupt at any time, in so many school districts. The apparent lack of system action in response to recognized racial problems on the whole suggests very low policy-making performance.

System action to deal with racial problems appears to be largely responsive, and at best, remedial rather than anticipatory and preventative. Indeed, in only one school district did school governors indicate that any action was taken in an attempt to minimize racial problems before such problems became critical. In all other cases, system action appears to have come only after the superintendent, or the school board, or most often, both the superintendent and the school board have recognized the severity of racial problems as is indicated in Table 5-9. The percentage of districts taking some system action increases from 0 percent where no racial problems are recognized to about one-quarter where either the superintendent or the school board recognizes racial problems to just over one-half where both the superintendent and the school board recognize racial problems. But it is also clear from Table 5-9 that recognition of racial problems is hardly assurance of system action. In just under one-half of the school districts where both the superintendent and school board do recognize racial problems, the school district has not moved beyond public relations action in response to the problem.

The eminence of the superintendent as the policy action initiator within the schools is striking in Table 5-9. Where the superintendent does recognize a problem, there is evidence of definite policy action if only public relations action. Even in the area of public relations action, the area in which we might expect the school board to excel beyond the superintendent, the superintendent demonstrates the ability to initiate such action quite readily. In contrast, in one-half of the school districts where the school board alone recognizes a problem, there is no policy action whatsoever. The figures do indicate that the school board can act alone but clearly not with the certainty of the superintendent. We suggested that the superintendent has a fundamental insensitivity to racial problems in the schools, but if there is to be action to deal with such problems, the superintendent is clearly the agent that should be alerted to such problems.

A model linking action type of policy to civil rights activity, white racial tension, and racial problem intensity while controlling for district racial structure is illustrated in Figure 5-8. The coefficients in the model suggest that while recognition of racial problems may be a necessary condition for action, pressure in the form of civil rights group activity is the most important factor influencing action in response to such problems (beta = .29). Two other findings are

Table 5-9
Policy Action and Racial Problem Recognition

		School Board	
		No Problem	Problem
S u p e r i n t e n d e n t	No Problem	No Action 100% (85)*	No Action 49% Public Relations Action 32% System Action 20% (35)
	Problem	No Action 0% Public Relations Action 71% System Action 29% (11)	No Action 0% Public Relations Action 44% System Action 56% (54)

*Number in parentheses is cell N.

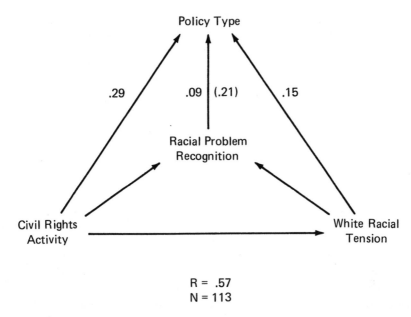

Figure 5-8. Policy Type and Three Key Factors. Note: Values given are standardized regression coefficients for predicting to Action type of policy and controlling for district racial structure (beta = .05). Value given in parentheses is for superintendent racial problem.

important here. First, among those school districts with some civil rights activity evident, the action policy is related to the level of civil rights activity ($r = .22$), suggesting that the intensity as well as the presence of civil rights activity has an impact upon policy.[23] Second, among those school districts in which the federal government had intervened to force desegregation, the action policy is also related to the level of civil rights activity ($r = .56$), suggesting that even under conditions of federal intervention civil rights activity has an impact upon policy. The goals of civil rights activity within the educational system may not necessarily be action policy as we have measured it. Civil rights groups often seek legitimation of grievances and attention to the special needs of nonwhite students as much as integration of the schools.[24] Our measures may therefore underestimate the total effect of civil rights activity on school policy. The importance of civil rights activity in moving the schools to action on racial problems is thus doubly underscored.

The coefficients in the model suggest a positive link between action policy and white racial tension (beta = .15), although the direction of the link is not entirely clear. White racial tension has little apparent effect in accounting for differences between school districts where racial problems are major issues under discussion and investigation but where no action is evident and school districts where action is evident (beta = .02). White racial tension thus does not appear to stem from action policy but rather appears to be associated more generally with the generation of race as a public issue. The possible effect of white racial tension, then, is to increase the likelihood of some public response by the schools to racial problems. That response may as well take the form of assurances that racial problems are not affecting education as any action to deal with the racial problems, particularly so given that white racial tension is so often a force of concern rather than opposition or action. We do caution, however, that while white racial tension here appears neutral on balance, in any single instance it may give support for, or more important, strong opposition against any action and particularly action leading to integration of the schools.

It is not clear that the schools can manage racial problems within the schools without changes in our entire society. Our findings suggest, however, that the performance of the schools as a whole in recognizing and acting on racial problems is far from satisfactory. This may well explain why racial problems continue to smolder under the surface, unattended, and threatening to erupt at any time in so many school districts. School governors often feel inhibited from taking necessary action within the schools because of public pressure. We agree that within our society, the rise of racial issues within the schools almost certainly assures some public pressure and community conflict. The paradox is that it appears that the schools are not recognizing and taking action to deal with racial problems until such problems balloon into public issues and political pressure is indeed brought to bear. This suggests that greater political involvement of the community, interest groups, and the school board and superintendent in educational policy-making may improve policy-making performance with regard to an issue like race, even if it also means greater conflict.

Summary

We have seen that most educational policy-making lies in the hands of the superintendent. Almost all action in the area of the educational program appears to be initiated by the superintendent and his staff in response to the problem priorities they recognize. Similarly, action on a more episodic public issue like race is more likely if the superintendent recognizes race problems as having a high priority. This situation can hardly be avoided if the superintendent is at all capable—assuming that we wanted to avoid it. The superintendent is in the position, as the full-time administrator of the schools and with the expert technical skills essential to administer the schools, to take necessary action to deal with problems that arise within the schools. We would hope that the superintendent would do so without continuous prompting from political elements. The point that has most concerned us, however, is just what the bases for establishing problem priorities are.

We found that the superintendent appears to give greater priority to strict educational problems like curriculum than to episodic problems like race that appear to concern the community more. This is to be expected given that the superintendent is charged with responsibility for the educational program whereas the community has little knowledge about or interest in the educational program. But more important, we found that the superintendent appears to have a very ethnocentric view of problems in the schools. Problems are identified and assessed from a narrow educational perspective that isolates educational functions within the schools from any political or social functions. Consequently, superintendent recognition of problems appears to have relatively little link to significant elements in the social structure. Superintendent recognition of race problems has less relation to district racial structure and superintendent recognition of curriculum problems has less relation to metropolitan complexity than either the community or the school board. There thus appears to be a fundamental disjuncture between the superintendent on the one hand and the school board and the community on the other hand in interpreting problems and setting problem priorities within educational policy-making.

We found that most interest group activity within the schools involves educationally related, establishment oriented interest groups, in particular PTAs. The traditional separation of education and politics provides a barrier to the entry of non-educationally related interest groups into educational policy-making. The more political an interest group appears, the less legitimacy it has within the schools, and the less potent it is as a political force. On the whole, interest groups have little impact on either the school board or the superintendent, although the school board appears slightly more receptive to interest group activity than the superintendent and to make more accurate interpretations of the representative character of interest group activity than does the superintendent. Interest group activity thus appears to play only a marginal role in linking the community on the one hand and the school board and the superintendent on the other hand within educational policy-making.

We found that if interest group activity can penetrate the school system, it can have a significant impact on policy-making, increasing school board and superintendent recognition of certain problems and moving the schools to action on such problems. Civil rights groups provide a key example of this. Buttressed by Constitutional provisions and court rulings lending legitimacy to their demands and organized around political (as opposed to technical) issues, civil rights groups appear to have a substantial impact on school race policy in at least some school districts. Where civil rights groups are salient to the school board and the superintendent, recognition of race problems and action to deal with such problems is most likely. Otherwise, race problems appear likely to be ignored, quite possibly until they explode into major public conflicts.

Contrary to some educator's fears, interest group conflict in educational policy-making is not necessarily dysfunctional. Indeed interest group conflict can contribute a spark of dynamism to educational policy-making, calling attention to new problems arising within the schools and broadening the perspective within which such problems are viewed. White racial tension together with civil rights activity appears to function in just this way. Rather than impairing action, the two different interest groups stimulate action.

We found that the school board plays a marginal role in representing the community in educational policy-making. School board members tend to be recruited from the educational supportive establishment and reflect the views of the educational establishment as much as the views of the community. The school board appears to have the most impact in educational policy-making when acting in a representative role in concert with an active and involved community on a public issue. The school board appears to have little impact when acting in a trustee role without community involvement or when strict educational or technical issues are involved.

Given the level of knowledge and involvement of the community compared to the superintendent and the apparent lack of structural or political linkages between the community, school board, and superintendent, it was not surprising that patterns of asymmetry were evident in the problems in the schools recognized by the community, the school board, and the superintendent. The superintendent recognized problems in the schools that were not evident to either the community or the school board, an indication of acceptable administrative autonomy. But the superintendent failed to recognize problems in the schools that were evident to either the school board or the community, an indication of unacceptable democratic failure. This failure appeared most predominant in the area of curriculum problems, reflecting the difficulty of political penetration into areas of basic education. The superintendent utilizes his technical educational expertise not just to assist in policy-making in the area of basic education but to monopolize policy-making in the area, effectively precluding political participation.

Educational policy-making is, to summarize, insulated from the political process: routinized, "technocratized," dominated by administration. Is such policy-making normal or functional for a community? Viewed in conservative terms as a process that minimizes tension and conflict, educational policy-making has worked rather efficiently. But apolitical educational policy-making is viable only if the school system is isolated from society, if educational functions are separated from political and social functions. This is obviously not the case. Moreover, there are signs that the demands placed upon the schools, the problems confronting the schools, may be taking increasingly external, episodic forms. Demands for increased participation in educational policy-making on the part of traditionally disfranchised groups are increasing. The issues raised, like civil rights, student rights, and local community control, are not easily converted from political issues to technical issues. Technology and expertise, which have given the administrator a monopoly of influence, may be losing some of their allure. Finally, values within the community may be gradually fragmenting, making it increasingly difficult for the schools policy decisions based upon monolithic values. This suggests that we may witness a change in the predominant mode of educational policy-making from administrative to political. Our basic model of educational policy-making allows for such change. Our findings indicate that the model will work, if uneasily and clumsily. Clearly, however, the difficult problem of integrating political and administrative concerns into educational policy-making will become more complex and more difficult than ever.

Appendix

During the summer and fall of 1968 the Survey Research Center conducted interviews with board members and superintendents in eighty-eight school districts throughout the continental United States. Because of the desire to link the school board study to a 1965 nationwide investigation of high school seniors, their parents, social studies teachers, and principals, a decision was made to study those boards having jurisdiction over the public secondary schools covered in the earlier inquiry. It should be stressed that this is not a representative sample of all school districts; rather it represents districts in rather direct proportion to the number of secondary students covered. Since most districts are rather small, a straight probability sample of all districts would have yielded a preponderance of small districts. Thus the sample may be strictly defined as those public school districts having jurisdiction over a national probability sample of high school seniors as of 1965. Although the changes in school district boundaries and population in the 1965-68 interim affect the representativeness of the sample for 1968 purposes, these changes were judged to be slight enough to permit the extraordinary utility of linking up the school board project with the earlier study.

In order to have enough districts from very large cities for analytical purposes, it was necessary to sample from that stratum beyond the rate set by the 1965 design. To this end the largest city in each of the thirteen largest Standard Metropolitan Statistical Areas (SMSAs), counting the New York-Northeastern New Jersey standard consolidated area as two SMSAs were surveyed. Having oversampled this stratum, it then became necessary to overweight the districts from the other three stratum used by the Survey Research Center in its classification of primary sampling units, *viz.*, the suburbs of these large SMSAs, other SMSAs, and non-SMSAs. All analyses reported in this chapter are based on weighted N's, but we have not let the inflated N's give the illusion of having more cases than are actually present. The weighting merely adjusts for oversampling of one stratum. To put the matter in perspective, here are the raw N's and the weighted N's for each of the four classes of primary sampling units by board members and by school districts.

	Raw N		Weighted N	
	Members	Districts	Members	Districts
Largest cities in 13 largest SMSAs	95	13	95	14
Suburbs in 13 largest SMSAs	84	13	181	28
All other SMSAs	171	30	358	59
Non-SMSAs	200	32	505	85
Totals	550	·88	1139	185

The 550 board members interviewed come from a potential total of 602, for a 91 percent response rate. All board members were interviewed in fifty-two of the eighty-eight districts. Of the boards contacted, all but two cooperated. In one case a similar district was selected as a replacement. In the second case and adjoining district in the same county, which was already in the sample, was doubleweighted since it would have been the appropriate substitute for the declining district.

Notes

1. While the literature on politics and education is growing at an impressive rate, systematic studies of interest groups have yet to appear in generally available form. Most of such studies are of the traditional case-descriptive variety, confining themselves to a single issue, a single group, or a single school district. Some of the more intriguing of these studies are: Rogers (1968), Gittell (1969), Iannaconne and Lutz (1970). Two recent comparative studies, each dealing with a single issue are Crain (1968) and Rosenthal (1969). Two projects deal directly with interest representation. They are: Smoley (1965) and Christie (1966). For an excellent effort to fit the various pieces together see Charters (forthcoming).

2. Daniel Lerner and Harold D. Lasswell (eds.), *The Policy Sciences: Recent Developments in Scope and Method* (Stanford: Stanford University Press, 1951), p. ix.

3. Ibid. Herbert A. Simon and James G. March, *Organizations* (New York: John Wiley & Sons, Inc., 1958).

4. Charles E. Lindbloom, *The Policy-Making Process* (Englewood Cliffs, New Jersey: Prentice-Hall, Inc., 1968); Charles O. Jones, *An Introduction to the Study of Public Policy* (Belmont: Wadsworth Publishing Company, 1970).

5. Ibid.

6. Lindbloom, *The Policy-Making Process*, p. 2.

7. Thomas Elliot, "Toward an Understanding of Public School Politics," *The*

American Political Science Review 52 (December 1959):1032-51; Paul Peterson and Thomas Williams, "Models of Decision-Making," in Michael Kirst (ed.), *State, School, and Politics* (Lexington, Massachusetts: Lexington Books, D.C. Heath and Company, 1972), pp. 149-168.

8. Roscoe Martin, *Government and the Suburban School* (Syracuse: Syracuse University Press, 1962); Marilyn Gittell et al., *Investigation of Fiscally Independent and Dependent School Districts* (Washington, D.C.: Office of Education, Cooperative Research Project No. 3237, 1967); David W. Minar, "Community Characteristics, Conflict, and Power Structures," in Robert Cahill and Stephen Hencley (eds.), *The Politics of Education in the Local Community* (Danville, Illinois: The Interstate Printers and Publishers, Inc., 1964); Alan Rosenthal, *Pedagogues and Power* (Syracuse: Syracuse University Press, 1969); Archie R. Dykes, *School Board and Superintendent: Their Effective Working Relationships* (Danville, Illinois: Interstate Printers and Publishers, Inc., 1965); C. Hines, "A Study of School Board Administration Relationships: The Development of the Eugene, Oregon, Superintendency, 1891-1944," *American School Board Journal* (1951); James D. Leorner, *Who Controls American Education? A Guide for Laymen* (Boston: Beacon, 1968); Elliot, *Understanding Public School Politics.*

9. Martin, *Government and Suburban School*; George Gallup, *How the Nation Views the Public Schools* (Princeton: Gallup International, 1969).

10. Lester Milbrath, *Political Participation* (Chicago: Rand McNally & Company, 1965); V.O. Key, *Public Opinion and American Democracy* (New York: Alfred A. Knopf, 1963).

11. Martin, *Government and the Suburban School*; Minar, "Community, Conflict, and Power."

12. Harmon Zeigler, Kent Jennings, and Wayne Peak, *Governing American Schools* (North Scituate, Massachusetts: Duxbury Press, 1973); also see Joseph Cronin, *The Control of Urban Schools* (New York: Free Press, 1973); Keith Goldhammer, *The School Board* (New York: Center for Applied Research in Education, Inc., 1964); Harmon Zeigler and Kent Jennings, "Avenues to the School Board and Political Competition," paper read at the American Educational Research Association, 1972; Louis H. Masotti, "Political Integration in Suburban Education Communities," in Scott Geer (ed.), *The New Urbanization* (New York: St. Martin's Press, 1968).

13. Minar, "Community, Conflict, and Power"; Martin, *Government and the Suburban School.*

14. James W. Guthrie and Edward Wynne (eds.), *New Models for American Education* (Englewood Cliffs, New Jersey: Prentice-Hall, 1971).

15. Robert L. Crain, *The Politics of School Desegregation* (Chicago: Aldine, 1968); Neil S. Sullivan, "Educational Leadership at the Crossroads," in R.L. Green (ed.), *Racial Crisis in American Education* (Chicago: Follet Educational Corporation, 1969); R.A. Dentler, "Barriers to Northern School Desegregation," *Daedalus* 95 (1966):45-63.

16. Ibid., esp. Crain.

17. Michael Kirst and Decker F. Walker, "An Analysis of Curriculum Policy-Making," in James Bruno (ed.), *Emerging Issues in Education: Policy Implications for the Schools* (Lexington, Massachusetts: Lexington Books, D.C. Heath and Company, 1972).

18. Arthur Bentley, *The Process of Government* (San Antonio, Texas: Principia Press of Trinity University, 1949); David Truman, *The Governmental Process* (New York: Alfred A. Knopf, 1951); Robert H. Salisbury, "An Exchange Theory of Interest Groups," *Midwest Journal of Political Science* 13 (February 1969):1-32; Earl Latham, "The Group Basis of Politics," in Heinz Eulau, Samuel J. Eldersveld, and Moris Janowitz (eds.), *Political Behavior* (New York: Free Press, 1956); Harmon Zeigler and Wayen Peak, *Interest Groups in American Society 2nd Edition* (Englewood Cliffs, New Jersey: Prentice-Hall, 1972).

19. Robert Salisbury, "Schools and Politics in Big Cities," *Harvard Educational Review* 37 (Summer 1967):408-424; Martin, *Government and the Suburban School*; Minar, "Community, Conflict, and Power"; Harmon Zeigler and Michael A. Baer, *Lobbying* (Belmont, California: Wadsworth, 1969).

20. Harmon Zeigler, Kent Jennings, and Wayne Peak, "Decision-Making Culture of the American Public Education," *Political Science Annual* (Indianapolis: Bobbs-Merrill, 1974).

21. Crain, *School Desegregation*; T. Bentley Edwards and Frederick Wirt (eds.), *School Desegregation in the North* (San Francisco: Chandler Publishing Co., 1967); Angus Campbell, *White Attitudes Toward Black People* (Ann Arbor: Institute for Social Research, 1968); Sheldon Stoff, *The Two-Way Street: Guideposts to Peaceful School Desegregation* (Indianapolis: David-Stewart Publishing Company, 1967).

22. Michael Lipskey, "Protest as a Political Resource," *The American Political Science Review* 62 (1968):1144-1158.

23. Crain, *School Desegregation*, finds the reverse but deals only with metropolitan cities where civil rights activity was fairly strong in all.

24. Ibid.

Bibliography

Bauer, R.A., I. Pool, and L.A. Dexter. *American Business and Public Policy.* New York: Atherton Press, 1963.

Bentley, A.A. *The Process of Government.* San Antonio, Texas: Principia Press of Trinity University, 1949.

Charters, W.W., Jr. *School Board Research Revisited.* Eugene, Oregon: Center for the Advanced Study of Educational Administration, University of Oregon, forthcoming.

Christie, S.G. "Political Pressures on the School Board Member." M.S. thesis. San Diego State College, 1966.

Crain, R.L. *The Politics of School Desegregation.* Chicago: Aldine. 1968.

Dye, T.R. *Politics, Economics, and the Public: Policy Outcomes in the American States.* Chicago: Rand McNally, 1966.

Francis, W. *Legislative Issues in the Fifty States: A Comparative Analysis.* Chicago: Rand McNally, 1967.

Froman, L.A., Jr. "Some Effects of Interest Group Strength in State Politics." *American Political Science Review* 60 (December 1966):952-962.

Gittell, M. *Confrontation at Ocean Hill-Brownsville.* New York: Praeger, 1969.

Gross, N. *Who Runs Our Schools.* New York: John Wiley, 1958.

Iannaconne, L. and F.W. Lutz. *Politics, Power and Policy: The Governing of Local School Districts.* Columbus, Ohio: Charles E. Merrill Co., 1958.

Milbrath, L. *The Washington Lobbyists.* Chicago: Rand McNally, 1963.

Olson, M.L., Jr. *The Logic of Collective Action.* Cambridge: Harvard University Press, 1965.

Rogers, D. *110 Livingston Street.* New York: Random House, 1968.

Rosenthal, A. *Pedagogues and Power.* Syracuse: Syracuse Univ. Press, 1969.

Salisbury, R.H. "An Exchange Theory of Interest Groups." *Midwest Journal of Political Science* 13 (February 1969):1-32.

Smoley, E.R., Jr. *Community Participation in Urban School Government.* Cooperative Research Project No. S-029. U.S. Office of Education, 1965.

Truman, D. *The Governmental Process.* New York: Alfred A. Knopf, 1951.

Zeigler, H. "Interest Groups in the States." In H. Jacob and K.L. Vines (eds.), *Politics in the American States.* Boston: Little, Brown, 1965. Pp. 101-147.

Zeigler, H. and M.A. Baer. *Lobbying.* Belmont, Calif.: Wadsworth, 1969.

About the Authors

Robert N. Spadaro, who received the Ph.D. in public administration and finance from the University of Georgia, is visiting associate professor of government and public administration at the Chinese University of Hong Kong. He is the former director of policy research for former Governor William W. Scranton of Pennsylvania, a former administrative aide to former Governor Winthrop Rockefeller of Arkansas, and a former research aide to the late Senator Robert F. Kennedy of New York. Dr. Spadaro has also contributed to several academic journals.

Thomas R. Dye, professor of government at Florida State University, received the Ph.D. in political science from the University of Pennsylvania. A former secretary of the American Political Science Association, Dr. Dye is the author of *The Irony of Democracy* (with L. Harmon Zeigler); *Politics, Economics, and the Public; Understanding Public Policy*; and *American Public Policy*.

Robert T. Golembiewski is research professor of political science at the University of Georgia. His publications include *The Small Group, Behavior, and Organization; Men, Management, and Morality*; and *Organizing Men and Power*. Dr. Golembiewski received the Ph.D. in political science from Yale University.

Murray S. Stedman, Jr., received the Ph.D. in political science from Columbia University. He is professor and chairman, Department of Political Science, Temple University. Dr. Stedman is the author of several published works, including *Urban Politics*.

L. Harmon Zeigler, professor of political science at the University of Oregon, received the Ph.D. in political science from the University of Illinois. A former Ford Foundation Fellow and Guggenheim Foundation Fellow, Dr. Zeigler is the author of several works, including *Interest Groups in American Society* and *Lobbying* (with Michael Baer).